The Beauty of Holiness

The Beauty of Holiness

Giotto's Passion Frescoes as a Prelude to the Artistic Afterlife of the Supper at Emmaus

BRIAN LESLIE BISHOP

Foreword by Gesa E. Thiessen

RESOURCE *Publications* • Eugene, Oregon

THE BEAUTY OF HOLINESS
Giotto's Passion Frescoes as a Prelude to the Artistic Afterlife of the Supper at Emmaus

Resource Publications
An Imprint of Wipf and Stock Publishers
199 W. 8th Ave., Suite 3
Eugene, OR 97401

www.wipfandstock.com

PAPERBACK ISBN: 978-1-5326-9877-4
HARDCOVER ISBN: 978-1-5326-9878-1
EBOOK ISBN: 978-1-5326-9879-8

Manufactured in the U.S.A. 01/02/20

. . . o, I have ta'en
Too little care of this . . .[1]

For all those who care and in particular for dear Jenny,
who cares unconditionally with such a generous heart.

For Sharon who spends her life caring for those
whose lives are fractured.

And for Sheena who when she was with us cared for the "Precious Earth" and helped young people to care also.

I am so proud of you all.

1. Shakespeare, *King Lear*, 3.4.36–37.

O worship the Lord in the beauty of holiness: fear before him, all the earth.[1]

1. KJV. Psalms 96: 9.

Contents

Illustrations

Foreword

SINCE THE 1980S, FAITH and the arts has become an important and widely recognized subject in theology. The numerous publications on the interdisciplinary relationship of theology and visual art, literature, music and film, etc. witness to the unprecedented development of this field of study with its overall aim of investigating how the arts are sources of revelatory-theological expression which can stimulate, challenge and expand both theological and art-historical insight.

While the imagination and images have concerned Christian theologians since the early church, in recent years, with the rapid expansion of this field, their role has been considered by a number of theologians, including Paul Tillich, Jane and John Dillenberger, Diane Apostolos-Cappadona, Horst Schwebel, George Pattison, Frank Burch Brown, David Brown, to name only a few.

Creation, revelation and faith, beauty, the role of the imagination and the search for meaning are at the heart of theological engagement with art. It is the power of the imagination that enables us to perceive *something* of the transcendent, to deal with and transform reality, to pray, and to disclose and discover glimpses of ultimate reality and of the eschaton.

Since Plato through history the imagination would at times be viewed with suspicion. Scholars, poets and artists have been well aware that the imagination inspires and is indispensable to making art, to science and scholarship, yet the imagination could be seen as dangerous, even demonic, when misused for instigating the most appalling atrocities in human history. - Still, we are often slow to acknowledge that the imagination is essential in any form of human living, knowledge, art, culture and technological developments. Without acts of the imagination, without vision, hope for transformation is unthinkable. Transformed being, glimpses of the eschatological kingdom of God realized through peace, justice, liberation and the care of creation, as well as eternity's ultimate transcendence and fulfillment need to be imagined. This can happen in the more systematic, conceptual work of the theologian, or in the immediacy of the sensuous work of art.

Brian Bishop's book must be commended for opening up to us a vista of imagination, a broad canvas, drawing us into an exploration of Giotto's works on the Passion in the Arena Chapel in Padua and taking these as the point of departure and anticipation of the theme of The Supper at Emmaus, depicted by a host of seminal artists, from Dürer to Titian and the Venetian painters, to Caravaggio, Rembrandt and Velasquez, amongst others. Beautifully written in a reflective style, yet informed by art-historical, theological and literary writings, the reader discerns the empathy and love he has for his subject. He begins his work by reflecting on the importance of hope. Today, we are living in politically and socially unstable times, aware that vast numbers of people on this globe are suffering from war, starvation, migration, disease and climate change, etc. In focusing on Jesus meeting and dining with his disciples *after* his resurrection, the author centers on realized hope, i.e. the risen Christ who has overcome death, the God who saves and liberates us from death into eternal life and communion with God. – This is a gracious book of Christian hope rendered in visual art.

Gesa Elsbeth Thiessen
Adjunct Assistant Professor School of Religion at Trinity College, Dublin, Ireland.
Visiting Scholar at Sarum College, Salisbury, UK

Preface

I THINK EVERYBODY HAS personal experience of the inadequacy of words. When confronted with bereavement, the expression, "there are no words," is often the best that we can do. Unimaginable atrocity such as that seen in the Holocaust or 9/11 also illustrate this point. In the latter case, the basic facts that summarize what took place—a group of human-beings took over the control of aeroplanes full of human-beings and deliberately flew them into high-rise buildings full of other human-beings—just renders speech inadequate. "*Es ist mir recht unheimlich geworden.*" Hans-Georg Gadamer, the German humanist philosopher whose life had spanned virtually the whole of the twentieth-century and who had so eloquently used words to convey the results of his accumulated wisdom was 102. He was asked for his thoughts on the atrocity of 9/11 and the above quotation was his response. The German words suggest that the world had become strange, even alien, to him: he wasn't at home here. He added that "people cannot live without hope; that is the only thesis I would defend without any restriction." For a lot of people the rallying cry of hope has become, "Follow the Science!" Gadamer had throughout his life paid great attention to scientific discovery in the twentieth-century. He was visited for the last time in 2012 by one of his former pupils who later became a colleague and he repeated his firm belief that without hope people cannot live. He went on to say that hope had become "this small," and he raised his hand and showed the tiny gap of light between his thumb and index finger. Christianity is, of course based upon the Gospel, the good news of hope revealed to the world at the Incarnation, the birth of Jesus. The eighteenth-century "Enlightenment" that placed the emphasis on reason and individualism rather than tradition made it difficult and, it would seem increasingly, virtually impossible to believe the Christian story. The language or the words that theologians inevitably deploy is very vulnerable to the forensic language that rationalist philosophers are able to use. But many people, particularly bright young people, use that rapier sharp language to analyze the atheistic philosophy that they have inherited. They unwrap this philosophy and discover that it is telling them that there is absolutely no point or purpose to life. Life is a purely random event. Essentially, I am nothing more than a bio-chemical reaction. If one of today's troubled teenagers seeks guidance from one of the many secular-humanist gurus available to them, that elephant in the room must be enormously difficult to tame. After all, it was only "perchance to dream" that prevented Hamlet from that devoutly-to-be-wished-for consummation of ending the life that had become pointless. But, if one is not awed by a dream . . .

The concept of me, a Christian, bandying *words* with Richard Dawkins, a highly-educated and fluently articulate atheist is ludicrous. The man would wipe the floor with me. It was with this knowledge that I decided to read his book *The God Delusion* in Ty Olwyn Hospice, Swansea. I was staying there with my wife, Jenny, as our daughter, Sheena aged forty-one, married with two sons aged eight and eleven was dying with cervical cancer. Clearly one's faith is tried in these circumstances and I can recall challenging Dawkins as I would not have the temerity to do face-to-face: "OK, Dawkins, do your worst!" As I had spent some time girding up my loins as it were, I was genuinely disappointed at the total lack of challenge to my faith that the book presented. I turned to the other matter that I was occupied with at the time. That was the completion of my master's dissertation: *The Theology of the Scrovegni Chapel Passion Frescoes* where I sensed that I was confronting "reality." This was 2007. I was sixty-nine, a retired English and Drama teacher who had spent the previous two-years working for a distance-learning theology master's from the University of Wales in the UK. My dissertation was accepted and I was awarded the degree the following summer. I, of course, dedicated the dissertation to Sheena's memory and the first part of this book is very largely that dissertation.

Unable to afford university fees to continue on this academic path, I continued to develop my pursuit of an understanding of the Gospel through art and this resulted in the publication by Wipf and Stock in 2017 of *The Continuing Dialogue*[1], an investigation into the artistic afterlife or lives of the five narratives peculiar to the Fourth Gospel and an assessment of their contribution to the understanding of that gospel. Graham Howes, Emeritus Fellow of Trinity Hall, Cambridge and author of *The Art of the*

1. Available on Amazon.

Sacred[2] reviewed *The Continuing Dialogue* in "Art and Christianity Today"[3] from which I quote.

> Bishop discusses each text and the artistic 'reading of it' with enviably clear language, an eye for both telling detail and overall composition and, above all, an unfailing ability (rooted one suspects in his career as a drama teacher) to provide explicit 'stage directions' to draw us painlessly towards significant pictorial and theological details. It is rare indeed that the crucial interaction of Word and Image in Christian art has been presented with such clarity and conviction.

Encouraged by such a generous response an idea was formed that would allow me to present my thoughts on Giotto's Passion Frescoes that had such a significant impact upon me to a wider audience. I could present them as a lead-in to a discussion of the artistic afterlife of that great triumphant event of the Christian story *The Supper at Emmaus.*

And so I set off on my personal road to Emmaus. It has been quite a trek. I have learnt so much and discovered afresh that as we concentrate on, in the oft repeated post modern mantra, "going forward," we lose so much if we do not also take time to look backward. This book is my attempt to share those uplifting, full-of-hope experiences with you.

Brian Bishop
Stratford-upon-Avon, 1st, November 2019.

2. Available on Amazon.
3. Winter 2017 edition.

Acknowledgements

I WOULD LIKE TO thank the many museums and galleries as well as private individuals who have offered encouragement and help and to those who have granted free use of some of the beautiful images seen in this book. Thanks to Professor Martin O'Kane who made the very generous comments on my Master's Dissertation that provided the initial encouragement that was the momentum needed to propel me forward and sustain me on the many occasions when energy was low. Thanks to Dr. Davide Banzano, Director of the Civic Museums of Padua for granting an extended pass to study the frescoes in the Scrovegni Chapel.

I have been very careful to credit all sources from which I have directly derived ideas and words. However, as I am subject to "senior moments," I may well have been less successful in this than I tried to be. If this is discovered to be the case, my sincere apologies to those offended.

Special thanks to my residential chief-whip for the support and wise comments based upon detailed and tiresome proof-reading. Jenny recently commented as she handed back yet more pages, "I'm always rather surprised to find that I rather enjoy reading what you have written." I'm still mulling that over.

Introduction

THIS BOOK IS BASED upon the belief that an artist's engagement with a biblical passage may be regarded as a discrete dialogue with that passage. The viewer of, or the participator in, the resulting artwork may develop understanding of the text upon which it is based. It may be a hermeneutical event.

The use of images in Christian worship has divided opinion for centuries. Byzantine Iconoclasm in the eighth and ninth centuries is well documented. Trying to arrive at the thinking behind it is more difficult. Theologically, it seems to have been based upon the *Old Covenant* and The Ten Commandments, in particular number two:

> Thou shalt not make unto thee any graven image, or any likeness *of any thing* that *is* in heaven above, or that *is* in the earth beneath, or that *is* in the water under the earth:[1]

Modern thinkers tend to look for sociological explanations. Sociology as opposed to theology seems to be a thicket in which they feel more at home. Arnold Toynbee suggests that the success of Islamic armies threatening the Byzantine Empires' eastern borders and, eventually, the very existence of Constantinople itself might have been attributed by the eastern church hierarchy to the aid of "the Lord, mighty in battle" and his approval of Islam's strict iconoclasm. Misogyny, a concept very much of our moment has been suggested. Evidently, female monks were disproportionally attached to images. Another theory, attractive to Marxist historians, is that class exerted an influence. The Byzantine Empire's non-Greek peoples from the east, so the argument goes, had their time and money exhausted in defending their eastern borders from attacks by their Arab neighbours; wealthier and more-leisured Greeks in Constantinople, the Balkans, and the Italian provinces were in a privileged position from which to indulge the niceties of their religious practices.

The unified church of Christendom was developing structural cracks.

1. KJV. Exodus 20:4.

This Church had been considered to be *societas perfecta*: one body, undivided. With seemingly unconscious irony, this idea is still chorused in protestant churches today as we sing the nineteenth-century hymn, "Onward Christian Soldiers," adopted by the Salvation Army as a processional accompaniment. The tune, again somewhat ironically, was composed by Arthur Sullivan who collaborated with W. S. Gilbert to present the famous comic operas. The third verse of the hymn boasts:

We are not divided
All one body we
One in hope and doctrine
One in charity.

Up until 1054 when The Great Schism took place, this was largely the case. From this tragic event onward matters deteriorated. The Iconoclastic legacy was that of enduring factionalism within the worldwide church. The Patriarch of Constantinople, Ignatius, was exiled in 858 and replaced by a high-ranking layman, Photius, who was rapidly ordained. Pope Nicholas resented what he regarded as his territorial integrity being threatened when the Southern Balkans adopted Greek practices and he refused to recognise the political appointment of Photius. This gave rise to Constantinople's counter accusation of heresy as Rome had independently added the *Filioque* to the creed. This doctrine states that The Holy Spirit proceeds from the Father *and* the Son, not from the Father alone. Difficult although it is for us to imagine today, historians tell us that this was a topic hotly debated by the common people in the market places of Constantinople at the time and not just by esoterical theologians. A reconciliation of convenience took place in 877 as Rome required military support against the Muslim armies in Sicily and southern Italy. Photius accepted Rome as *primus inter pares* and the Greek influence amongst the Bulgars was allowed to continue. The fundamental issue seems to have been whether the church as a whole should accept the conciliar government favoured by Constantinople or the monarchical approach of Rome.

The Great Schism took place in 1054 when the patriarch of Constantinople, Michael Cerularius, closed Latin churches in the city in response to pope Leo in Rome imposing the Latin rite on the Greeks of southern Italy who took their authority from Constantinople. Cardinal Hubert visited Constantinople from Italy on a mission that was poorly received. He left a papal bull of excommunication on the high altar of *Hagia Sofia* citing the threefold heresy of the greek doctrine on the procession of the Holy Spirit being solely from the Father; the marriage of greek priests; and the use of leavened bread for the Eucharist. Pope Leo was duly excommunicated in return. It was not the mutual excommunication itself that was unique, sadly, this had happened before, it was its enduring quality. [2]

The Fourth Crusade of 1204 was the event that finally closed the door to reconciliation. In 2001, Pope John Paul II addressed Christodoulos the archbishop of Athens:

> It is tragic that the assailants who had set out to secure free access for Christians to the Holy Land, turned against their own brothers in the faith. The fact that they were Latin Christians fills Catholics with deep regret. How can we fail to see here the *mysterium iniquitatis* at work in the human heart?

The terrible events of the carnage and desecration of *Hagia Sophia* are matters of long-standing historical record. The division between the eastern and western Church was firmly entrenched from that tragic time.

2. This mutual excommunication was not revoked until 1965.

PART ONE

Giotto's Passion Frescoes in The Scrovegni Chapel.

I SHALL USE STAGE directions when writing about the paintings: left and right are from the characters' perspectives; upstage is to the back of the painting and downstage to the front. This seems entirely appropriate to me as from Cavallini and Giotto onwards painting has tended to present dramatic situations that engage the viewer imaginatively in the manner of stage presentations.

Approaching the Scrovegni Chapel,[1] one is in no way prepared for the splendour of the interior. The simple brick building is itself unremarkable. It is a barrel-vaulted rectangular room the size of which is not imposing. As White observes, both inside and outside one is struck by the simplicity of the structure. There is practically no internal architectural decoration. It is as if it has been designed by a painter, perhaps Giotto himself, to provide "no competition from the building."[2] Upon this "canvas" Giotto employs: "Competent realism, strictly limited depth, and absolute subordination to the needs of the narrative scenes."[3] The "strictly limited depth" is a crucial point here. The two *coretti* either side of the chancel arch clearly demonstrate Giotto's competence in three-dimensional representation. Had he chosen to use this competence when painting the frescoes, the undermining of the integrity of the wall's surface would have seriously disturbed the overall harmony of the interior. Whether or not Giotto was the architect as

1. NB. The Scrovegni Chapet is built on the site of a Roman arena. The land was owned by the Scrovegni family and it was their private chapel. It is referred to as The Arena Chapel and also the Scrovegni Chapel interchangeably.

2. White. *Art and Architecture in Italy*, 311.

3. Ibid.

well as the decorator of the Chapel, the use of space is remarkably harmonious. As Harrison writes:

> The sense of overall spatial integration is furthered by the even tenor of colouring maintained throughout the individual scenes, and by the consistent scale adopted for the foreground figures."[4]

The intense blue of the arched roof is a powerful integrating factor: the unity with the blue of the sky in the individual frescoes encloses the space to create a sense of entering a discrete and potent world. Approaching the altar from the West door, one is embraced by the ambience of color and tranquillity before the eyes focus on specific images.

4. Harrison. *The Arena Chapel*, 99.

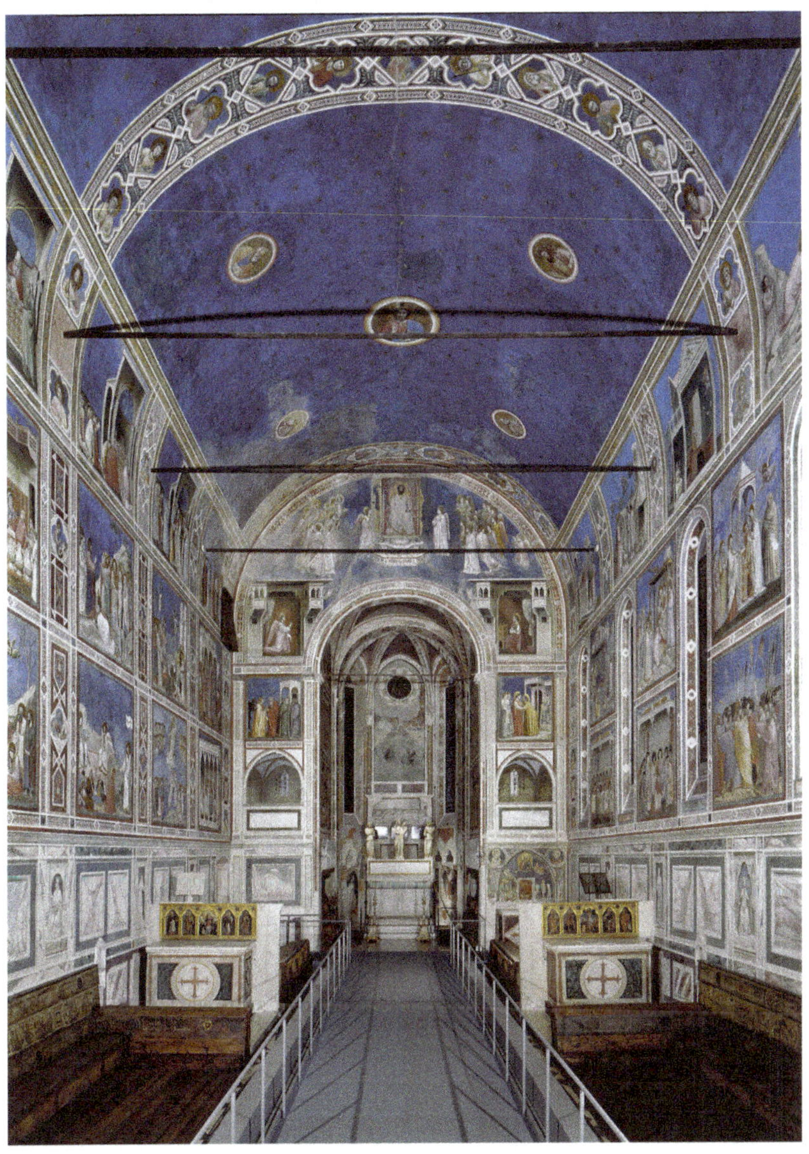

Fig. 01 Approaching the chapel from the west door.
By courtesy of the Municipality of Padua-Department of Culture.

One is immediately aware of "the solemn hush and the implicit reverence"[5] of which Offner writes. It draws one in and predisposes the senses to an act of worship. The worshippers' eyes would first have focused on Giotto's magnificent crucifix which was suspended over the nave and is now in the adjacent *Museo Civico*.

5. Offner. "Giotto, non-Giotto," 96—113.

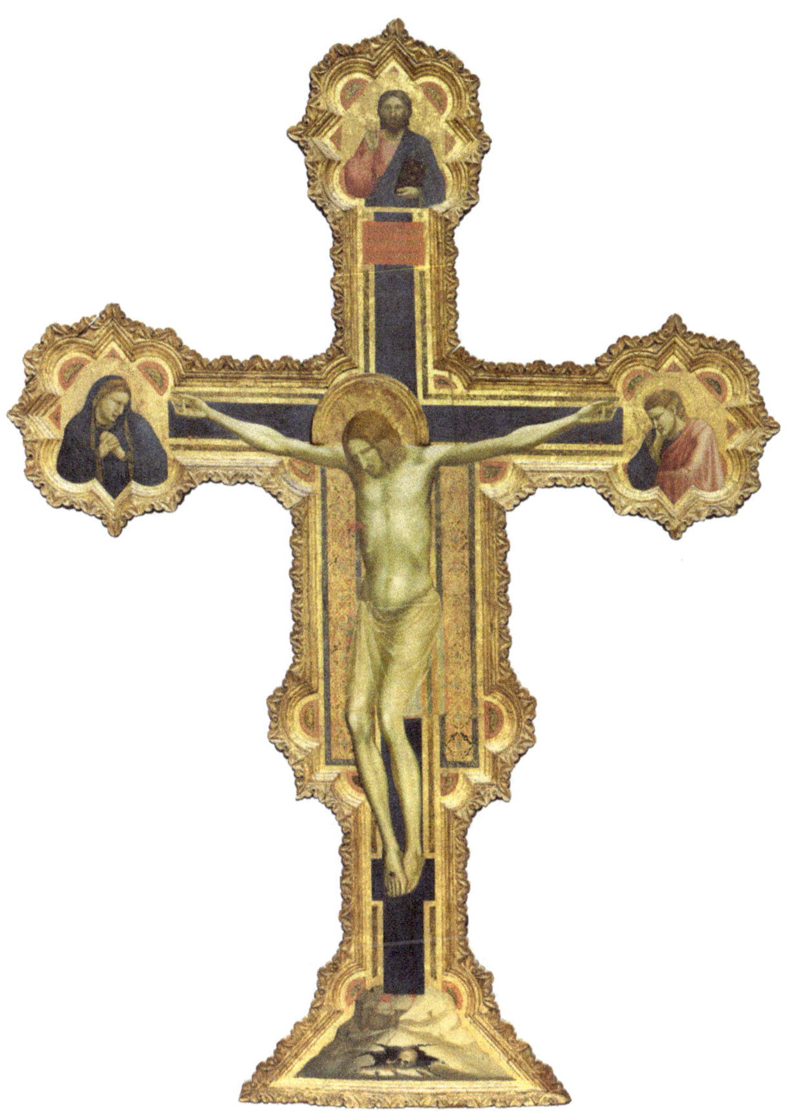

Fig. 02 Crucifix.
By courtesy of the Municipality of Padua-Department of Culture.

The gaze is moved aloft to where the eyes focus on the image of God the Father dispatching the angel Gabriel to initiate his salvific mission. The juxtaposition of these two images would have charged the space with spiritual energy for the devout as right there, at the top of the chancel arch—"the liturgical centre of the chapel"[6]— is the image of the compelling event which underpins the claims for the possibility of the infinite being conveyed in the finite world: the Incarnation. The Annunciation with which the site had long been associated spans the space between the top of the chancel arch as Gabriel kneeling to the left greets Mary who kneels to the right. This introduces the viewer/worshipper to the great overriding theme which dominates the individual representations of the Frescoes: God's redemptive purpose as expounded by the scriptures canonical and apocryphal heard from the pulpit of the Chapel. Gary Radke writes of Giotto's splayed construction rupturing the plane behind which all the rest of the divine narratives seem to take place. He sees this as paralleling the manner in which, at the Incarnation, the Divine breaks through the veil separating our finite world from the Eternal.[7] As Derbes and Sandona point out, the fact that the "innocent eye" is lost to us is not necessarily a matter of regret.[8] The creative response of an earlier viewer might well be an inspiration to consider alongside that of the artist.

But what of the individual illustrations on the north and south walls of the chapel: are they no more than illustrations of narratives to which the priest might draw the attention whilst expounding the scriptures? Might they be considered to have a theological force of their own with which the viewer might become engaged? Looking particularly at the Passion frescoes, I suggest that there is more available than illustration. Perhaps what we witness in the Scrovegni Chapel is part of that process "from historical truth to the *heart* of present-day man"[9] of which Barth writes when discussing Lessing. Lessing himself writes of moving from gross to net with the whole edifice of Christian religion as the gross from which the net of Christ himself[10] may be distilled. Giotto, it might be argued, presents some of that distillation on the walls of the Chapel. Dixon takes a postmodern stance suggesting that the analysis of a work of art is:

6. Derbes. *The Cambridge* Companion, 198.
7. Radke, "Giotto and Architecture," 76–102.
8. Derbes. Ibid., 97.
9. Barth. *Protestant Theology*, 254 original emphasis.
10. Ibid., 255.

> . . . a reciprocation, dialogue, discourse, intercourse where the self, or all the participant selves, and the work of art are mutually defined.[11]

But before the participation of the viewer is possible there are two necessary preconditions: the act of contemplation and the acceptance of the proposition that the inspiration claimed for purveyors of the word is also available to purveyors of images. The first of these—contemplation—requires time and a conducive atmosphere. These are difficult to find in current western culture both secular and religious where time is somewhat ironically regarded as precious, which commonly means of monetary value—"time is money!"—and church doors are commonly locked for "down time."[12] It is, I suggest, only by withdrawing from the world of *bisynesse* in an act of contemplation that we may fully respond to that which the frescoes have to offer. The prevalence of frescoes on monastery and convent walls and particularly in the cells of monks and nuns suggests that this practice recommended itself to the devout. Without this time to contemplate, the Chapel is reduced to an art gallery and the frescoes to art objects. Impressive as they are in such a context, they are not fulfilling their intended function as permanent presences in sacred space. It seems to me that only under such conditions is their proper role capable of being fulfilled. Under these circumstances, it is possible to argue that there is a coherence at work in the imagery of the Scrovegni Chapel Passion Frescoes just as it is to argue that there is in the words and imagery of the Fourth Gospel Passion Narrative. Here, in short, is another way of approaching or understanding the person of Jesus.

Perspectives regarding the position of Giotto in art history have changed considerably. Boccaccio writing midway through the fourteenth century is effusive regarding Giotto's truth to nature:

> Giotto, was so extraordinary a genius, that there was nothing Nature, the mother of all things, displays to us by the eternal revolution of the heavens, that he could not recreate with pencil, pen or brush so faithfully, that it hardly seemed a copy, but rather the thing itself.[13].

11. Dixon. "Painting as Theological Thought."

12. Visits to the Scrovegni Chapel are now limited to fifteen minutes for environmental reasons. I was granted a pass which allowed me to stay for two-hours a day for one week.

13. Hagiioannu. "Giotto's Bardi Chapel," 28–47.

However, Maginnis reminds us that praise in such terms was derived from the Ancients:

> Astonishing naturalism . . . was the highest praise writers of antiquity had to offer . . . the elevation of naturalism was not a report on fact, but a propagandistic device.[14].

Offner,[15] in 1939, turned the focus to narration that, for him, predominates over verisimilitude.[16] However, it appears that until quite recently the Paduan frescoes themselves excited little critical response with critics from Vasari to Ruskin paying them scant attention. "The Arena Chapel," states Maginnis, "is, fundamentally, an early twentieth-century discovery made possible by the dethronement of *mimesis* which was led by Picasso,"[17] allowing us to see what is there rather than obscuring it with preconceptions. White suggests that it was late thirteenth-century sculpture that would have had a major influence upon Giotto and in particular the work of Nicola and Giovanni Pisano and Arnolfo di Cambio. As Viladesau points out, such an influence is highly probable as for a long time in the West sculpture was the major visual art. It was also able to develop relatively independently as "religious sculpture was not a major part of the Byzantine iconic tradition."[18] The presence in the Chapel of Giovanni's *Virgin and Child* and two candle-holding angels argues for Giotto's intimacy with contemporary sculpture. Giotto is likely to have seen Giovanni Pisano's pulpits at Pistoia and Pisa. Kenneth Clarke refers to Giovanni as "one of the great tragic dramatists of sculpture,"[19] and maybe it was this dramatic quality that moved and inspired Giotto. The emotional expression of Giovanni's work so powerfully communicated inspired another artist working in the same medium more than six hundred years later. In the introduction to *Giovanni Pisano*, Henry Moore sees the energy of Giovanni's figures being expressed as an inner state of being rather than in external action.

> He used the body to express his deep philosophical understanding of human nature [and] human tragedy.[20]

14. Maginnis. *Painting in the Age of Giotto*, 202.
15. Offner, *Ibid.*, 96–113.
16. Maginnis. Ibid., 85.
17. Ibid. 86.
18. Viladesau. *The Beauty of the Cross*, 143.
19. Clark. *Civilisation*, 85.
20. Moore in Ayrton. *Giovanni Pisano*, intro.

It is this understanding and sense of empathy with the human condition that one responds to in Giotto's Scrovegni Chapel Frescoes. Giotto is always on our side as confused, struggling human beings; he never preaches as one with superior insight. Those who communicate their insight verbally often find it difficult to avoid giving the impression of somehow being set apart. Giotto's theology does not wag the finger, rather it holds the hand. But it was not only the visual language of this sculptural work with the greater naturalism of the forms and dramatic narrative that would have excited Giotto.

White suggests that as sculpture became increasingly independent of architecture, it was representative of

> a transition from the world of the medieval craftsman to that of the self-conscious modern artist.[21]

To the craftsman's skill in using tools to manipulate his material has been added the emotion of the man who conceived the idea. Giotto, White implies, continued to build upon the achievements of the sculptors of the half-century preceding him. The *zeitgeist* was clearly conducive to artistic depiction of human emotion in the world of everyday experience. Within this context Giotto demonstrated

> extraordinary ability to find a formal counterpart in terms of paint and colour for the intangibles of spiritual and psychological states whether by conscious planning or by intuitive means.[22]

Just as the Tuscan vernacular was dignified by the thirteenth-century poets to become the national language so Giotto's ability to reveal what was beneath the surface of his human subjects took painting in a new direction giving it a dignity that elevated it to the heights previously exclusively occupied by poetry. Prior to Giotto, the serious criticism that poetry attracted was not directed towards painting. Writing towards the end of the fourteenth-century, Fillipo Villani states:

> He showed himself so far a rival of poetry that keen judges consider he painted what most poets represent in words.[23]

Such thinking suggests that the work of Giotto invited a response appropriate to an artist rather than an artisan or mere producer of illustrations

21. White. John, *Art and Architecture*, 76.
22. Ibid., 315.
23. Villani. Cited Harrison ibid., 101.

of religious texts. Here was work that appeared to be vehicles for religious emotions and concepts. One becomes aware of being absorbed into a timeless purposefulness. Everyday experience and the religious experience merge. Painting has become "*a cognitive practice.*"[24] It appears that Giotto was in Rome in the 1290's where he is likely to have seen Pietro Cavallini's mosaics depicting scenes from the life of Mary in Santa Maria at Trastevere. Here, Cavallini attempts to represent figures in space and perhaps this would have suggested the limitations of the mosaic technique in dealing with the complexities that challenged the newly emerging artists. Cavallini himself moves away from mosaic to fresco. Bellosi points out that in Byzantine art "the only true reality was considered to be that of the spiritual world."[25] By contrast, there seems to be a validation of sense experience in the Scrovegni frescoes: a recognition that we live in a *real* world. Bellosi continues to suggest that "the coherent conception of space"[26] in Giotto's frescoes enhances this sense of reality and it was seen as something innovative. Paul Hills[27] suggests that one of Giotto's innovations was in depicting the direction of light as uniform to the painting as a whole rather than specific to objects or persons depicted within the painting. So there is an interesting overlap here. Giotto shows the light within the frescoes falling from the window in the west wall as it naturally does. This, as Hills observes, creates an illusion of space that invites the viewer to respond to the figures contextually. That is, they are seen as responding to one another in a dramatic presentation. Malroux identifies a sense of theatre rather than an obsession with naturalism in the Scrovegni frescoes. He makes reference to a movement of great significance in contextualizing Giotto's work:

> The gradual transmutation of communal worship into private worship, and of the liturgical drama into the mystery play.[28]

A papal edict of 1210 forbade the clergy to act on a public stage and the responsibility of writing and performing what were devotional aids was gradually assumed by the laity. What were liturgical embellishments such as the tenth-century *Quem Quaeritis* and distant representations of biblical

24. Harrison. Ibid.,102, original emphasis.

25. Bellosi. Cited, Viladesau, ibid.,142.

26. Ibid.

27. Hills. Cited, Harrison, ibid.,100.

28. Malraux. *The Metamorphosis of the* Gods, 335/6.

events began to develop into something more robustly connected to the mundane world outside the church door. In this atmosphere, it seems likely that the individual members of the congregation whilst engaging in acts of common worship began to develop religious mental landscapes of their own and a sense of personal responsibility for their spiritual condition. The papal bull granting indulgences for visitors to the Arena Chapel[29] supports this impression. In the bull the faithful are reminded that they should "visit in the spirit of humility" and also that they visit as part of "the universal community of the faithful."[30] Thus they were engaging in both a personal act and one that expressed solidarity with the community both local and worldwide. These developments would, perhaps, suggest more mundane imagery than a celibate church hierarchy contemplated as devotional aids. From the middle of the thirteenth century books of hours were available to the aristocracy but fresco painting on the surface of the church walls has a universal appeal and it is accessible to all. Reflection upon the immanent rather than the transcendental nature of God is, no doubt, what Cennini has in mind when he writes in 1390 that Giotto "translated painting from Greek into Latin."[31] The subject matter of the Passion Narrative depicted by Giotto, as Hegel tells us, is not capable of being represented by

> the classical plastic ideal . . . Christ scourged, with the crown of thorns, carrying his cross to the place of execution, nailed to the cross, passing away in the agony of a torturing and slow death–this cannot be portrayed in the forms of Greek beauty.[32]

It is interesting to note that some 700 years before Giotto, Gregory the Great, writing to the Bishop of Marseilles, appears to applaud what Giotto was to do.

> To adore a picture is one thing, but to learn through the story of a picture what is to be adored is another. For what writing presents to readers, this a picture presents to the unlearned . . . in it the illiterate read.[33]

Perhaps we would go a little further today when referring to the Paduan frescoes to bring both the learned along with the unlearned into

29. March,1304.
30. Cited Stubblebine, 105.
31. Cited, Malraux. Ibid., 341.
32. Hegel. Excerpt in Thiessen, ibid., 195.
33. Cited, Thiessen, Gesa Elsbeth, (ed.), *op. cit.*, p. 47.

the frescoes' ambit. As Viladesau reminds us when writing on Giotto's *Crucifixion* in Padua, the faces and attitudes of the characters, "allow the viewer not only to recall the narrative but to enter into the psychological action."[34] The sense of ones own dignity as a human being is something of great comfort that might be taken from or "read" in the frescoes as one is brought face to face with the fact that puzzles the mind—the Incarnation. It is God himself walking among us as a human being. I think that this is fundamental to Giotto's innovation and whilst Anne Derbes and Mark Sandona may well be correct in assuming "a complex range of responses"[35] to the frescoes, the suggestion that the capacity to respond to "the fullness of (their) meanings"[36] was only given to "the educated elite"[37] seems to require restating. The educated elite may have the advantage, if it is thought to be such, of being able to articulate their response, but that is not quite the same thing. It is arguably the case that "the fullness of (their) meanings" might well be missed by the complexities of the educated elite.

Dixon suggests that "only Paul and Augustine among the verbal Theologians so dominate history as did Giotto."[38] He sees Giotto as introducing personality into the human/religious drama that he depicts on the walls of the Srovegni Chapel.[39] Giotto, shaped by his time as he inevitably was, "spoke" to those who participated in his frescoes with a new voice. It was a voice that told of the necessity of human involvement in the Divine Plan. Malraux sums matters up succinctly:

> If Giotto did not 'invent painting' as Vasari thought, he invented a certain kind of painting; and though the mastery of illusion was not his *raison d'etre*, its evolution, up to the end of the Baroque era, marched side by side with that of the mastery of illusion.[40]

Throughout the fifteen frescoes under consideration there is a unifying sense of the *otherness* of Jesus. Those close to him and also casual bystanders are invariably puzzled by what they are witnessing. "Who is this man?" appears to be the unspoken question. Frequently, there is a palpable

34. Viladesau. Ibid.,140.
35. Derbes, and Sandona in *The Cambridge Companion,*197–220.
36. Ibid., 220.
37. Ibid.
38. Dixon. "Painting as Theological Thought."
39. Dixon. Ibid.
40. Malraux. Ibid., 340.

tension sensed from Giotto's depictions. Jesus is a disturbing presence and this appears to be a deeply felt experience of the artist conveyed by the empathy with which he depicts the confusion in the responses of his characters. Something clearly has to be surrendered if the tension is to be released and Mary and Martha in *The Raising of Lazarus* demonstrate this as they kneel at the feet of Jesus in worship.

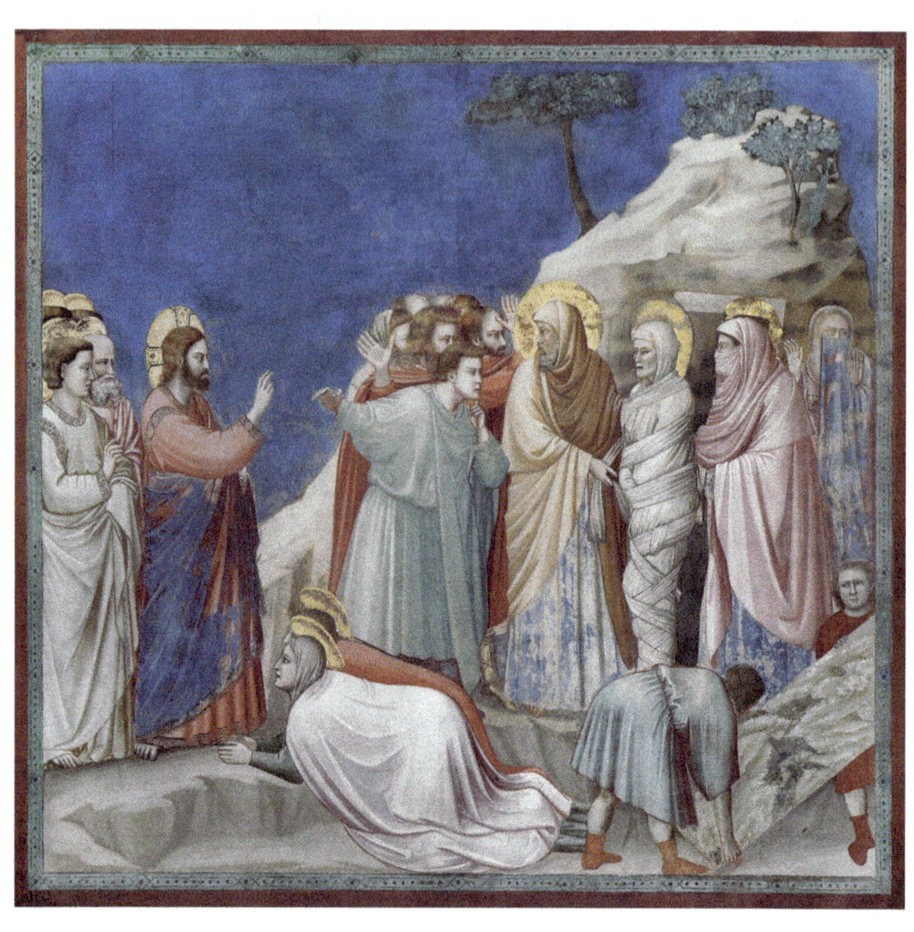

Fig. 03 Raising of Lazarus.
By courtesy of the Municipality of Padua-Department of Culture.

When participating in—as opposed to merely watching—any drama, we have to suspend our disbelief in the improbable presentation of events presented simultaneously that took place in different historical time, so here. All around Mary and Martha there is confusion. The disciples stare in wonder and mystification. The people surrounding Lazarus are in some agitation with the figure in the centre of the picture, one hand to his chin and the other pointing towards Jesus seeming to be questioning the meaning of what is taking place and the manner of man who has brought it about. The two young lads downstage-left[41] have a man's job to do. As they move the heavy marble slab from the entrance to the tomb, they appear completely absorbed in the practicalities of the occasion and pay no attention to its significance. The figure of Jesus is the calm central presence although effectively calm*ing* only for Mary and Martha. This point is emphasized by the fact that Jesus is isolated in the composition of the fresco by being presented against the blue background of the sky whilst the central, agitated group is framed by the triangular rocky background. The rock divides the picture in two diagonally. Mary and Martha fall at the feet of Jesus and worship he whom Martha has earlier confessed "the Son of God, the one coming into the world."[42] They are the knowing ones, possessors of holy wisdom. Viewed from the believer's perspective, they are the ones who respond appropriately. They are, in that moment of adoration, isolated from the stench of death to which masked women react. They are unaware of the confusion of the group surrounding Lazarus, the mystification of the disciples, and the backbreaking labour of the two boys. They are in another world. This iconic experience of other otherworldliness is experienced by characters within the drama portrayed on the walls and therefore recommended to the viewer/worshipper as an appropriate response for them also. Giotto appears to be predominately concerned with the impact of Christ's presence and action on the characters within the narrative. These characters are marked out by gesture rather than being rendered as three-dimensional beings who impose their physical presence on the viewer. The realism of the work lies in the representation of human emotion rather than in naturalism of figure drawing. There is little sense of body beneath outer garment. Mary and Martha are shapes rather than figures as is the bent back of the boy to their stage-left. The presentation of Lazarus is of great interest. He is not, as one might expect, the focus of attention. The two recently-bereaved and

41. See opening paragraph to Part One.

42. KJV John 11: 27.

grieving sisters have turned their backs to him. Were it not for his opened eyes, there is nothing to indicate that he is alive. The grave cloths enhance the sense of an object rather than a sentient creature. His presence in the construction has the effect of a dramatic device, a catalyst rather than a participating presence. The man, Lazarus, will die again. His resurrection is of itself rather pointless. *The* Resurrection to which it points is the significant moment. This is quite literally underlined by the fact that *The Resurrection* fresco is directly beneath *The Raising of Lazarus* on the north wall of the chapel. It is, then, what it tells us about Jesus that is of significance and Mary and Martha fall to their knees in recognition of this. We are, then, presented with the human world of process and change. This earthbound world of mutability which is symbolized by the rocky frame is invaded by the eternal and permanent, symbolized by the background of sky, to which only Mary and Martha know how to respond. There is a sense of unease as if the characters are out of their comfort zones. We can perhaps more easily identify with the rock-framed group being ourselves more at ease with the familiar rather than the challenge of the extraordinary. The two boys moving the heavy weight make what is perhaps the most telling human comment as they escape the need to respond by "burying" themselves in hard physical work.

The centrality of Jesus in the frescoes and his separateness is noteworthy. He is

> the formal centre of gravity . . . mediator of revelation, the representative of the supranatural idea, who gives a depth-content (gehalt).[43]

A viewer may well sense a didactic purpose relating to the governing theme mentioned earlier—God's redemptive purpose in the Incarnation—and conveyed by the central image above the chancel arch. God incarnate must needs be separate even as he walks among us and that agonizing mystery is very movingly conveyed in *Noli Me Tangere*.

43. Tillich. "One Moment of Beauty," 59.

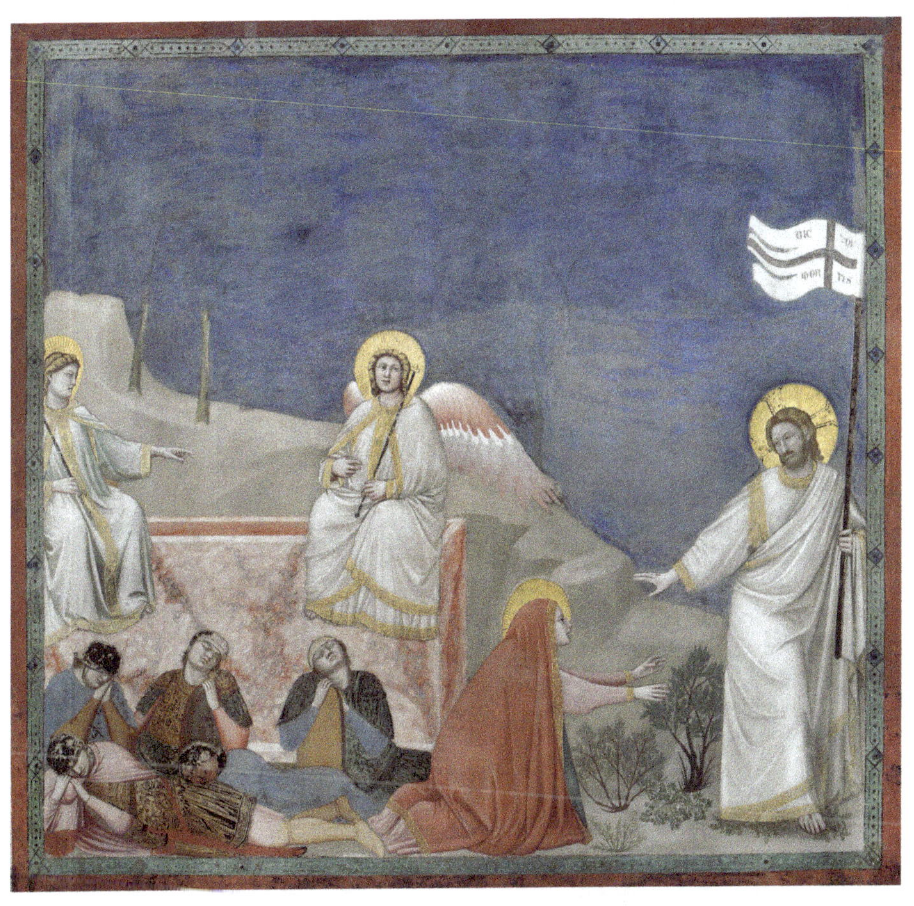

Fig. 04 *Noli Me Tangere.*
By courtesy of the Municipality of Padua-Department of Culture.

The relationship between the kneeling Mary Magdalene and the risen Christ is very powerfully rendered. Earlier, I referred to the suggestion of White that contemporary sculpture was an influence in the formulation of Giotto's ideas.[44] The depiction of *The Thirsting Woman* by Arnolfo di Cambio compares with the depiction of Mary in Giotto's fresco in a way that makes White's point compelling.

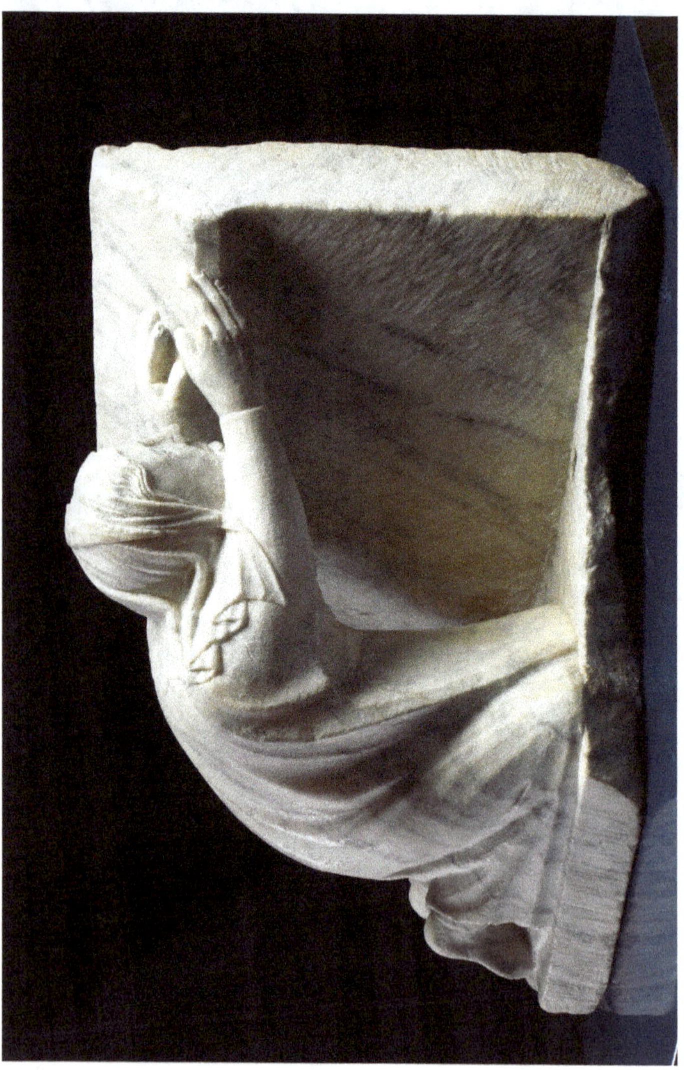

Fig. 05. Arnolfo di Cambio. Thirsting Woman.

44. See notes 18.

The attitude of profound human thirst for water in Arnolfo di Cambio's sculpture becomes in Giotto's fresco the attitude of spiritual thirst for living water of which Jesus speaks in the Fourth Gospel.[45] Mary appears to have her weight forward almost off balance as if her outstretched hands have missed their grasp. The palms are downward not outstretched in entreaty. Claudio Bellinati remarks:

> Some observers believed that the stretching out of arms in the 'Noli me Tangere' was rooted in the beautiful sacred plays which the Middle Ages offered in such refined feeling and depth of devotion.[46]

This gesture of a grasp beyond the reach is certainly a very poignant depiction of the human condition as represented by Mary on the day of the Resurrection. The outstretched hand and the compassionate face of Jesus demonstrate infinite sympathy for Mary's sense of infinite loss. The predicament of someone bereaved discovering their loved one is alive only to be told that reunion is not possible is difficult to comprehend in words but Giotto does so visually and very movingly. One recalls Martha's response in the Fourth Gospel when told by Jesus that Lazarus, her brother, will rise again. She dismisses what she takes as a reference to the Parousia as small comfort. It is a very human moment that demonstrates the gulf that there often is between faith in a spiritual dimension and the warmth and comfort of a bodily presence.[47] This gulf is given pictorial representation here: Mary is trying to grasp the fact that the man she has come to adore is no more an earthly presence and, until the comfort offered at Pentecost, she is entirely bereft. Jesus who has lived as a man empathizes with Mary and this empathy is conveyed by his expression. Such a representation of the departing Jesus "speaks" very eloquently to the viewer contemplating the mystery of the Incarnation. As Monsignor Bellinati suggests, the viewer is involved in a kind of "choral participation" with the "perennial humanity" of the scene.[48] In another human touch the soldiers sleep soundly with lolling heads and collapsed bodies. The miraculous moment passes them by. They are not condemned. They are simply tired. One is reminded of Richard Offner's observation regarding the frescoes in general:

45. KJV John IV 10.
46. Bellinati in Deganello. *Giotto*, 7.
47. John 11: 24.
48. Bellinati. Ibid., p.7.

> Nowhere is human frailty so frankly postulated and so graciously condoned, and nowhere the doctrine of brotherly love so nobly affirmed.[49]

Perhaps a sense of coherence may be further demonstrated by reference to three other frescoes: *Christ Before Caiphas*, *The Scourging of Christ*, and *The Ascent to Calvary*.

49. Offner. Ibid., 261.

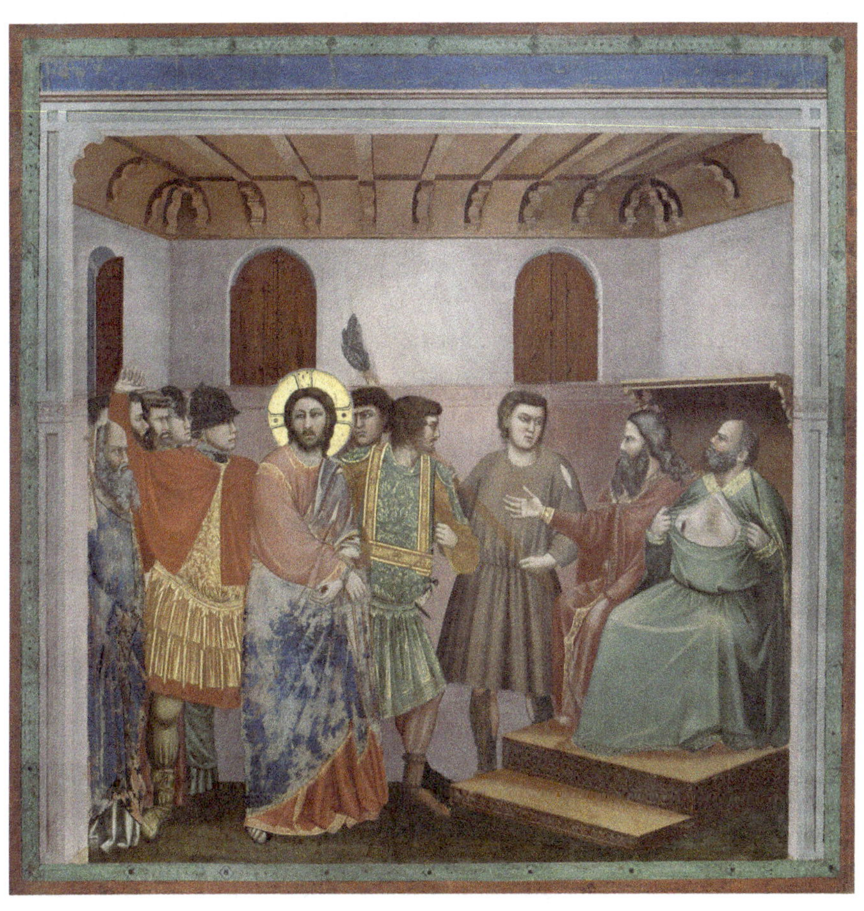

Fig. 06 Christ before Caiphas.
By courtesy of the Municipality of Padua-Department of Culture.

In *Christ Before Caiphas*, Giotto sets the figure of Christ slightly forward of the action taking place behind him. He is thus placed with bound hands, in isolation, downstage-centre. Giotto draws our attention to the commotion caused by this quiet "impotent" figure. Caiphas rends his garments in pantomimed horror, his jutting chin and arrogant expression displaying a truculent resentment at this upstart rather than genuine horror. The effect is that of a rude gesture rather than spiritual outrage. The priest at the side of Caiphas is issuing instructions to the soldier to the stage-left of Jesus. The young soldier to the stage-right of Jesus seeks to curry favour by raising his right hand to slap the face of Jesus. Nobody is impressed by what, in the circumstances, is a pathetic and cowardly act. The lookers-on to the stage-right of the picture stare bovinely as the drama unfolds. This drama is being directed, paradoxically, by the character least actively involved, Jesus. He stares out beyond the viewer of the fresco to a place beyond our understanding. The composure of Christ's face is remarkable and the interpretation of Bruce Cole is difficult to understand: "the human part of His nature faces the coming martyrdom with fear."[50] The juxtaposed face of the soldier partly obscured by Christ's halo and surely intended as a point of contrast *is* clearly worried and confused. Jesus is not engaged with the events within the box-like enclosure. There is a sense of pent-up energy ready to burst out but not in any violent way. This is the paradox that causes the confusion and commotion. Violence they can handle. The characters are nonplussed: they have encountered nothing like it. They are not equipped to deal with it and it infuriates them. It is Christ's submissive gaze that dominates the picture and disturbs the viewer both within the fresco and outside of it as the humility of Jesus disturbs Peter in The *Washing of Feet.*

In *The Scourging of Christ* Jesus, now handed over to the Roman authority, is surrendered to a bunch of thugs eager for their task.

50. Cole. *The Scrovegni Chapel*, 100.

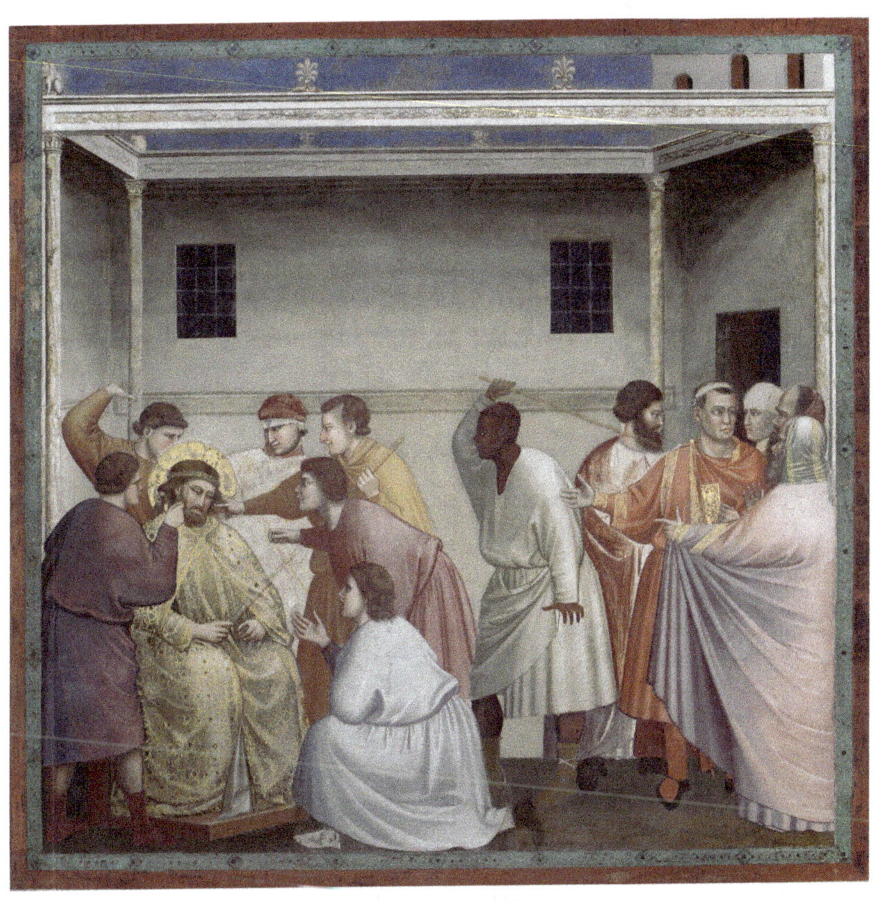

Fig. 07 Scourging of Christ.
By courtesy of the Municipality of Padua-Department of Culture.

Although in the Gospel accounts these are soldiers, Giotto reduces them to something less dignified. The contrast between the braggadocio of Caiphas in the previous Fresco and the troubled countenance of Pilate as he appears to be appealing to the priests is noteworthy. It is as if he is suggesting that they leave it at that, but the priests are not to be swayed. The scourging itself, in particular the mockery, is what Giotto concentrates upon. The black figure highlighted by his white garment almost touches Pilate with the backward swing of his cane. It is as if he is demonstrating like a lecturer with a pointer that this vacillation of Pilate, results in this mob rule. The black figure is of particular interest and in danger of misconstruction by modern viewers. Professor G K Hunter points out that it would be a mistake to bring our own modern sensibilities about 'color' to a depiction of this period. The color black and its association with evil and death[51] does not derive from animosity towards the ethnically dark-skinned races: it is traditionally to be found in the culture of these races as well as that of lighter-skinned races.

> The most celebrated picture in which this tradition appears is *The Scourging* by Giotto in the Arena Chapel in Padua. In this the negro (sic.) scourger stands alone brandishing his rod above the head of Christ. Among the many monographs devoted to Giotto no one seems to have pointed to the tradition with which I am here concerned.[52]

Thus, in Giotto's fresco, the figure of evil bridges with his rod the space between the ugly mob and the authority. It is like a lightning rod connecting the indecision of Pilate and the sophistry of the priests directly to the ugly brutality of the mob. As a matter of fact the black figure, in human terms, is quite a handsome fellow, certainly in comparison with the gargoyles tormenting Christ. The ugliness of sin is written upon human faces. Jesus is robed in mock regal garments with a "sceptre" of mock authority. His beard is tweaked from either side as his tormentors stare into his eyes looking, no doubt, for the sign of fear that will satisfy their cruelty. It is not to be as the inward focus of Jesus's eyes remains, as in the previous fresco, on a greater reality that, as it is beyond the understanding of the ignorant mob, places

51. Cf. description of "the Evil Forest" in chapter 10 of Achebe's *Things Fall Apart*.

52. Hunter. *Dramatic Identities*, 37. The point is relevant, of course, to the blackness of the devil in *The Pact With Judas*.

Jesus beyond their grasp. This is surely not a "slumped and unconscious"[53] figure. The composition of this fresco is remarkable. White observes:

> (The group does not) congeal into a solid entity, a sort of complex single figure, (it is) a gathering of physically separate but dramatically connected individuals.[54]

This effect is enhanced by the use of colour with Jesus and Pilate picked out in gold and red as the contrasting representations of power and glory. The startlingly white-robed black figure is the fulcrum of the construction. Jesus is isolated in his submissive role with such dignity that, once more, one is, if not sympathetic to the tormenters, at least deeply embarrassed for them.

53. Cole. Ibid., 102.

54. White. Ibid., 327.

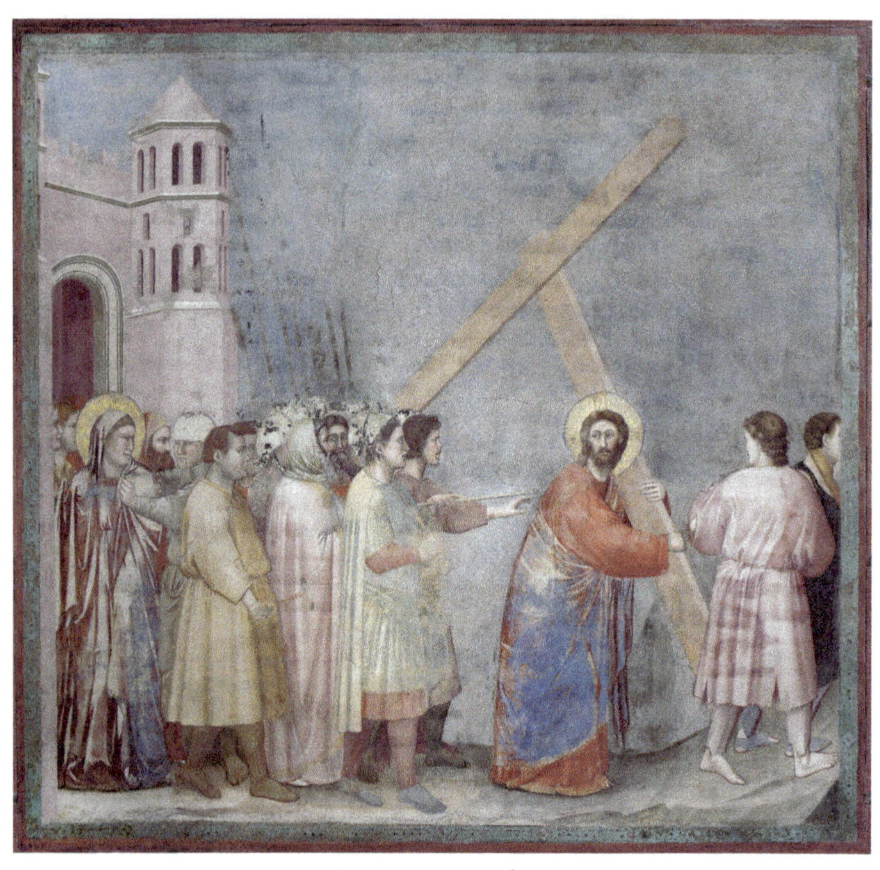

Fig. 08 Ascent to Calvary.

By courtesy of the Municipality of Padua-Department of Culture.

The gates of Jerusalem at Jesus's back in *The Ascent to Calvary* mark the sharp contrast with the *Entry to Jerusalem* where Jesus moves towards those same gates amidst gestures of acclamation. Here he is being goaded forward like an animal to slaughter carrying his own cross as we are told in the fourth Gospel. The same serene face that appears in *Christ before Caiphas* looks out over the shoulder of the viewer to a place beyond as if oblivious of the brutality that threatens him. As one of the soldiers rudely manhandles a grieving Mary, the followers are portrayed by Giotto as men who "know not what they do."[55] One of the figures leading the way half turns to Jesus as if to contemplate the face of a man about to die. One can only imagine his confusion at what he actually sees. The fresco is badly deteriorated but there may be discerned what was once a "forest" of spears in the background similar to that seen in *The Betrayal*. Thus, once more, we are presented with images of earthly power contrasting with what appears to be impotence willingly embraced. The word "embraced" is difficult to avoid when one looks at the way Giotto shows Jesus holding the cross. There is certainly no attempt to depict a tortured body straining under an intolerable burden as, for example, in Tiepolo's eighteenth-century version. There is a spirituality about the figure all the more effective by being isolated in the midst of figures from the very familiar "here and now" world of the viewer's experience. In these three frescoes, the position of Jesus is made all the more poignant by the fact that the disciples have deserted their master. Only in the last of the three, *The Ascent to Calvary*, does Mary the mother of Jesus appear at a sorrowing distance to the stage-right of the fresco. In *The Crucifixion* and *The Lamentation* it is the women who are prominent in the fullness of their grief, the apostles returning to prominence to witness the Ascension and to receive the Holy Spirit at Pentecost.

55. KJV. Luke 23:34.

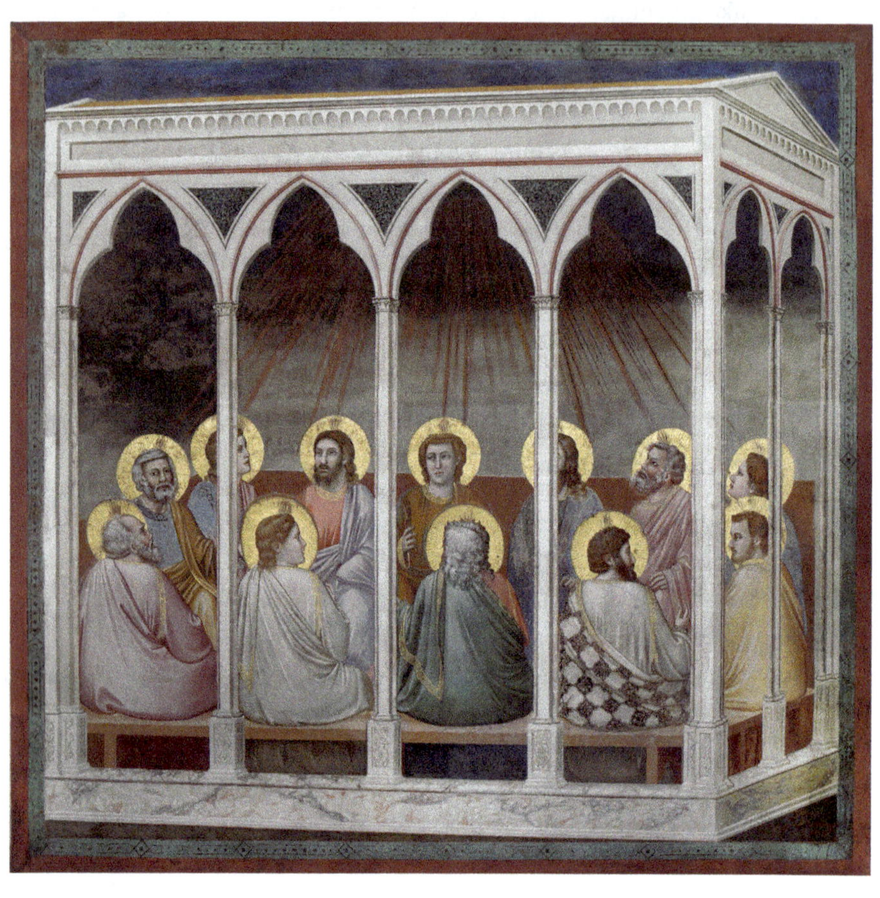

Fig. 09 Pentecost.
By courtesy of the Municipality of Padua-Department of Culture

In the final fresco of the cycle, *Pentecost*, the apostles are presented as a rather subdued group. One is somewhat surprised by the absence of expressions of ecstasy or elation. There is, rather, a sense of apprehension with the apostle on the stage-right, thought to be Peter, appearing to be looking out at the viewer. The visited apostles certainly do not appear to be "filled with new wine."[56] Perhaps they are better described as responding with "consolation and fear . . . irreducible ambiguity."[57] Giotto, captures the sublime moment when the Apostles are empowered for their daunting task. It is a profoundly sensitive "reading" of the moment. The empowerment—the consolation is accompanied by the awful burden of responsibility—the fear. The initial surprise at viewing the fresco is shown to be shallow as one "participates"[58] in it. Another initial surprise is the solidity with which the loggia is depicted with base, pillars, and pediment presented in solid perspective. However, there are no back or side walls depicted. It is as if the downward rays of the descending spirit have broken through this solid structure and the division between earth and heaven has been torn asunder as with the veil of the Temple at the Crucifixion. Apart from the two Apostles to the stage-left of the fresco, separated by the corner pillar, there is no verbal communication. They appear to be lost in their own thoughts as the weight of the responsibility of ordination bears down upon them along with the gift of the Holy Spirit. In fact, the atmosphere created by Giotto is quite remarkable. There is a palpable mood of apprehension. The Apostles have crosses to bear and will have to be sustained by faith. The sense of "am I up to it?" is, after the initial surprise, a most moving and human aspect of this fresco. Seen in this light, perhaps the outward looking gaze of Peter, the *rock* on whom the Church is to be founded, may be imaginatively penetrated. Is he remembering the third crow of the cock that so recently reminded him of the insecurity of human resolution as he looks out on the world to be evangelized? Looking at this fresco one is aware of the sense of what Otto so tellingly names

> creature-consciousness or creature feeling . . . the emotion of a creature submerged and overwhelmed by its own nothingness.[59]

56. KJV. Acts 2: 13.

57. Taylor. *Disfiguring*, 19. Taylor is here describing the Romantics' response to nature: that which makes it, for them, sublime.

58. See note 39.

59. Otto. Ibid., 11.

The *Pentecost* fresco that faces the seats that were reserved for the Scrovegni family and the fresco with Judas clutching his moneybag to their right on the chancel arch, present a tremendous challenge. The gift of the Holy Spirit has to be received. It is there for all, but it requires the active participation of the receiver just as the frescoes as a whole require the active participation of the viewer/worshipper. The consoling arms receiving Judas in the fresco to the right of the Pentecost fresco are ever there as the easier option. One gift has to be taken or the other may not be refused.

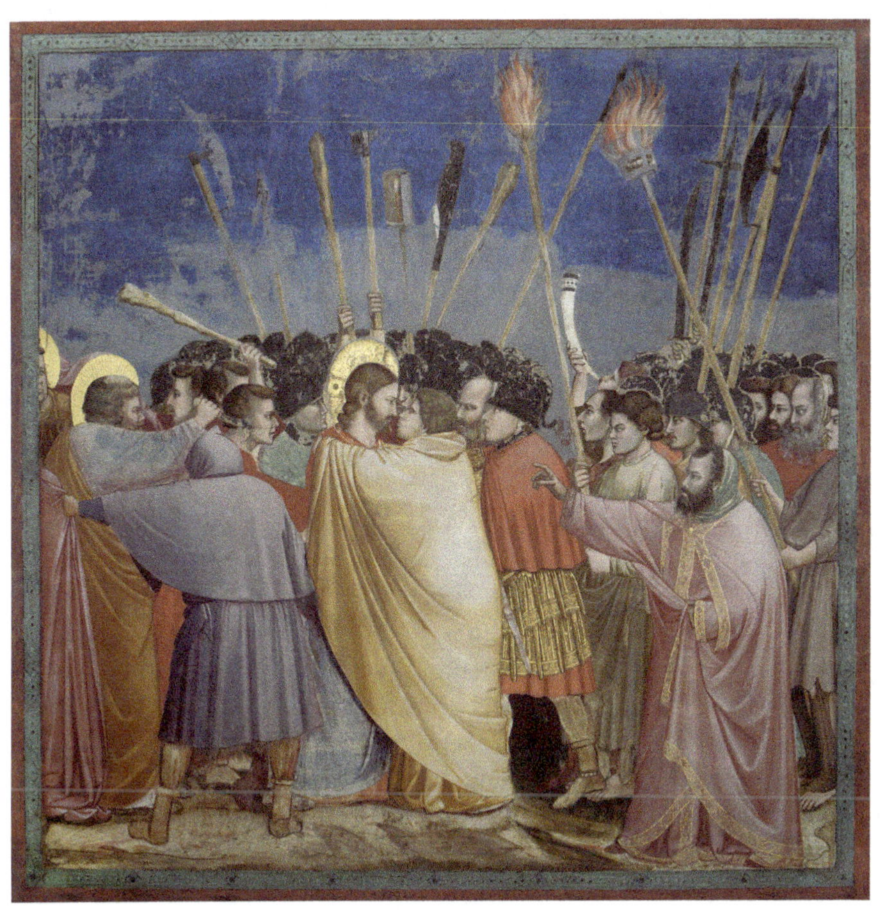

Fig. 10 The Betrayal.
By courtesy of the Municipality of Padua-Department of Culture.

This leads into a consideration of the moral weight or the moral purpose of the Passion Frescoes. I would like particularly to focus here on *The Betrayal* and the way in which a response is evoked by the organization of the picture. The central bulk formed by the cloak of Judas as he wraps it around Jesus predominates and is extended to the stage-right by the hunched back of the hooded enforcer attempting to restrain Peter. There is a great sense of drama conveyed by this fresco as a forest of threatening staves, spears, and clubs surround the central pair and raised lanterns illuminate the act of betrayal according it ironic celebrity. There is also, as with *The Scourging*, a very cleverly arranged current of dramatic energy across the front of the picture as the bearded high priest to the downstage-left of the picture points out Jesus and carries our eyes across to Peter as he cuts off the servant's ear.[60] The servant appears remarkably unconcerned which is hardly a naturalistic touch. Clearly, Giotto did not wish to distract from the central event by including heightened drama to the stage-right. The allusion makes the character point without interfering with the dramatic point. This contrasts with Menabuoi's depiction of the same scene in the Baptistry of the nearby cathedral. Here, the servant has been forced to the ground and the incident is placed forward of Judas and Jesus vying for the viewer's attention. The hooded thug in Giotto's fresco, has his back to the viewer and is thus a shape of dull colour setting off the enfolding cloak of Judas. He grabs unceremoniously at a cloak presenting a strong image of a bullying dictatorship. Remove the pointing figure from the downstage-left position and we have Jesus and Judas rather artificially surrounded on three sides only. As it is, they are in the middle of a throng yet completely visible as an isolated unit. In dramatic terms, the fourth wall is there but it is transparent. Judas enfolds Jesus in his robe. The two figures thus present one mass with the emphasis focused on the eye contact between the two. Jesus calmly fixes Judas with a steady gaze and motionless lips as Judas with puckered lips looks furtively up into those penetrating eyes. It is quite amazing, given the overwhelming show of power that Giotto is careful to present, that it is Judas with whom the viewer empathizes rather than Jesus, the one ostensibly threatened by the power. Judas is the one in whose shoes we would least like to be. The picture's final didactic triumph is the bitter irony of the figure who blows the shofar. This was sounded at various moments of both danger and triumph. Perhaps Giotto had in mind: "With trumpets and the sound

60. Further evidence of an amalgamation of Gospel accounts: only John names Peter, but John omits the Judas kiss.

of the horn make a joyful noise before the King, the Lord."[61] This is clearly not in the mind of the blower. The drama of the scene is not so much conveyed in suggested action as in tableaux-like being. It is not so much what Judas is *doing* as what he *is* that is conveyed. Maginnis suggests with some force: "The figures of the Arena remain non-naturalistic, almost symbolic embodiments of inner states."[62] We are not looking at two men at the centre of the fresco so much as at an idea or maybe an "ideogram."[63] What that idea is, I suggest, chills the heart of the viewer/worshipper in a non-verbal way, as does the back of the hooded figure to the stage-right. It chills with a frisson of recognition of an ever-present earthly force that viewers have to contend with on the spiritual journey that they are undertaking here and now. With this realization, pillorying the historical figure of Judas is not appropriate. It would be nonsense to suggest that by removing the figure of Judas from the picture, all would be well. The spirit that has entered Judas—whatever name one chooses to put upon it—would remain. To put a name to that spirit distances it and makes its force manageable. But we cannot anatomize an impression made by a painting. We experience it in a manner irreducible to words and herein lies its potency. In this particular fresco, the focus is on the exchange of looks between Christ and Judas. I suggest that this is the moral force of the fresco. We could perhaps suffer the threatening forest of staves and spears more easily than that look and our moral purpose is to avoid it being directed at us. Words may also evoke such a moral purpose as illustrated in Luke's Gospel. When Jesus is taken from Gethsemane to the high priest we are told, "And the Lord turned and looked upon Peter,"[64] as he denies Jesus for the third time. The empathy with Peter is difficult to avoid as we are invited to imagine the force of that look. The skill of the artist enables him to aid our imagination here in the Scrovegni Chapel but, I suggest, Luke and Giotto are engaged in a similar theological activity.

61. KJV. Psalms 98: 6.

62. Maginnis. Ibid., 88.

63. See note 73.

64. KJV. Luke 22: 61.

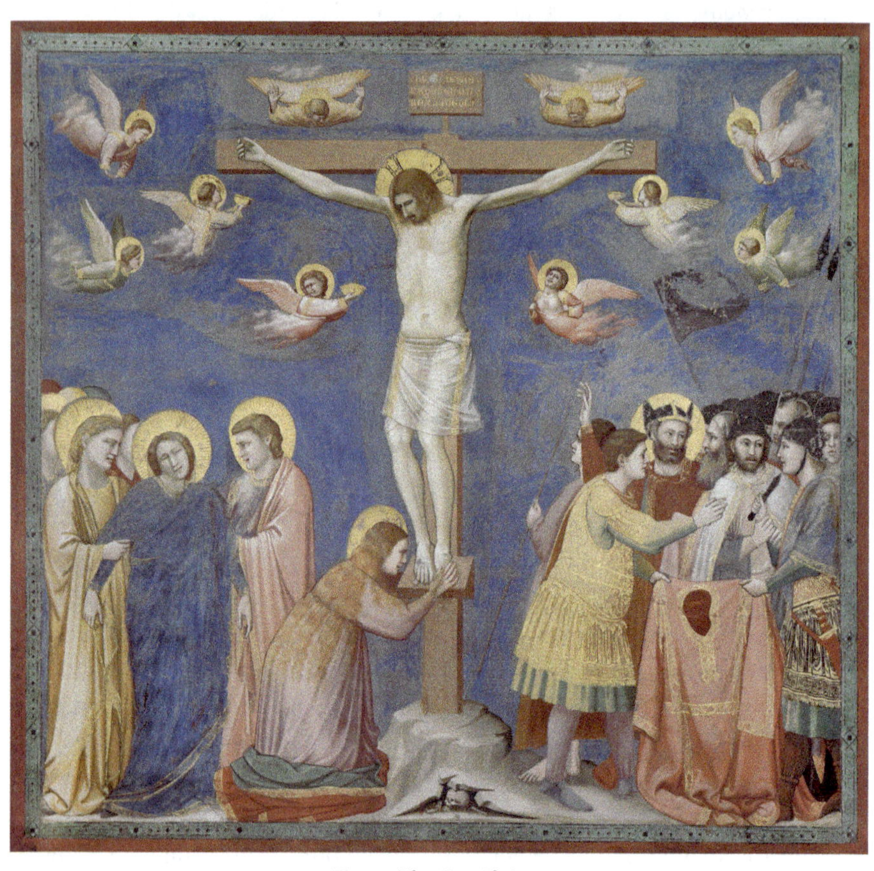

Fig. 11 The Crucifixion.
By courtesy of the Municipality of Padua-Department of Culture.

The Crucifixion, apart from being a very powerful portrayal of the central event of the redemption narrative, also presents the challenge of the centurion's raised hand. It is with the act of recognition that is also the challenge for the pilgrims at Emmaus that the redemptive relationship is formed. Thus Giotto accords the centurion a halo. This fresco is composed of three groups with the whole dominated by the figure of the crucified Christ on a cross that extends from top to bottom of the fresco dividing it into two. As Viladesau observes, "In some ways the representation is still iconic."[65] He goes on to explain that it is iconically arranged as there are different elements of the narrative represented simultaneously and there is an absence of scenery. Beneath the cross are the remains of the old Adam signifying the inauguration of a new, or re-newed, covenant. The figure of Christ with lank, sweat-drenched hair is very sensitively realized. The pallor and delicacy of touch that is emphasized by the transparent loincloth contrast in a very moving way with the human figures either side of the cross. Here, the richness of colour of the cloak falling around Mary Magdalene's knees at the foot of the cross and Christ's robe over which the soldiers argue to the stage-left, emphasize the otherworldly nature of the central event. The robe is shown to have real weight as it hangs from the soldiers' hands and it is this material world that preoccupies them. Giotto does not at this moment shrink from depicting the allure of this world. The figure of Mary Magdalene with her beautiful hair is another instance of this. However, as she caresses rather than wipes the feet of Jesus with her hair we have another example of the self-abnegating adoration that runs throughout the frescoes and it separates her from the two human groups. To the stage-right is the fainting figure of Mary the Mother of Jesus supported by two haloed figures one of whom is thought to be John. This tableaux-like grouping contrasts with the group to the stage-left who are so engaged with their dispute that they disregard the central event. The spears and the flag present an ironic depiction of earthly power similar to that of *The Betrayal.* The centurion whose haloed head appears between the disputing soldiers attempts, unsuccessfully, to draw their attention to the figure on the cross whom he has recognized as the Son of God. However, a common spear-carrying soldier looks up into the face of Jesus as he, maybe, contemplates the task of piercing his side. Perhaps the most remarkable feature of the fresco is the flight of angels that appear to spiral around the crucified savior. The artistic technique is, of course, amazing. The two foreshortened angels at the top

65. Viladesau. Ibid., 140.

centre and the figures depicted in profiled perspective create this spiralling movement and the truncation by cloud of their bodies provides a solution to the less successful presentation of angels in Cimabue's "Crucifixion" in the upper church of San Francesco in Assisi. But the artistic technique that renders the ethereal quality of the angels aside, it is the weight of overwhelming grief that dominates the fresco's impact. Here, in the representation of the angel at the downstage-left of the group is a rending of garments to contrast with the theatricality of Caiphas in *Christ before Caiphas*. Cole states: "One (angel) rends his garments in exactly the same way as does Caiphas in 'Christ before Caiphas.'"[66] I think not. Here, an observation of Harrison comes to mind. He makes reference to Giotto's: "ability to show . . . how *people* look . . . *under certain dispositions*."[67] The different dispositions of Caiphas and the Angel could not be more sharply contrasted. The overall range of the angels' facial features, the three angels collecting the blood of Christ in goblets, the face of the Virgin, and the presentation of Mary Magdalene evoke an overwhelming and palpable response to the central cosmic event. The centurion clearly is moved by what he experiences and it is this response that beatifies him as he attempts to communicate his experience to the soldiers. They, absorbed in their task of dividing up the spoils, ignore him. The response of Mary Magdalene is very clearly made at the centre of the fresco. It is in this free choice that the moral purpose of the fresco may be grounded. Time and again, Giotto presents the viewer with a similar choice.

Perhaps Maginnis somewhat overstates the case in objecting to the classification of Giotto as a naturalistic painter. There are some wonderful naturalistic touches in the Arena Chapel. *The Nativity of Mary*, for example, in the top left-hand corner of the north wall presents two maidservants who are immediately recognizable as naturalistic representations of domestic activity. The one on the stage-left cleaning the baby's eye with the tip of her finger connects with the sense experience of anyone who has ever cared for an infant. However, Maginnis is surely right when he says,

> Giotto . . . sought to embody universals, not so much universals behind physical forms and shapes, as of ideas emotions, psychological states . . . in tempered illusion, he employed an economy of

66. Cole. Ibid., 107.

67. Harrison. Ibid., 102. original emphases.

> means that spoke more eloquently to ideas for being less encumbered by appearances.[68]

One has only to walk a few hundred yards to observe the frescoes of Menabuoi in the Baptistry of the Cathedral for the point to be illustrated by contrast. Menabuoi's *Crucifixion* that dominates the east wall of the Baptistry and is magnificent in its own way substantiates Maginnis' point. "Encumbered" is a word difficult to avoid when contemplating the fresco; similarly "eloquent" comes readily to mind when contemplating the *ideas* in Giotto's *Crucifixion*. However, the sheer hubbub of the Menabuoi depiction is surely nearer to what a camera would have recorded.

Within the Passion Cycle at the Scrovegni Chapel, the point that Maginnis makes can be further illustrated by one or two examples.

68. Maginnis. Ibid., 101.

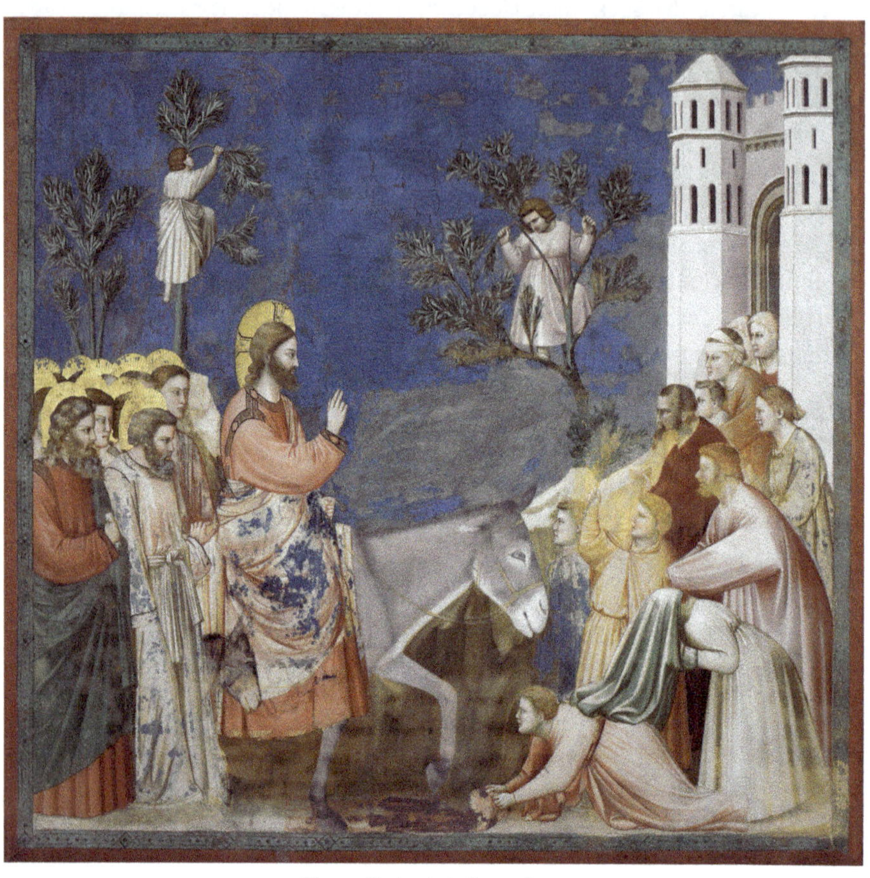

Fig. 12 Entry into Jerusalem.
By courtesy of the Municipality of Padua-Department of Culture.

To the stage-left of *The Entry into Jerusalem,* in a line running parallel to the donkey's neck, we are presented with three stages of a devotional gesture. The first figure to the extreme stage-left pulls at his sleeve, the bent figure in front of him struggles to remove the garment from his head, and, finally, the kneeling figure lays his garment in the path of the donkey. It is a great doxological moment presented as, it were, in slow motion. The interest is in emphasis rather than naturalism here and Giotto makes the sacrifice of naturalism repeatedly.

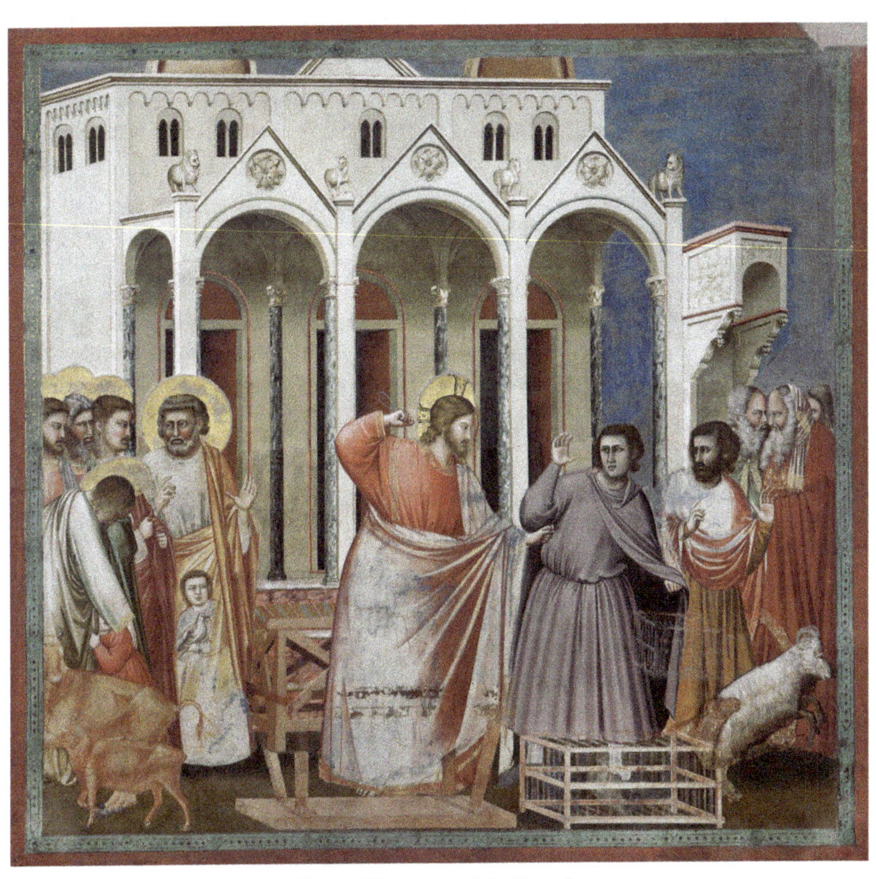

Fig. 13 Cleansing of the Temple.
By courtesy of the Municipality of Padua-Department of Culture.

In *The Cleansing of the Temple*, the Fresco is dominated again by the central figure of Jesus. However, this is not the calm figure of the preceding frescoes but an angry and alarming figure. There are no adoring figures in this fresco. The right hand of Jesus is not raised in blessing but it is clenched into a threatening fist that holds a whip. The animals flee not so much in elation at freedom but in fear and alarm at the chaos. The cow to the stage-right of the picture risks a most unlikely backward glance of incredulity or maybe it is an equally unlikely caring glance at its calf. Most movingly, Giotto depicts a young, horrified child holding a dove with a calming hand. The child shelters beneath the robe of Peter who holds his hands up in amazement. As Harrison points out, the deterioration suggests *a secco*[69] work. It is clearly a detail added as a refinement[70] and it is evidence of the "*cognitive practice*"[71] of which Harrison also writes. Another child buries its face in the robe of another disciple. These elements of compassion seem to contrast with the divine anger and represent the world with which we are more comfortable and expect always to be reflected in face of God. The fresco suggests that this expectation is unsound. Divine compassion has its limits or, at least, is not always decipherable by human understanding. There is a pervading sense of awe in both the human and the animal world. Radke draws our attention to,

> The dramatic energy of Christ driving two sheep off to the end of the (north) wall . . . propelling the narrative forward to the chancel wall and *The Pact with Judas*.[72]

This privileges the viewer/worshipper with an insight into the wrath of Jesus that confuses the characters within the fresco itself. The fresco has, to quote Rudolph Otto, a "numinous quality." Reflecting upon God's wrath, Otto writes:

> We are not concerned with a genuine intellectual 'concept', but only with a sort of illustrative substitute for a concept. 'Wrath' here is the 'ideogram' of a unique emotional moment in religious experience.[73]

69. A retouching technique where pigments are mixed with plaster and then applied over dry plaster whereas frescoes are painted on to wall-applied damp plaster and thus become part of the wall.

70. Harrison. Ibid., 99.

71. See note 83.

72. Radke. Ibid., 90.

73. Otto. Ibid., 19.

The human characters in this fresco, I suggest, are involved in a religious experience which Giotto realizes in a manner that is beyond words. The disciple to the stage-right of the fresco in whose robes a child buries its face is overcome by the "supra-rational"[74] nature of the experience. Here, Giotto depicts the "tremenda majestas or 'awful majesty'"[75] of Jesus. The solidity of the Temple edifice supported on marble pillars makes ironic comment upon the scene being enacted before it. As White points out:

> Giotto's architecture, like his landscapes, is always more than a mere attribute or habitat, and always plays a positive role in building up his unified and meaningful design.[76]

Here, the earthly power which has overtaken it and turned it into "a den of thieves"[77] is alluded to by the upturned table of the money lenders in the foreground. This earthly power is to enjoy its empty triumph in the crucifixion of the man who confronts it. This man appears to be doing his best to bring that "triumph" about. The two bearded figures, presumably temple elders, who whisper conspiratorially at the extreme-stage-left of the fresco can almost be heard articulating that very point. Thus two kinds of authority are represented in this fresco, that of the world and that of the kingdom over which Jesus claims to rule. The lions and horses mounted on the pillars of the Temple façade allude to Venice and to the vicissitudes of earthly power traceable in the history of the St. Mark's horses. As Venice sinks inexorably beneath the waves, the point is reinforced for modern viewers.

There are two frescoes in the group under consideration which do not feature Jesus as the central figure: *Pentecost* where he is replaced by the Holy Spirit descending; and *The Pact with Judas,* where he is replaced by a devil.

74. Ibid.

75. Ibid., 20.

76. White. Ibid., 320.

77. KJV. Matthew 21: 13.

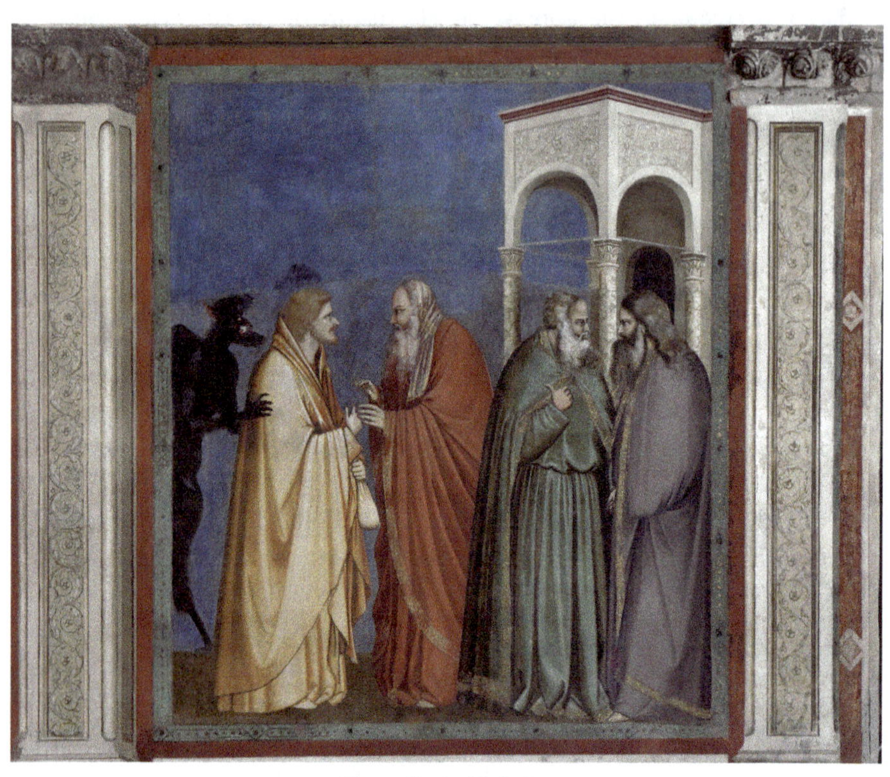

Fig. 14 Pact with Judas.
By courtesy of the Municipality of Padua-Department of Culture.

The construction of the latter, with two inward-facing couples effectively conveys the aura of conspiracy, as hand gestures communicate that which cannot be heard. The reassuring hand of the devil on the shoulder of Judas contrasts with the hand with which Judas nervously clutches the bag of silver. The fear in his eyes is difficult to avoid. The calming hands of the priest facing Judas correspond with those of the devil behind Judas and make the point that evil is carried out by seductive human agency. The presence of evil in non-human form conveys the enormity of the deed that Judas contemplates. The contemptuous jerk of the thumb by the figure with his back toward Judas "speaks" of the isolation of disloyalty. Judas does not invite respect from those with whom he would ingratiate himself any more than with those whom he has betrayed. He literally has only one way to turn as the entry to the Temple is barred by the bulk of the three bearded figures. The pictorial power of the presentation of this idea still retains its frisson. As with the account of Judas' attempt to return the money and repent,[78] so in this fresco, we empathise with Judas in his terrible isolation. We are all in danger of losing our soul in an attempt to gain the world. Never did the lure of money seem less appealing as the dead weight of the coinage hangs from Judas's left fist. The positioning of the fresco on the left pilaster of the chancel arch leading to the altar and the sarcophagus of Enrico Scrovegni is of great significance in the chapel dedicated to the Virgin in propitiation for the sins of the family who made money breed.[79] Judas clutching the bag of barren silver to his stomach stands facing the fresco of *The Visitation* on the opposite side of the archway. The contrasting atmosphere of the two visits could not be greater as Mary visits her cousin Elizabeth to share the wonder of their fruitful wombs. Here we have joy and love and life contrasting with fear and hate and death. As the Scrovegni approached the altar at mass they were painfully reminded of the unwise choices they had made. The same contrast would present a grim warning to other worshippers.

78. Matthew 26: 3–5.

79. If this is accepted as the motivation.

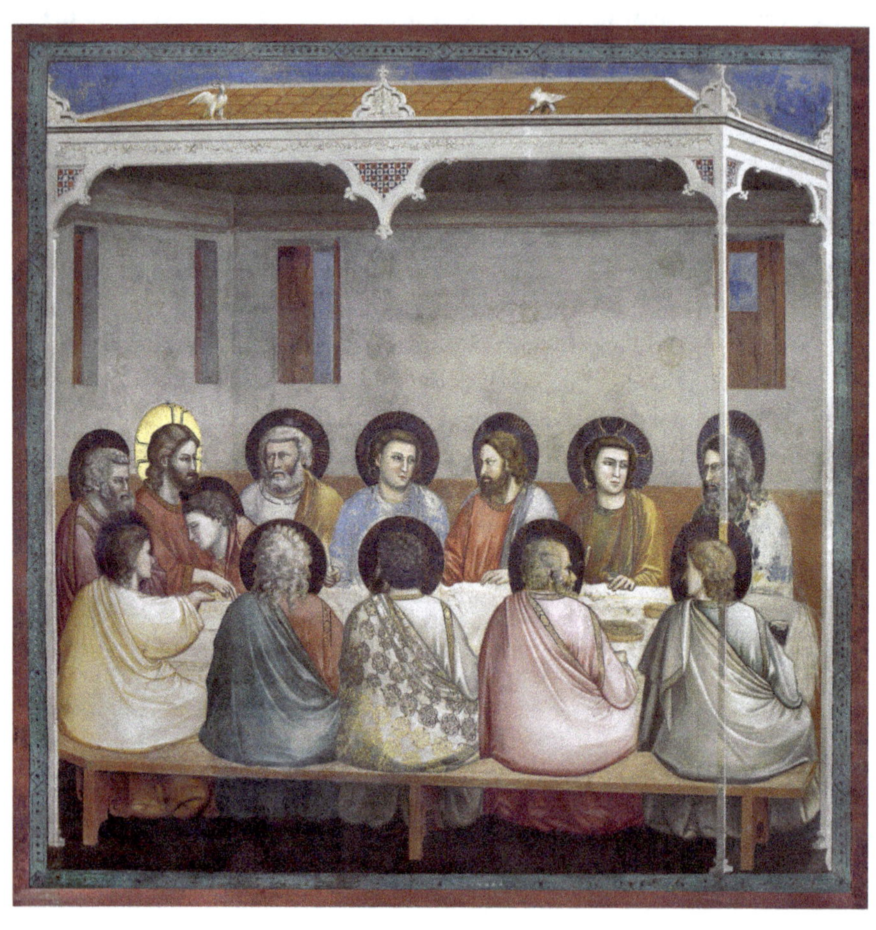

Fig. 15 The Last Supper.
By courtesy of the Municipality of Padua-Department of Culture.

Perhaps the imaginative penetration of the artist is nowhere more apparent than in *The Last Supper*. It is almost as if Giotto is there and senses the quiet, claustrophobic setting. The very formal representation with its precise geometrical arrangement appears to be based on the account found in all four Gospels. Judas, extreme-stage-right with his back towards the viewer, dips the bread into the bowl thus identifying himself as the one to betray Jesus. The fact that *The Pact with Judas* precedes this fresco, apart from the position that this accords it on the arch, perhaps favours the account in the Fourth gospel where we are told that the devil had already entered the heart of Judas.[80] Giotto's emphasis appears to be on the atmosphere of despondency amongst the disciples apart from John who rests, eyes shut, on the breast of Jesus. Peter stares distractedly at Jesus: what is to become of them when Jesus is betrayed to the Roman authorities? There is no confident looking forward to the Parousia here. The loggia in which the disciples are confined is like a prison through which the light of Pentecost is yet to burst. It is the dark night of the soul that would have "spoken" to and still "speaks" to every believer. An historical accident gives a potency to the image today which was not available to the original viewer and could not have been foreseen by the painter: corrosion has blackened the originally gold haloes of the disciples whilst the halo of Jesus, painted in pure gold, remains brightly shining.

80. KJV. John 13: 2.

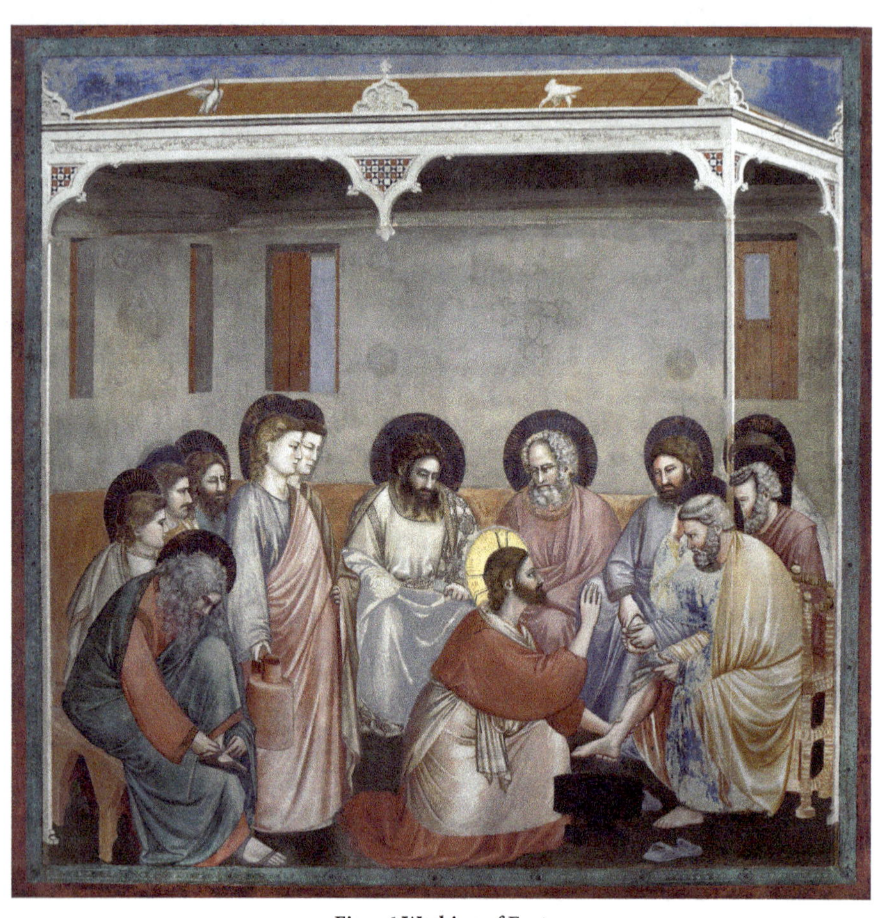

Fig. 16 Washing of Feet.
By courtesy of the Municipality of Padua-Department of Culture.

The Washing of Feet is extremely interesting from the theological point of view. The foot washing only appears in the fourth Gospel. Giotto chooses to place it alongside the depiction of the actual supper at which the Eucharist is established. The supper itself does not feature in the Fourth Gospel as it does in the other three. Clearly, this is not a problem for Giotto: he presents it as another aspect of the understanding of Jesus. The foot washing is depicted as taking place in the same loggia with the two feeding doves on the roof in the same position. The lesson of humility—the humility that reaches its apogee in the Crucifixion—is dramatized as Jesus washes his disciples' feet. Peter is told that the understanding of the action will come later. Peter who is having his feet washed looks uncomprehendingly at Jesus. This eye contact is depicted in an extremely powerful manner. It is a profound, searching gaze that penetrates to Peter's soul. All other looks are inward. Giotto clearly engages with the fact that the disciples are told in the Fourth Gospel that understanding will come later. They have to trust these words and the difficulty of doing so is clearly portrayed. Apart from the position of Jesus, there is nothing slave-like about him. He is depicted with a remarkable dignity as he raises his right hand in blessing with all the majesty with which Giotto depicts him in *The Entry into Jerusalem*. The tension of the occasion is palpable in Giotto's presentation. As with the previous fresco, the formality of the setting helps to convey the sense of sacramental solemnity. The enclosed, confined space furthers the sense of a pent-up need to burst out which builds until the final fresco of the series, *The Ascension*. There is an overwhelming sense of an imminent apocalyptic moment.

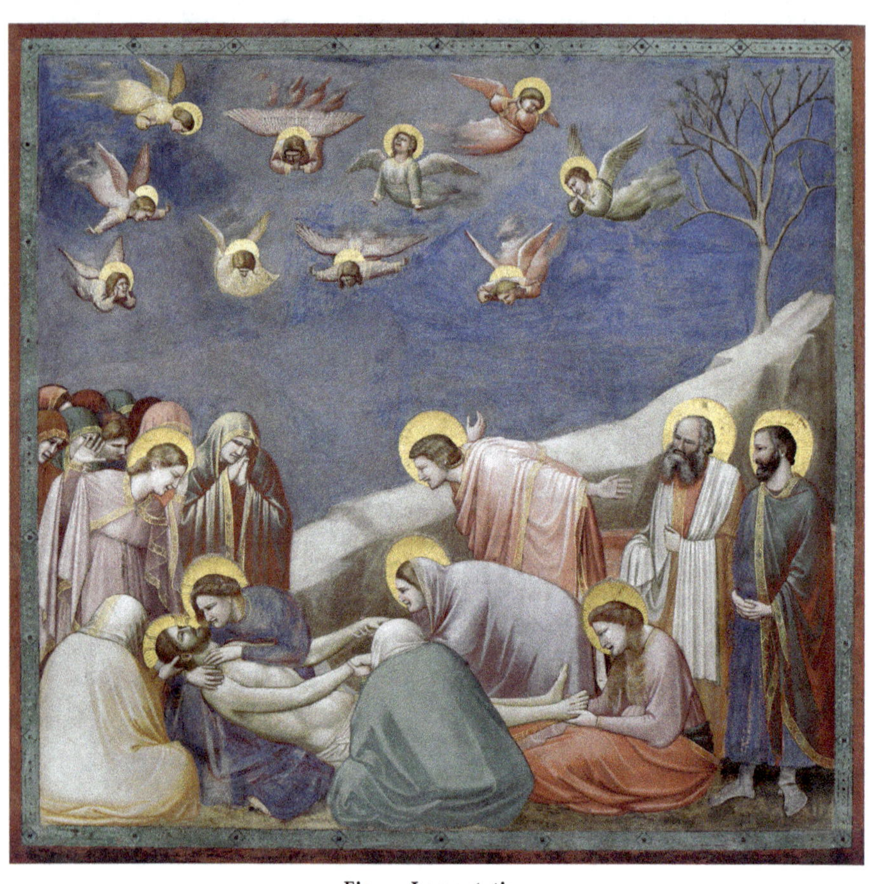

Fig. 17 Lamentation.
By courtesy of the Municipality of Padua-Department of Culture.

The Lamentation is outstanding for the way in which the attention is focused on the image of Mary cradling the dead Christ. All eyes converge on that point and the backdrop of the barren rock slopes down to the same point. The bare tree at the top right of the rock is like a Samuel Becket set and conveys a sense of a world bereft. It is not so much landscape imitation but more "an accompaniment to the death of Christ."[81] There are no divergent groupings here but as White observes, the psychological content of the fresco is increased by,

> the subtlety and variety of individual reaction to a dramatic event . . . Except upon the [extreme-stage-right], each member of a single, rhythmically connected group is an individual entity.[82]

The figure of the Virgin, eyes shadowed with grief, at Christ's head is balanced at the feet by the figure understood to be Mary Magdalene whose head is at an angle of helpless grief. A pious woman cradles the hands of Christ completing a picture of reverential lament for the sacred body. At this point it is interesting to recall Bishop Kallistos's observation concerning the doctrinal significance of icons:

> Icons are necessary and essential because they protect the full and proper doctrine of the Incarnation. While God cannot be represented in His eternal nature . . . He can be depicted simply because He 'became human and took flesh.' Of Him who took a material body, material images can be made. In so taking a material body, God proved that matter can be redeemed. He deified matter, making it spirit-bearing, and so if flesh can be a medium for the Spirit, so can wood or paint, although in a different fashion.[83]

In this particular fresco the protection of "the full and proper doctrine of the Incarnation" is deeply felt. The sense of the precious nature of Christ's body conveyed by this trio is overwhelming. The group of grieving women to the stage-right is complemented by the restrained grief of the two men to the stage-left taken to be Joseph of Arimathea and Nicodemus. The latter is of some significance when we recall Malraux's statement:

> The spirit of Byzantine theology is embodied in Christ's conversation with Nicodemus as recorded in the Gospel of St. John.[84]

81. Malraux. Ibid., 335.

82. White. Ibid,. 327.

83. Ware. *The Orthodox Church*, 33–34.

84. Malraux. Ibid., 146.

The backs of two hooded figures at the front of the fresco have a featureless solidity about them that does not detract from the focus but, rather, enhances it. The one to the stage-right makes up with the head and shoulders of the Virgin an arching frame for the head of Christ, producing a virtual icon within the fresco. The one to the stage-left overcomes the aesthetic awkwardness of having to depict across the centre of the fresco the full stretch of body of the crucified Christ. The figure with arms swept back at the centre of the fresco thought to be John appears with this gesture to be related to the angelic ecstasy of grief above. The angel above him looks down in a similar abandoned manner and earth and heaven seem at that point united in sorrow. The attitudes of grief depicted by the angels are, as in *The Crucifixion*, remarkable. The central angel is particularly impressive as it forces its body backwards in an agony of childlike sorrow. It is almost impossible not to be moved by and drawn into the sheer weight of grief that this fresco carries. Whilst it is true that the warmth of the Virgin's embrace suggests a mother gazing at her dead son, there is also a restraint and sense of wonder. This is, surely, not a full transportation "from the timeless into Time, from God's world to the world of man"[85] of which Malraux writes with reference to what he sees as the shift from the appeal to the community of Byzantine art to the appeal to the individual of Gothic religious art. As far as the context of this fresco is concerned, we are still in the historical time of Giotto as described by Tillich:

> In the time of Giotto, relation to transcendent reality gave meaning, centre and content to personal life . . . every individual participates in a communal movement created by loyalty to a transcendent reality.[86]

We, today, find ourselves in a world where "the centre cannot hold."[87] Tillich seems to suggest that in the circumstances of Giotto's time, the center was so firm that it was not possible to make a spiritual appeal to the individual without in a real sense also appealing to community loyalty. Maybe we are witnessing a different approach to this representation—an artistic world in transition. But it is not yet fully an individual rather than a community appeal that is being made as, it might be argued, it is today. In *The Lamentation*, Giotto clearly depicts a sacred event to be contemplated

85. Malraux. Ibid., 296.

86. Tillich. *On Art and Architecture*, 63.

87. Yeats. *The Second Coming*.

by the church community *as well as* by the individual worshipper whose loyalty to that community was an inextricable part of what he or she was.[88]

88. See Note 30.

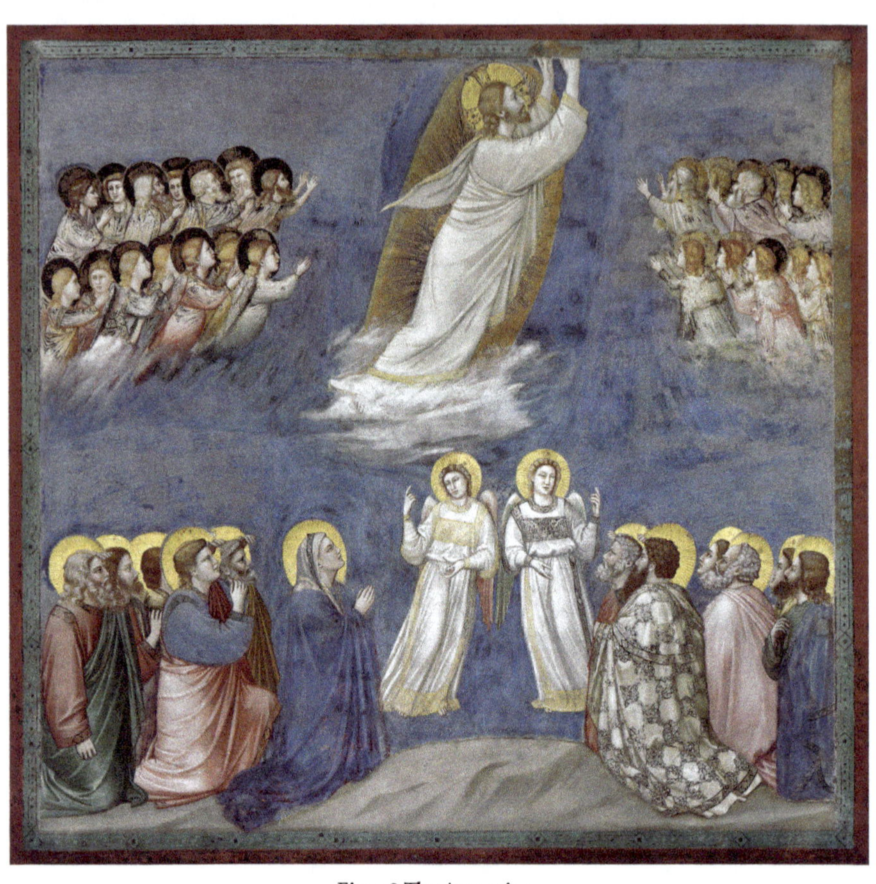

Fig. 18 The Ascension.
By courtesy of the Municipality of Padua-Department of Culture.

The final release of the pent-up energy identified in some of the earlier frescoes is achieved in *The Ascension*. There is a great sense of weightlessness conveyed by the Savior and the angels and saints to either side which may be contrasted with the burden of earthly weight given to Jesus in *The Scourging*. This is achieved also in the figures of the two pointing angels even though here they are fully drawn. They sway above the ground creating a sense of perspective with Mary and the Apostles who are firmly rooted to the ground in front of them. As Christ's hands disappear through the top of the fresco, the faces of the ground-based figures are composed but mystified. It is as if Giotto suggests that where rational understanding is elusive, adoration is the only appropriate response. There is a cruciform arrangement to the structure of the fresco with the two angels and the ascending Savior forming the upright and the saints and angels the crosspiece reminding believers of the life-giving source of their faith.

CONCLUDING REMARKS.

Richard Harries tells us that the integrity of the artist dictates that the work of art will not only please the eye but "will convey a truth which may disturb."[89] Creative disturbance perhaps describes the presence of Jesus as presented by Giotto in the Passion Frescoes of the Scrovegni Chapel. These are offered to the viewer/worshipper for their contemplation. They may not present a system of theoretical principals or a rational analysis of faith, but they do have theological force as profound studies of the defining moments of Christianity that, as Dixon tells us, the viewer/worshipper has had the opportunity to experience "in his (sic) own flesh."[90] In the quiet contemplation of them one experiences a sense of tranquillity and inspiration that often proves elusive when contemplating words. The agitation of questions regarding competing interpretations and the source and reliability of words is avoided when contemplating the visual imagery here presented. It is a tranquil and harmonizing experience that accompanies the viewer as he or she goes out once more to the busy world. To quote Dixon again, perhaps this experience would be not of "ecstasy" but of "joy."[91]

The dignity made available to humanity through the Incarnation is deeply felt in the Scrovegni Chapel and in that sense it makes a profound

89. Harries. *Art and the Beauty of God*, excerpted, Thiessen. Ibid., 354.

90. Dixon, "Painting as Theological Thought."

91. Ibid.

theological statement. The contemplation of visual images may lead to a place where true or right worship is possible, and that, surely, is a function of theology. This, of course, begs the question: what is true or right or proper worship. I suggest that frescoes may contribute to this sense of properness. Of course, response to visual images is a private matter. It cannot be catechized and is therefore not capable of the central control that may be exerted over verbal responses. In the Foreword to the book of the television series, *Civilization,* Kenneth Clark writes:

> I cannot distinguish between thought and feeling and I am convinced that a combination of words and music, colour and movement can extend human experience in a way that words alone cannot do.[92]

It is this extension of human experience, this merging of thought and feeling that, I suggest, is realizable by contemplation of and participation in the images in the Scrovegni Chapel.

Western naturalistic developments were parallel developments to those initiated by Giotto and not Giotto's *raison d'etre*. He is not usefully seen as a step along this naturalistic road. A more telling contrast between the iconic tradition and western art is that of artistic freedom. This concept of individual artistic inspiration affecting interpretation of material did not flourish in a culture where pattern books existed to guarantee fidelity to inherited forms. The icon is, Viladesau observes, as it always has been "dictated by tradition, rather than by aesthetic impulses of the artist."[93] This, of course, is the point alluded to by Viladesau when he comments on the influence of sculpture upon Giotto. This had developed in the West almost independently as it was not part of the Byzantine iconic tradition.[94] Byzantine tradition sees the icon as dealing not with the world through which we are passing but rather with the world to which we journey. The icon invites awe and worship. It is a mystical experience. As George Pattison writes: "The flesh which it reveals is a flesh whose desires and passions have been vanquished and subjugated."[95] One thinks with human affection of Giotto's soldiers in *Noli me Tangere*. Such human affection is not evoked by the world of the Byzantine icon. And, just as there is a danger in the western

92. Clark. *Civilisation*, XV.

93 Viladesau. Ibid.,55.

94. See note 70.

95. Pattison. *Art, Modernity and Faith,* excerpted, Thiessen. Ibid., 242.

tradition of over familiarising the divine, perhaps there is a danger in the eastern tradition of losing the vision of what Jurgen Moltmann refers to as,

> the glory of God (that) manifests its brightness on this earth in the face of him who was crucified by its laws and powers."[96]

If we do this, we can so easily "inwardly emigrate(d) into liturgy."[97] This would lead to a place where we lose sight of an obligation to challenge the values of the society in which we find ourselves here and now. In the words of Bonhoeffer to which Moltmann refers:

> We have no right to chant in Gregorian mode if we fail to cry out for the Jews."[98]

Perhaps a tradition that emphasizes the essential unreality of this world may be used as an escape for passing by on the other side. However, this would be a misunderstanding. Leonid Ouspensky points to the inevitability of such misunderstanding but he sees it as by no means confined to iconography.

> Both theology and iconography are faced with a problem that is absolutely insoluble—to express by means belonging to the created world that which is infinitely above the creature.[99]

Ouspensky sees value in this failure as it demonstrates our insufficiency as human beings and emphasises the virtue of the spiritual exercise involved in striving towards immutable content whether in word or image rather than actually realizing it. One is reminded, here, of the famous dictum of Lessing:

> If God were holding all the truth that exists in his right hand, and in his left just the one ever-active urge to find the truth, even if attached to it were the condition that I should always and forever be going astray, and said to me, "Choose!" I should humbly fall upon his left hand and say: "Father, give! Pure truth is surely only for thee alone.[100]

96. Moltmann. "Theology and Joy," excerpted, Thiessen. Ibid., 336.

97. Ibid. 337.

98. Ibid.

99. Ouspensky *The Meaning of Icons,* excerpted Thiessen, ibid., 345.

100. Lessing. Cited Barth, ibid., 265.

We are engaged on a quest whether in the eastern or western tradition, and whether through verbal or visual media. The humility that Ouspensky realizes for us is, perhaps, encouraging for the possibility of tolerance and understanding that it accommodates.

PART TWO

The Supper at Emmaus.

In the previous section I have attempted to participate in bible-based art within the Scrovegni Chapel at Padua. In the following pages, I have attempted to apply this method of active participation to Renaissance and Post-Renaissance art based upon the great post-Crucifixion event, the supper at Emmaus.

With the fall of Constantinople to the Ottoman Empire in 1453, many eastern scholars moved to the West and Rome became the centre of the western church. Until the Protestant Reformation[101] the church worldwide was split two ways: western Catholics, and eastern Orthodox. The political situation in the East was, of course, radically transformed in 1453. However, in 1454 the sultan, Mehmet II, allowed the election of a new patriarch to be the head of the entire Christian jurisdiction in the Turkish empire. Tax and justice for what was effectively a ghettoed community was also devolved to him. The other eastern Patriarchs were subject to his domination. His canonical and spiritual authority was augmented to include political power as well. Within the christian ghetto he was thus emperor as well as patriarch strictly controlled, of course, by the Sultan. The new patriarch, clearly relishing his newly acquired powers, dressed so as to impress them upon anyone who cared to view his splendid person. His mitre resembled a crown and eagles adorned his robes. The conciliar approach to matters theological was clearly not on the top of his agenda. But the church survived as an institution within the ottoman empire albeit in a somewhat truncated form.

This uneasy calm was completely shattered some sixty-years later by the earthquake that was the Protestant Reformation. This divided the

101. Usually dated from the time Martin Luther published his ninety-five theses in 1517.

western church and was a catastrophe from which it has yet to recover. The reformers thought—with very good reason—that the church had become corrupt and needed to be purified. They suggested that the focus on the Bible—God's Word—had been diverted towards an emphasis on church tradition and pious deeds. In particular they were scandalized by the popularity of the sale of indulgences. Often these were fraudulent relics attached to which there was the promise of absolution of sins. The message as seen by the reformers was that you could buy your way into the kingdom of heaven. This was blatant heresy and it needed to be stamped out. Much stamping followed. Luther's succinct rallying cry was *sola scriptura*. Only in God's Word to be found within the pages of the Bible was the path to salvation revealed. These ideas were not particularly of that moment. They had been expressed many times before. However, what was most decidedly of that moment was the printing press. Martin Luther and his followers were very adept at using it. Johannes Gutenberg had revolutionised the world of woodblock printing by providing a type-based printing press system in the first half on the fifteenth century. By the early sixteenth century this development had been refined and it facilitated the spread of ideas at a low cost and great speed. This brought about an era of mass communication. If we think of the overwhelming impact of the internet today with all of its mixed blessings, we may have some idea of the propaganda potential with all of its attendant positive and negative power available to Luther and his fellow reformers. Idolatry and the fear of it became an obsession of the reformers and it unleashed passionate violence that became an irresistible destructive force directed against artistic representation of the sacred. The two following examples demonstrate the extreme ugliness of the passions unleashed by careless words. In 1566, Antwerp Cathedral boasted over seventy altars adorned with magnificent works of sacred art. On the twentieth of August that year the British royal agent, Richard Clough entered the Cathedral after it had been visited by an iconoclastic mob. This is what he wrote:

> I went into the church (the cathedral) with ten thousand others. It looked like a hell, as if heaven and earth had gone together, with fallen images and beating down of costly works, so that in fine I cannot write to you in ten sheets of paper the strange sight I saw there, organs and all, destroyed! They have left not a place to sit on in the church.

Six years after this desecration, in 1572, a catholic mob committed the dreadful atrocity of The Saint Bartholomew's Day Massacre that began in Paris and spread to the provinces with thousands of protestants brutally massacred.

Throughout the sixteenth century in Europe a protestant revolt against the tradition of catholic art continued unabashed. The Council of Trent, met in Trento in northern Italy in twenty-five sessions between 1545 and 1563. This was an ecumenical council of the catholic church meeting in response to the Protestant Reformation. This is often referred to as the Counter Reformation or as the catholic church thinks of it Catholic Renewal accepting as it did the validity of some of the accusations being leveled against it. Clarification and emphasis of catholic doctrine were undertaken. In addition, biblical art was required to be clear and compelling in the presentation of the central events of the faith and also to be conducive to piety.

Along the way of these historical events, Thiessen suggests that we have lost the holistic vision:

> The retrieval and development of a theological aesthetics and the interest in mystical theology in recent decades may also be seen as an acknowledgement of a 'poetic poverty' in much (modern) theology.[102]

Theologically, the word and the image have a long history of being accorded equal authority. But, Harrison observes,

> It is part of the prejudice of our culture that the scientific and the rational are of a different order from the intuitive and sensuous.[103]

Postmodern thought questions this division and suggests that, perhaps, Theological Aesthetics has more of a contribution to make than the approach of positivism might lead us to believe. Andreopoulos[104] sees a relationship between what he identifies as "the modern fragmentation of the self" and what he further identifies as "the death of (western) art" both of which have developed from "the separation of the intellect from the heart." Bishop Kallistos Ware clarifies this concept:

> 'Heart' in this context is to be understood in the Semitic and biblical rather than the modern Western sense . . . the totality of the human person . . . the absolute centre.[105]

102. Thiessen. Ibid., 12.

103. Harrison. "The Arena Chapel," 102.

104. Andreopoulos. *Art as Theology*, 64.

105. Ware. *The Power of the Name*, cited. Andreopoulos. 47.

What is being urged by some current theologians, then, is not a new approach but a "retrieval and development." Burch Brown observes that it is important to remember that aesthetic and religious values are distinct. Were this not so, a viewer without religious sensibility would not be able to respond aesthetically to Giotto.[106] Quite clearly, profound pleasure in viewing the frescoes at the Scrovegni Chapel is not restricted to believers. However, I suggest that the response of non-believing viewers would be missing something of the totality of the frescoes under consideration: in Dixon's terms, they would be "spectators" rather than "participants." Alex Garcia-Rivera argues for the fundamental reality of transcendental Beauty. He observes that the Wisdom literature makes the assumption that aesthetic value is introduced into the world with God's act of creation: "*Aesthetic value is an intrinsic reality of the cosmic order*."[107] Genesis tells us,

> And God saw every thing that he had made, and behold, it was very good.[108]

George Pattison claims that "art anticipates . . . the return of the world to that created fullness in which we may declare, with God, that it is all 'very good.'"[109] The aesthetic experience allows the individual to see through to that essential goodness. He or she is able to see that although the circumstances of life may be cursed, the overarching reality is blessed. John Keats's journey through the Odes comes to mind here. The terrible vision of the third stanza of *Ode to a Nightingale* where this world is a place where we "sit and hear each other groan"[110] is transformed through the aesthetic vision to the tranquillity of *Ode to Autumn*.

> Where are the songs of Spring? Ay, where are they?
> Think not on them, thou hast thy music too,
> While barred clouds bloom the soft-dying day,
> And touch the stubble-plains with rosy hue;
> Then in a wailful choir the small gnats mourn
> Among the river sallows, borne aloft
> Or sinking as the light wind lives or dies;
> And full-grown lambs loud bleat from hilly bourn;

106. Burch Brown. *Religious Aesthetics*, 97.

107. Garcia-Rivera. "Creator of the Visible and the Invisible," 49, original emphasis.

108. KJV. Genesis 1: 31a.

109. Pattison. *Art, Modernity and Faith* excerpted Thiessen, ibid., 243/4.

110. Keats. *Ode to a Nightingale*.

Hedge-crickets sing; and now with treble soft
The red-breast whistles from a garden-croft;
And gathering swallows twitter in the skies.[111]

The sense of order and purpose is, perhaps, a useful working definition of the aesthetic experience as it applies to theology. Perhaps this might also be extended to suggest that the aesthetic experience has a contribution to make to the morality of worship.

> If the chief end of humanity is to glorify God, the completed act of worship will certainly have a moral value for the worshipper because the act accomplishes what is proper.[112]

Artistic reflection on the sublime moments of the life of Jesus, in particular the Passion of our Lord where what human wisdom regards as the very antithesis of the Divine—impotence and humility—is manifested, may provide, for us, glimpses into the penetralium. Whether or not Paul Tillich attributed more of his theological understanding to pictures rather than to books as has been suggested,[113] he certainly identified the central challenge of communicating the christian message as that of focusing on what he called, "the right stumbling block."[114] The categorical verbal statements dismissed by Dawkins as "dialectical prestidigitation,"[115] are perhaps more satisfactorily addressed by the words of Gregory, Bishop of Nyssa in the fourth century :

> Every man (sic.) who commits his (sic.) interpretation of the ineffable light to words is really a liar, not because of any hatred of truth, but because of the weakness of his(sic.) description.[116]

The Journey used as a metaphor appeals to the popular imagination. We are all on a journey so we are told constantly. Frequently, this image is used to encourage individuals to regard the difficulties or upsets that they might be experiencing as temporary; they are part of our procession towards some vague destination at which we are fated to arrive.

111. Keats. *Ode to Autumn,* last stanza.
112. Stiles, "In the Beauty of Holiness," 31–35.
113. Dillenberger. *Paul Tillich,* 151.
114. Tillich. "Ultimate Concern," last paragraph.
115. Dawkins. *Delusion,* 108.
116. Gregory of Nyssa. *On Virginity,* cited Thiessen, ibid., 25.

> Reality TV shows depend on the language of *the journey*, that voyage of personal discovery that culminates in revelatory self-knowledge or a sought after prize, whether that be a contract with Simon Cowell or a taste of kangaroo testicles.[117]

It is this journey that marks us out as individuals, special and unique, therefore it must be endured. If we endure to the end of this journey, we may look forward in Winston Churchill's words to "broad, sunlit uplands" or in Vera Lynn's words ". . .bluebirds over the white cliffs of Dover," depending on one's taste.

Luke's' account places two of Jesus's disciples on a road journeying from Jerusalem to Emmaus.

LUKE CHAPTER 24, VERSES 13 TO 32 KING JAMES' VERSION (KJV)

13 And, behold, two of them went that same day to a village called Emmaus, which was from Jerusalem about threescore furlongs.

14 And they talked together of all these things which had happened.

15 And it came to pass, that, while they communed together and reasoned, Jesus himself drew near, and went with them.

16 But their eyes were holden that they should not know him.

17 And he said unto them, What manner of communications are these that ye have one to another, as ye walk, and are sad?

18 And the one of them, whose name was Cleopas, answering said unto him, Art thou only a stranger in Jerusalem, and hast not known the things which are come to pass there in these days?

19 And he said unto them, What things? And they said unto him, Concerning Jesus of Nazareth, which was a prophet mighty in deed and word before God and all the people:

20 And how the chief priests and our rulers delivered him to be condemned to death, and have crucified him.

21 But we trusted that it had been he which should have redeemed Israel: and beside all this, to day is the third day since these things were done.

22 Yea, and certain women also of our company made us astonished, which were early at the sepulchre;

117. Victoria Segal, The Sunday Times *Culture* March 11th. 2018. The introduction to a preview of the BBC's commitment to increasing its religious-themed offerings.

23 And when they found not his body, they came, saying, that they had also seen a vision of angels, which said that he was alive.

24 And certain of them which were with us went to the sepulchre, and found it even so as the women had said: but him they saw not.

25 Then he said unto them, O fools, and slow of heart to believe all that the prophets have spoken:

26 Ought not Christ to have suffered these things, and to enter into his glory?

27 And beginning at Moses and all the prophets, he expounded unto them in all the scriptures the things concerning himself.

28 And they drew nigh unto the village, whither they went: and he made as though he would have gone further.

29 But they constrained him, saying, Abide with us: for it is toward evening, and the day is far spent. And he went in to tarry with them.

30 And it came to pass, as he sat at meat with them, he took bread, and blessed it, and brake, and gave to them.

31 And their eyes were opened, and they knew him; and he vanished out of their sight.

LUKE CHAPTER 24, VERSES 13 TO 32 NEW REVISED STANDARD VERSION (NRSV)

13 Now on that same day two of them were going to a village called Emmaus, about seven miles from Jerusalem,

14 and talking with each other about all these things that had happened.

15 While they were talking and discussing, Jesus himself came near and went with them,

16 but their eyes were kept from recognizing him.

17 And he said to them, "What are you discussing with each other while you walk along?" They stood still, looking sad.

18 Then one of them, whose name was Cleopas, answered him, "Are you the only stranger in Jerusalem who does not know the things that have taken place there in these days?"

19 He asked them, "What things?" They replied, "The things about Jesus of Nazareth, who was a prophet mighty in deed and word before God and all the people,

20 and how our chief priests and leaders handed him over to be condemned to death and crucified him.

21 But we had hoped that he was the one to redeem Israel. Yes, and besides all this, it is now the third day since these things took place.

22 Moreover, some women of our group astounded us. They were at the tomb early this morning,

23 and when they did not find his body there, they came back and told us that they had indeed seen a vision of angels who said that he was alive.

24 Some of those who were with us went to the tomb and found it just as the women had said; but they did not see him."

25 Then he said to them, "Oh, how foolish you are, and how slow of heart to believe all that the prophets have declared!

26 Was it not necessary that the Messiah should suffer these things and then enter into his glory?"

27 Then beginning with Moses and all the prophets, he interpreted to them the things about himself in all the scriptures.

28 As they came near the village to which they were going, he walked ahead as if he were going on.

29 But they urged him strongly, saying, "Stay with us, because it is almost evening and the day is now nearly over." So he went in to stay with them.

30 When he was at the table with them, he took bread, blessed and broke it, and gave it to them.

31 Then their eyes were opened, and they recognized him; and he vanished from their sight.

It is what we might call something of a trek: we are told that Emmaus is sixty furlongs from Jerusalem, roughly seven-and-a-half miles or twelve kilometres. This is no metaphorical journey. We do not know why they are going to Emmaus. Whatever the reason, the events that take place on the journey and at the supper in which it culminates result in a dramatic change of plan. They rush back to Jerusalem with their miraculous news. Maybe they just needed to get away from Jerusalem. Their world was in turmoil. In the cataclysmic words of W. B. Yeats writing about another Easter.[118]

> All changed, changed utterly.

The one whom they had *trusted* to be "he who would have redeemed Israel"[119] had betrayed them. The NRSV replaces *trusted* with *hoped*. This weakens the impact. These men are devastated as only people whose trust

118. *Easter 1916*.

119. KJV. Luke, 24–21.

is betrayed can be. Hope not being fulfilled is a daily human experience: we *hope* for sunshine and it rains. The betrayal of trust is the stuff of dramatic tragedy. *Hamlet* is the epitome of this. Hamlet loses his ideal: his absolute trust in the love and fidelity between his mother and father. His world has become,

> an unweeded garden/ That grows to seed. Things rank and gross in nature/ Possess it merely.[120]

How much greater must have been the depth of despair that the two disciples are experiencing. They are trying to escape from it but it clings to them. It is almost tangible. If we compare the two versions of verse seventeen, we see that the KJV has the stranger *seeing* the sadness of the two disciples as clearly as he sees their physical activity: "...ye walk and *are* sad." The NRSV tells us, " They stood still, *looking* sad."[121] The difference here is profound. Again, one recalls *Hamlet.* In the KJV version, the two disciples "...have that within which passeth show."[122]It is the innermost essence of their being, not a facial expression. They *are*. Not, they *look.* And, of course, the privileged reader knows who the stranger is and we would expect him to see this inner truth. Verse sixteen is very intriguing:

> But their eyes were holden that they should not know him.

It is as if the Emmaus moment has to be experienced at a non-physical level. After all, at verses twenty-three andtwenty-four, the angelic message has been delivered to the disciples by the women who had actually come from the empty sepulchre. After the experience of living with the earthly presence of Jesus, it seems that the disciples have a limited understanding of the person or his words. In the *Farewell Discourse*, Jesus says,

> I have yet many things to say unto you but you cannot bear them now.
> Howbeit when he, the Spirit of truth is come, he will guide you into all truth.[123]

They will move from human knowledge to spiritual wisdom. The breaking of bread when the physical presence of the stranger disappears from the disciples' sight is the moment replicated in the christian church at the Eucharist. This is the moment when " their eyes were opened and they

120. Shakespeare. *Hamlet,* 5: 2, 135–7.

121. My emphases.

122. Shakespeare. *Hamlet,* 1: 2, 85.

123. KJV. John 6:12/13.

knew him." The NSRV renders this as "their eyes were opened and they *recognised* him." The narrator in KJV is not writing about physical eyesight whereas the writer in NRSV seems to be so doing. They *knew* him, they experienced him as they had not when he was physically present to them. The message that they are compelled to take back seems to rivet the attention of the listeners.

> They told what things were done in the way and how he was known to them in the breaking of bread.

If, as the idiomatic expression has it, "seeing is believing," the earthly departure of Jesus must leave future generations bereft, unless they experience the *Emmaus Moment*. This may be made available to us in the celebration of the *Eucharist*. It may also be conveyed by inspired artists in a way that is beyond the power of words.

PAINTINGS OF THE ROAD TO EMMAUS.

There are many more pictorial depictions of *the Supper at Emmaus* than of the subject that Duccio chooses: *the Road to Emmaus*. The supper is an event: the journey is a process. The essence of this process is the utter despondency bordering on despair of the two pilgrims. This is perhaps the territory that is more accessible to poetry rather than visual art. The two pilgrims have received the women's report but their faith is not sufficient to accept it. This realization may be a contributing part of their despondency rather like that of Peter at the third cock-crow when he is confronted with the inadequacy of his human condition.[124] T. S. Eliot famously found an affinity with the two pilgrims on the road to Emmaus. In 1922 as he sought to navigate his own journey through the waste land of the post world-war-one world and his tragic marital circumstances, Eliot enters the minds of the two pilgrims:

> He who was living is now dead
> We who were living are now dying[125]

How may such a condition be conveyed in the silent drama that painting was in the process of becoming?[126]

124. KJV. Matt. 26: 75: *And he went out and wept bitterly.*

125. Eliot. *The Waste Land.*

126. I shall use stage directions when writing about the paintings, i.e., left and right

June ninth 1311 saw the completion of a double-sided altarpiece for the high altar of Siena's Cathedral. It was approximately four metres high and five metres wide and it was paraded around the central Piazza del Campo with great ceremony before taking its place in the Cathedral. The painter was Duccio di Buonosegna.[127] Duccio's fame as master was only rivalled by his younger Florentine contemporary, Giotto.[128] The Maestà[129] as the altarpiece is known derives its title from the central figure of the Virgin enthroned in majesty. The reverse comprises narrative scenes from the life of Christ. The only comparable work at the time was Giotto's fresco cycle in the Arena or Scrovegni Chapel in Padua. The front and the back of *The Maestà* were separated in 1777 and some of the individual narrative scenes were sold. So the powerful effect that must have been presented to the congregation and the celebrants during the mass when it was situated below the rose window in the apse[130] can only be imagined. The audacity of the inscription that Duccio painted in gold letters on the marble dais of the Virgin's throne may be seen as an illustration of the thinking behind the protestant animus against religious art in churches.

> *MATER S(AN)L(T)A DEI SIS CAUSE SENIS REQUIEI SIS DUCIO VITA TE QUIA PINXIT ITA*
>
> O holy Mother of God, may you grant peace to Siena and long life to Duccio because he painted you thus.

The suggestion, of course, is that good works may curry favour, via the saints, with the deity. In Orthodox tradition Icons were not signed. The iconographer was to regard himself as a mere channel of divine light. This doctrinal difference aside, Duccio, as a painter, appears to be a bridge between Byzantine formality and the developing western tradition that was in the process of breaking off into other directions. Keith Christiansen draws our attention to Duccio's,

---

are from the characters' perspectives. Upstage is to the back of the painting and downstage to the front. This seems entirely appropriate to me as from Cavallini and Giotto onwards painting has tended to present dramatic situations that engage the viewer imaginatively in the manner of stage presentations.

127. 1255/60—1318/19.

128. 1266/7—1337.

129. Majesty.

130. Also designed by Duccio some twenty years previously.

> dazzling sense of pattern and colour, the keen sense of narration, the manifest interest in the investigation of spatial problems and the lyrical beauty of the figures.[131]

Duccio explored the expressive possibilities of painting without cutting himself off from the spirituality of Byzantine conventions. Lorenzo Ghiberti a century later was to produce the magnificent bronze Gates of Paradise doors for the Florentine Baptistery upon which the "keen sense of narration" is developed to an awe inspiring level of perfection. What Ghiberti had come to regard as the degenerate Byzantine tradition has now been discarded by Ghiberti. However, Duccio's spirituality is still grasped or conveyed by conventional elements. Duccio undertakes the challenge of depicting the process of *the road* by placing his depiction not as an isolated representation but as part of a sequence on the back of the Maestá. This would have been the surface viewed by the celebrants of the mass. The distant congregation was confronted by the splendour of the Virgin in Majesty. In this way the differing needs of two viewing groups were simultaneously catered for. The congregation had their spirits uplifted by the vision of the Madonna and Child with saints and angels as they awaited the miracle of the mass. The celebrants as they prepare for their awesome role are able to contemplate the images of Christ's suffering, humiliation, and *Crucifixion* followed by the sequence of the *Deposition*, *Entombment*, *Resurrection*, the angel addressing the women in the empty tomb, the *Road to Emmaus*, and, finally, *Noli Mi Tangere*.

131. Christiansen. *Duccio and the Origins of Western Painting*, 20.

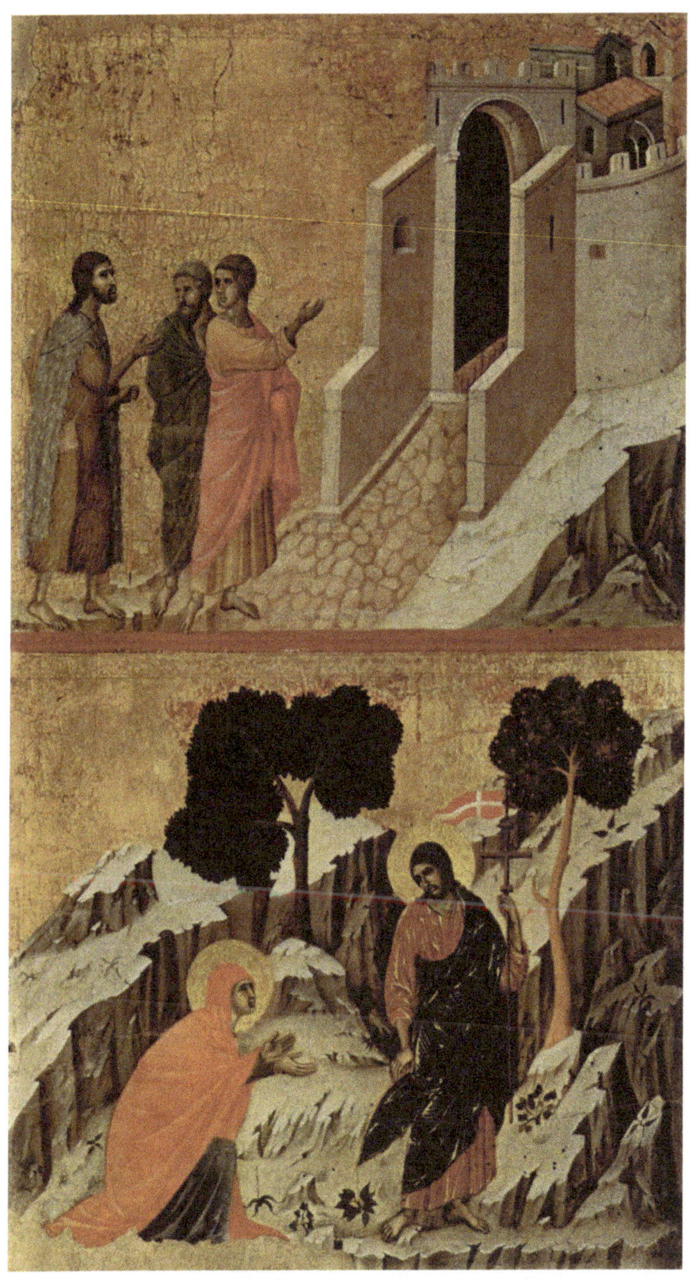

Fig. 19 Duccio di Buoninsegna ***The Road to Emmaus*** **(1308–11)**
Opera Della Metropolitana, Siena.

Within this context, rich in dramatic detail, the sparse presentation of *the Road to Emmaus* is eloquently poignant. The beautiful, harmonious colors available in egg tempera are employed to full effect here. The green and red of the pilgrims cloaks contrast with the dull brown and hirsute drapery of the mysterious stranger with his pilgrim's hat slung over his back, all against a rich background of yellow ochre and gold. The man in green peers deeply into the face of the stranger who has caused his heart to burn within him. He is visibly disturbed as he touches the back of his comrade as reassurance that he remains in the world of here-and-now where, paradoxically, he feels more at home. He cannot quite let go. At least his wasteland is familiar territory. He is such a sympathetic, human character in this predicament, one that we all experience in varying degrees. His experience recalls the words of Agrippa to Paul: "Almost thou persuadest me to be a Christian."[132] The celebrants of the mass by following the logic of the sequence must have received confirmation of the vital nature of the celebration over which they are about to preside. They are, in a way, about to complete the sequence set up by the paintings by the breaking of bread at which their faith tells them Christ becomes present. The dramatic welcoming gesture of the red-cloaked figure as he invites the stranger into the security of the enclosed city is hugely symbolic. The welcoming of the stranger is an obligation in Judeo-Christian tradition. In Matthew, it is presented as the distinguishing mark of the faithful:

> For I was an hungered, and you gave me meat; I was thirsty, and ye gave me drink; I was a stranger, and you took me in.[133]

Duccio's painting is divided into two sections: stage right[134] has the three pilgrims outside the city walls. It is as if the two disciples are inviting the stranger in from the disordered outside to the order and discipline of the city. Duccio represents this city by sharply delineated geometrical shapes. This motif of the sharp and salutary divide between the wilderness and the comfort and convenience of civilization is a persistent one in western literature. There is the storm-ravaged wilderness in which Lear meets with "unaccommodated man" and learns with Gloucester:

> . . . Full oft 'tis seen
> Our means secure us and our mere defects

132. KJV. Acts 26: 28.

133. KJV. Matt. 25: 35.

134. See note 126.

Prove our commodities . . . [135]

And in the twenty-first century in Sergio de la Pava's breath-taking epic novel *A Naked Singularity*[136] we are presented with Casi who is a public defender. Working in Manhattan, Casi identifies humanity in the drug-addled wilderness of the streets that is not catered for in the civic and cultural life of the city. Here, "civilization" is underpinned by Law devoid of Justice. Of course, the spiritual template for this idea is Christ's forty days in the wild. Duccio presents us with two characters who are not the same at the end of their journey. But they are not yet aware of just what has changed them and they are disturbed.

Cremona is a city in Lombardy, northern Italy. It is the capital of the province of Cremona. Here, Altobello Mellone[137] painted *The Road to Emmaus.*[138]

135. Shakespeare. *King Lear,* 4: 2, 22–24.

136. de la Pava. *A Naked Singularity.*

137. Mellone's dates are uncertain. It is thought likely that he was born around 1490. He was painting between 1517 and 1535.

138. Now in The National Gallery, London.

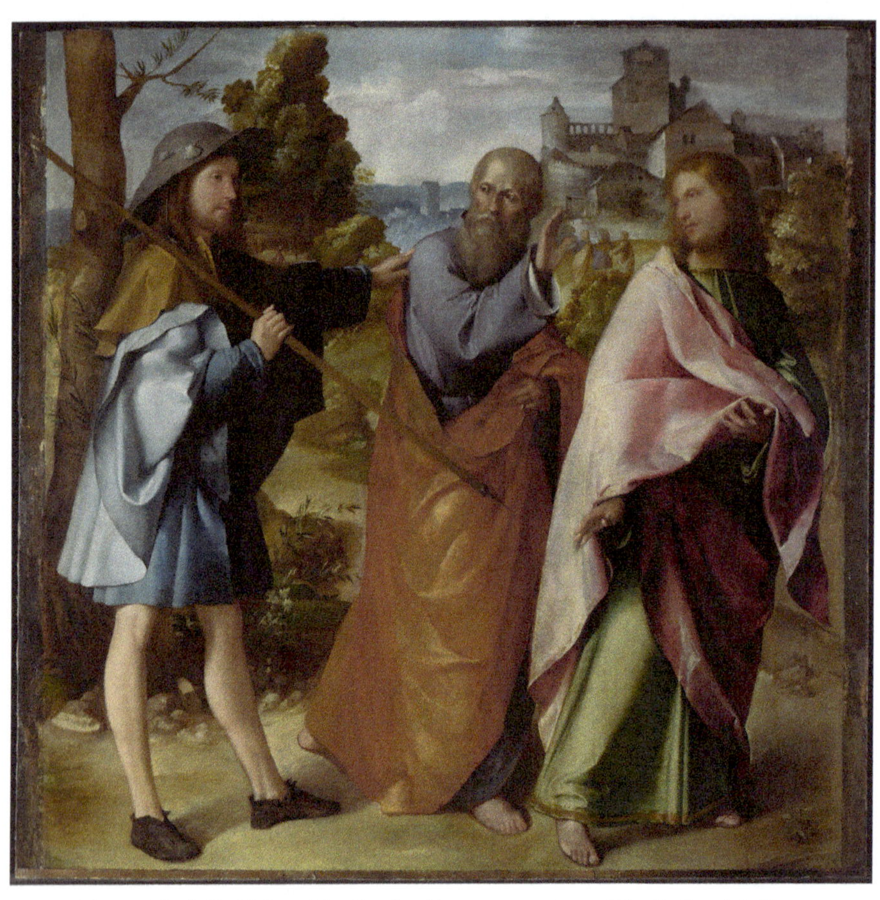

Fig. 20 Altobello Melone *The Road to Emmaus* courtesy of the National Gallery (London) Picture Library.

It is of a similar moment to that of Duccio's painting with the same title. I have drawn attention to the difficulty of painting a process rather than an event. Duccio captures this idea of process by featuring his work as part of a sequence of paintings that convey a sense of the burden that the two disciples have carried along the road. Altobello achieves a similar effect by showing the condition of the two disciples in sharp contrast to that of the pilgrim/Christ figure. The disciple stage left has a face telling of utter weariness indicative of total spiritual exhaustion. He looks at the pilgrim so wearily and devoid of hope that it is almost palpable. The central figure pulls away from the touch of the pilgrim/Christ with a mixture of apprehension and anger in his expression. He has just been lectured and called a fool and slow of heart when perhaps he felt entitled to a more gentle response to his predicament. Perhaps this is an example of what is now referred to as "tough love." It does seem to be at odds with the modern counselling approach. He seems to be asking, "Is this another con-man?" The pilgrim/Christ stands out as something "other." His eyes are focussed on the middle distance, not on the disciples. He is very formally dressed and of a rather rigid and forbidding appearance. His pilgrim's hat and staff are precisely placed as if awaiting a superior's inspection. The disciples seem to be pondering the question that is the central hermeneutical issue of the gospel: "Who is this man?" How are we to understand the life of Jesus. There is an expressive quality about the work that recalls that of late gothic painters like Duccio and Giotto. The body positioning and the sidelong glances are very eloquent of inner emotion. What Freedberg refers to as Altobello's "hard-shelled lucidity of form"[139] perhaps detracts from the naturalism of the former elements. Again, Freedberg has a succinct phrase that expresses this response: he suggests that Altobello conjoins "power of ornament and expressive sense."[140] The sense of the journey is also captured by the gothic device of representing scenes that took place earlier in time than that of the painting's main focus. The city into which the Jesus figure is invited is shown on the same plane as the two disciples in Duccio's painting. Here, in Antobello's work, it is to be seen in the distance behind the foreground figures. The three figures are distantly depicted journeying towards it. The invitation offered to the Christ figure in these two road paintings is an invitation to enter into the muddle and confusion of our worldly endeavour to order our lives. It hardly needs to be stated as we look at our present

139. Freedberg. *Painting in Italy*, 252.

140. Ibid.

predicament that this endeavour is subject to repeated disintegration. The "road" paintings seem to illustrate the worldliness of grace,[141] the suggestion that Christ may be found in the midst of our muddle.

141. This expression was presented to me in an essay by one of my students. She suggested that the character of Marmeladov in *Crime and Punishment* was used by Dostoevsky to illustrate the worldliness of grace. I suggested that the student had borrowed the phrase and that she should cite the source (I had Graham Green in mind). She claimed that the phrase was her own. I have been unable to find another source for the phrase. If I have done the student an injustice, I apologise unreservedly. In the unlikely event that she is reading this, if she contacts me, I will gladly acknowledge her contribution.

PAINTINGS OF *THE SUPPER AT EMMAUS*

Pre sixteenth century

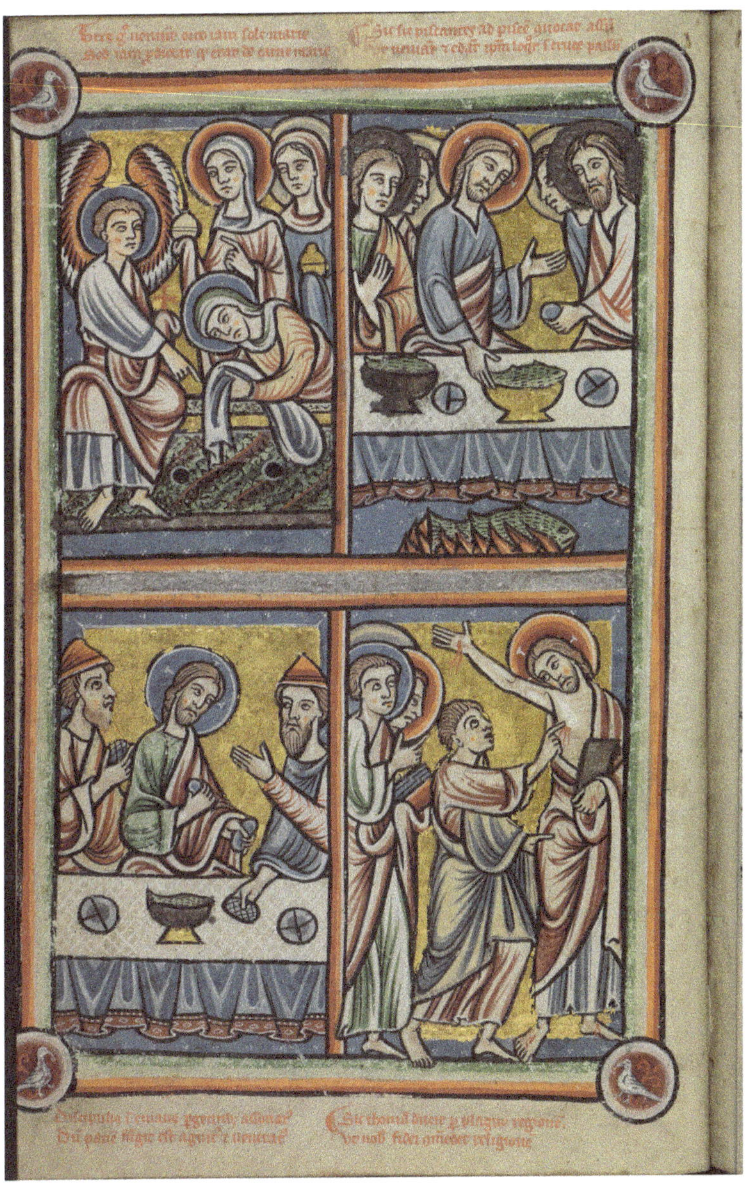

Fig. 21 Medieval Pictorial Bible *The Supper at Emmaus and scenes from the Life of Christ* **courtesy KB national library of the Netherlands.**

Dating from 1190–1200 we have a French pictorial bible from the Benedictine abbey of Saint Bertin. The relevant page of the bible is divided into four sections. At the top left we have the preparations for the anointing of the feet of Christ. Thus the sacred significance of this biblically recorded act that escaped the disciples,[142] is celebrated here. To the right is the Last Supper; bottom right depicts Thomas who refused to believe in the Resurrection without tactile proof; and bottom left is the Supper at Emmaus. The theological emphasis of early depictions of *The Supper at Emmaus* is on the disciples' recognition of Jesus or, as the KJV bible expresses it, the knowledge of Jesus. In fact, the illustrations tend to be entitled *The Disciples Recognize Jesus* rather than *The Supper at Emmaus*. The stylisation of the illustrations is clear. We do not receive a sense of personality. However, the events are elevated by stylistic presentation to an ethereal level. In the Benedictine Abbey example, this is aided by the three nails of Christ's crucifixion being enclosed within the nimbus that surrounds his head. We are transported not to a historical moment but to the spiritual essence of a historical moment into which we gain access by contemplation of the work. In *The Recognition* the two pilgrims defer to the central figure. No words are required. They are speechless before that which they have encountered as the bread is broken. Although that moment has been addressed in differing ways in western art as circumstances changed, the potency of medieval or Byzantine presentation may still be experienced by present-day viewers.

142. The Fourth Gospel attributes the protest at the waste of money to Judas Iscariot. The other three gospels are less specific.

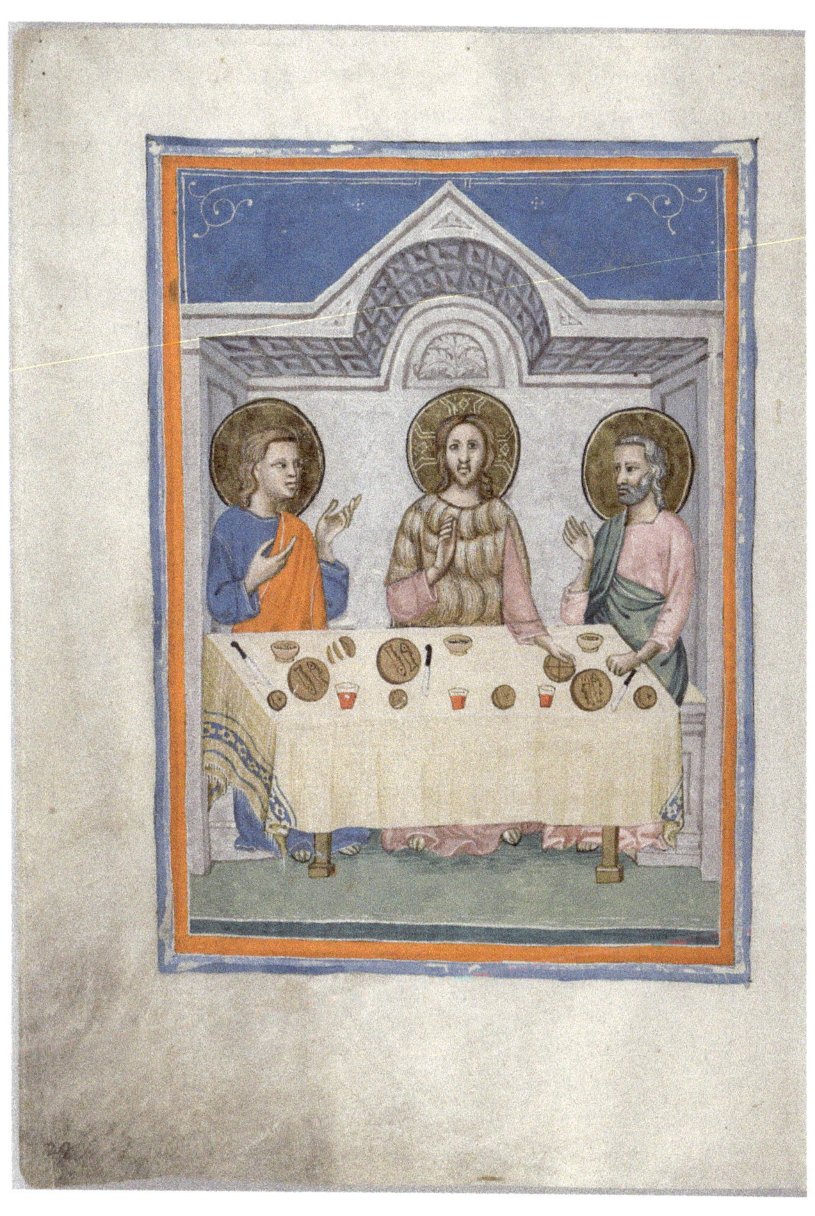

Fig. 22 Pacino di Bonaguida. *The Disciples Recognize Jesus from Scenes from the life of Christ and of the Blessed Gerard of Villamagna* **Italian (Florence) 1315–1325)** NY Pierpont Morgan Library MS M643, fol. 14v courtesy KB national library of the Netherlands.

Some hundred years later, Pacino di Bonaguida[143] painted a similar scene for an illuminated manuscript in Florence. Clearly, limitations were imposed upon miniaturist painters requiring them to concentrate upon a precise moment of time rather than the development of that moment afforded to painters on a broader canvas such as Giotto. But Pacino was clearly influenced by his Florentine contemporary, Giotto. The stately beauty and the colour aesthetics of Pacino's work recall the frescoes of Giotto in The Arena Chapel at Padua. Approximately one hundred years after Pacino's work the master of Catherine of Cleves produces another example in the Netherlands.

143. Florence 1315–1325.

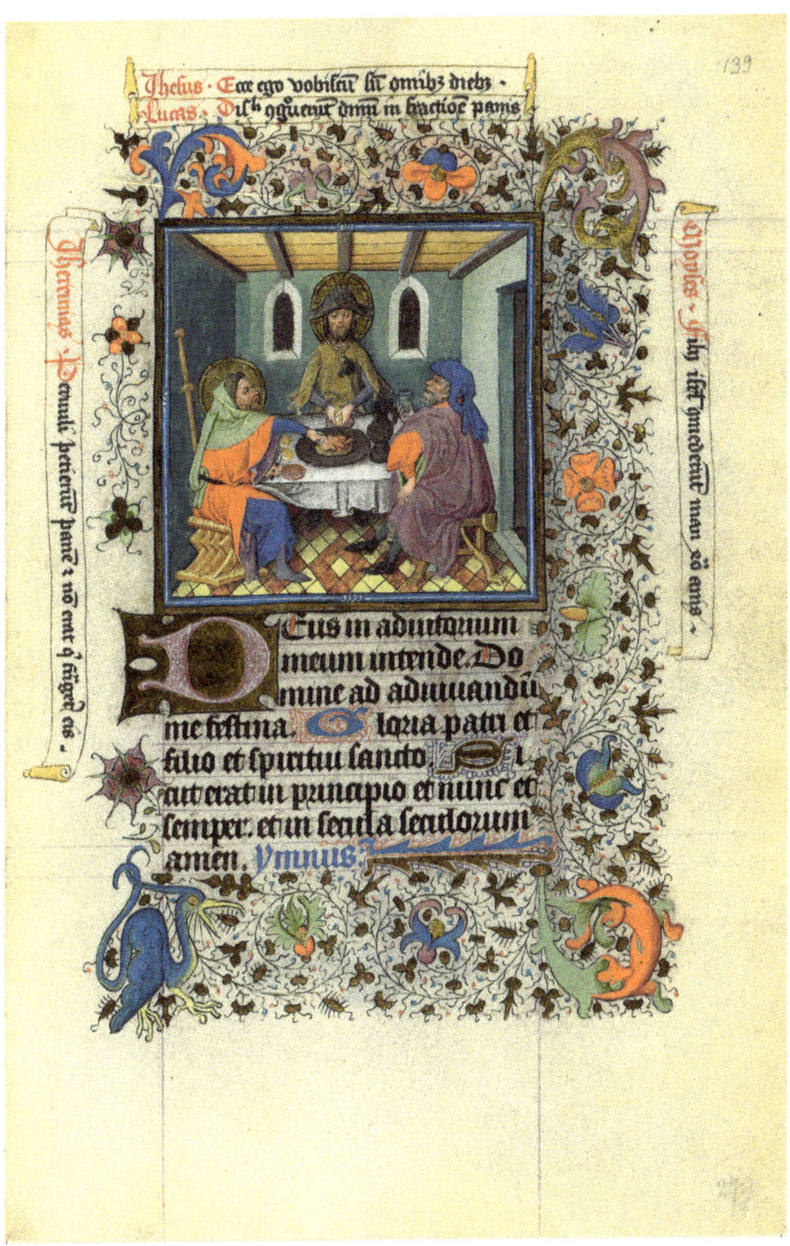

Fig. 23 Master of Catherine of Cleves. *The Disciples Recognize Jesus from The Hours of Catherine of Cleves* **Dutch (Utrecht) c. 1435–1445.**

NY Pierpont Morgan Library MS M945, fol. 139ra courtesy KB national library of the Netherlands. ©Facsimile Edition of *The Hours of Catherine of Cleves* (MS M. 917 and MS M. 945), 2010 Faksimile Verlag.

There is a clear development slowly taking place with the example from France humanizing the features of the participants somewhat. But the gestures and poses retain a degree of stylisation that has been abandoned by Duccio in Siena one hundred years earlier. The Dutch example presents us with two disciples of artisan appearance and manner as the stage-right character who has been given a halo reaches out in a rather unmannerly fashion to grab a handful of meat before the bread arrives. It is a much more down-to-earth presentation typical of the period known as the Northern Renaissance. So within these regional variations, Duccio stands out as an innovator albeit that Ghiberti felt that he had not quite freed himself from inherited tradition.

The Sixteenth Century

Albrecht Dürer[144] was an artist who exerted great influence upon renaissance artists. His output both as a printmaker and painter was prodigious. After travelling in Italy early in the sixteenth-century, Durer began work on a cycle of woodcuts known as *The Small Passion*. The full cycle of thirty-six woodcuts was published in 1511 and republished continuously until the twentieth-century. It proved to be extremely popular in Europe being published in Venice in1512 with an Italian text.

144. Nürenberg 1471–1528.

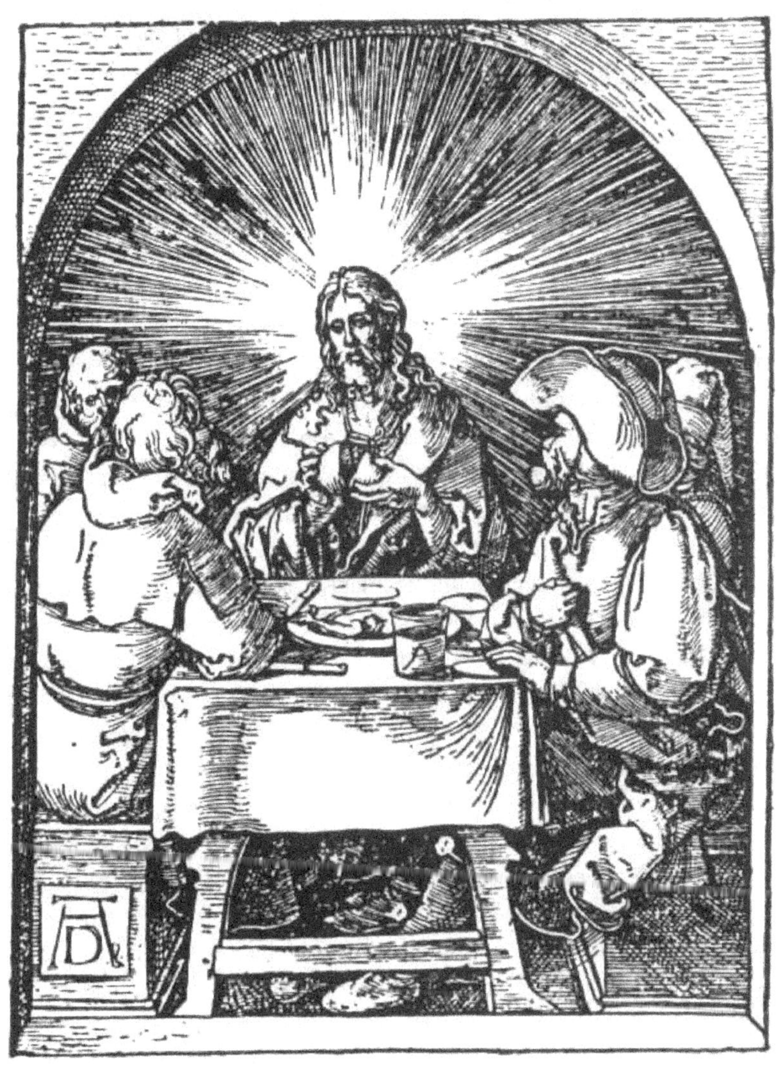

Fig. 24 Albrecht Dürer. Creative Commons CCO License.

The woodcut of *Christ and the Disciples at Emmaus*[145] appeared about fifty years after the image in *The Hours of Catherine of Cleves* but it has closer affinity with it and the Gothic tradition than it does with the Italian influences apparent in Duccio's paintings of the same period. The-stage left disciple in particular seems to be related to the earlier depiction with his coarse features and rough demeanour. In fact, the whole presentation with the rough-hewn table and rudimentary utensils speaks of life lived at the basic level of physical comfort. The expression of the two disciples and the third background figure tell of a harsh existence unrelieved by the comforts of life. The Christ figure fits in with this impression. The appearance is of a *man of sorrows and acquainted with grief*[146] who empathises with those whose human condition makes understanding and belief a huge challenge. He is very much at one with them but also apart—other. This *otherness* Dürer depicts with a spectacular burst of radiance emanating from the presence of Christ as he breaks the bread. It is presented like an explosion from which the disciples do not recoil but simply stare, silent, teased out of thought. It is a very potent, hypnotic image, eloquent in its silent simplicity.

Shortly after producing the small passion cycle, Dürer met Martin Luther in Augsburg just after Luther had circulated his ninety-five theses. Dürer became a devoted follower of Luther whose emphasis on the essential nature of faith in spiritual progress was clearly exercising Dürer as he worked on this image before the meeting with Luther. Luther appears unwittingly to have given verbal expression to Dürer's imagery. If we go back to the biblical text of the meeting on the road to Emmaus, it is clear that it is the failure of faith that Christ identifies and for which he roughly chastises the pilgrims. What I find very significant in the image created by Dürer is that he seems to focus on a holistic response to the gospel. He avoids the temptation that many of us fall into of hurling a text at a situation that supports a particular extreme point of view. The figure of Christ is here one upon whose lips harsh words of judgement do not easily sit. It is the message of care, understanding and empathy permeating the gospel that Dürer communicates.

Marco Marziale was employed by the Venetian republic and worked under Giovanni Bellini as a pupil and as an assistant on the decoration of the great council chamber of the Doge's Palace. His dates are uncertain but he was known to have been active from 1492–1507 in Venice. He was part of the early Renaissance in western art.

145 .Whereabouts unknown.

146. KJV Isaiah 53: 3.

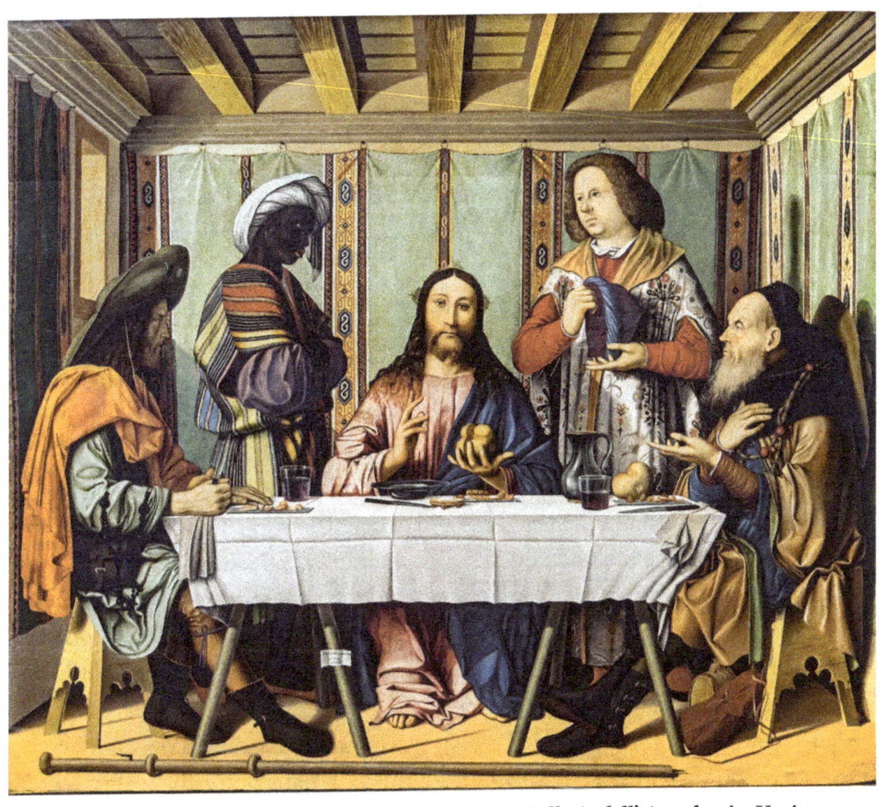

Fig. 25 Marco Marziale *Supper at Emmaus* **1506 Gallerie dell' Accademia, Venice.**

It may be of interest to look back at Altobello Melone's *Road to Emmaus*.[147] Marziale was working in Germany where he met and was an influence upon Melone. It is thought that Melone may have been Marziale's pupil. It is possible to see Melone's Christ/Pilgrim figure in the style of Marziale's painting of *The Supper at Emmaus*.[148] Marziale's figures appear stiff and posed and of rather coarse features. It appears that Marziale had himself been influenced by the northern renaissance painters and in particular by Dürer. The straight-ahead, distant stare of Christ recalls that of Dürer's famous *Self-portrait in Fur Collared Robe*.[149] The two disciples in the Emmaus painting are very rigidly posed and show little sign of hearts let alone ones that have burned within them. The attendant to Christ's stage-left looks rather like a waiting bureaucrat with a briefcase under his arm. The black waiter splendid in turban and robes looks on patiently. There is a stillness and discipline about the painting that contributes to a solemnity that later painters discarded, often dramatically so. To modern eyes, Marziale's approach may appear to pull against rather than enhance the subject matter. The biblical account of the reappearance of Christ suggests that he breaks into and disrupts the old order. The measured formality of Marziale's presentation and very detailed attention to the textiles and décor suggest that Marziale's focus is not centered on the emotion conveyed by the biblical account. An interesting anecdote perhaps illustrates this point regarding the nature of and the response to the work of Marziale. Evidently, John Ruskin asked a friend who was visiting Venice in 1872 to make a detailed drawing of the decoration on a tablecloth that appears in one of Marziale's paintings in the city. Ruskin used this as a pattern for the wallpaper in his study in the English Lake District.

Tiziano Vecellio[150] or, as he is known worldwide, Titian, was born in the region of the Veneto about seventy miles to the north of Venice. He worked in Venice and eventually died there. He was influenced by Giorgione and he is thought to have been a pupil of Giovanni Bellini. His pedigree as a member of the Venetian School is impeccable. The love of light and color characterises the venetian painters of the Renaissance and Titian is widely regarded as their greatest master. Titian developed the style of painting that he had inherited to a more dynamic level.

147. Fig. 20.

148. Gallerie dell' Accademia, Venice.

149. 1500 now in The Alte Pinakothek, Munich.

150. c.1488–1576.

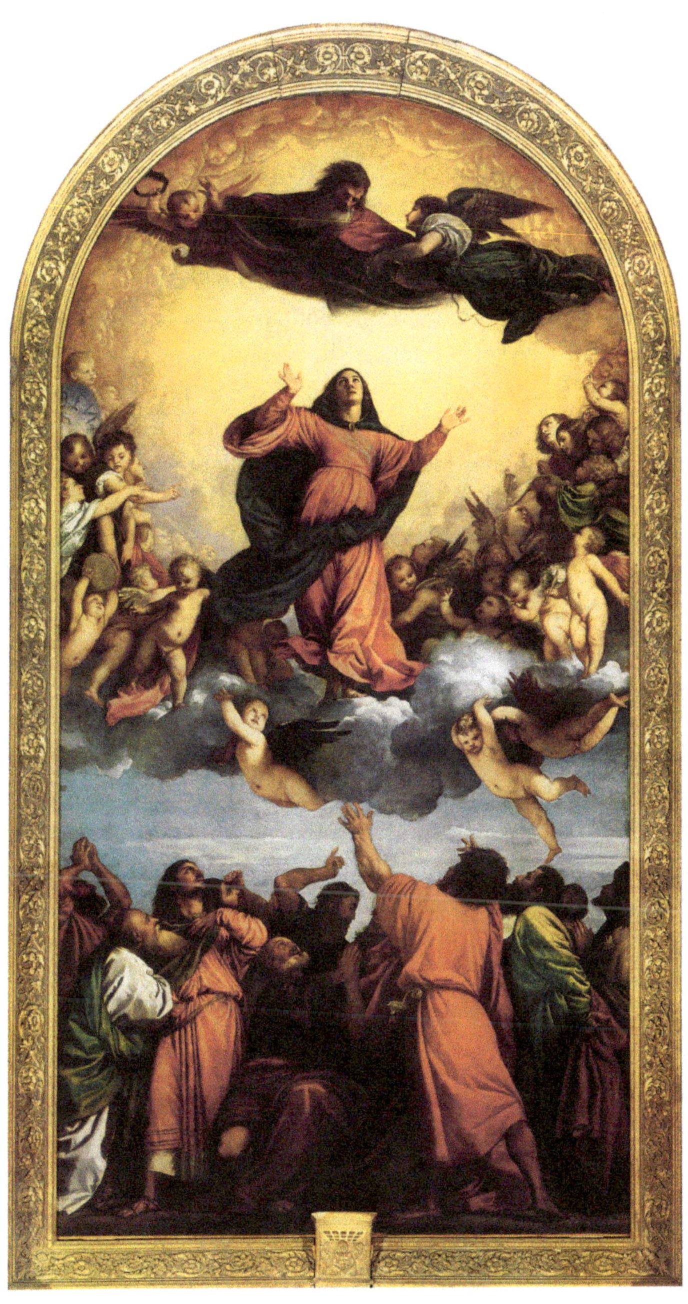

Fig. 26 Tiziano Vecellio known as Titian ***The Assumption of the Virgin*** **1516–18 Santa Maria Gloriosa dei Frari, Venice.**

With grateful thanks to Fr. Apollonio for granting me permission to use this image.

This is demonstrated magnificently in *The Assumption of the Virgin.*[151] The painting conveys a sense of breaking free. It is as if Titian now in his early thirties is asserting his independence from earlier classical influences. There is a dramatic agitation in the painting. The Apostles looking up are arranged as a stage tableau might be arranged to convey to an audience in a freeze-framed moment an iconic image of confusion, excitement and awe. The downstage centre-left figure reaches with outstretched hands as if fearful of the Virgin falling to earth. Indeed, the two putti supporting the cloud upon which the Virgin is borne aloft do appear to be under considerable strain and in need of assistance. The figure stage-right clasps his hands in wonder. The bearded figure next to him stoops for protection beneath the more vigorous younger man who himself appears to be entranced. The figure next to him shields his eyes against the light and the central figure points upwards and exclaims to his companion. The perspective is adjusted for each of the three groups of figures. The group of the Apostles is closest to us the audience or viewers of the painting. The central group featuring the Virgin is further back, and God the Father is further back still. In this way we are drawn inwards and upwards. The movement is, of course, emphasised by the magnificent use of colour so beloved by the venetian painters The red of the cloaks worn by the stage-centre-right and left Apostles is picked up by the robe of the Virgin and the stage-left shoulder of God the Father. The high drama, agitated energy and turmoil of the painting mark a departure from the calm, still presentation of high-renaissance painting which was a style that Titian had inherited. However, the control remains. There is a disciplined plan behind the presentation of turmoil.

151. 1516–1518 Santa Maria dei Frari, Venice.

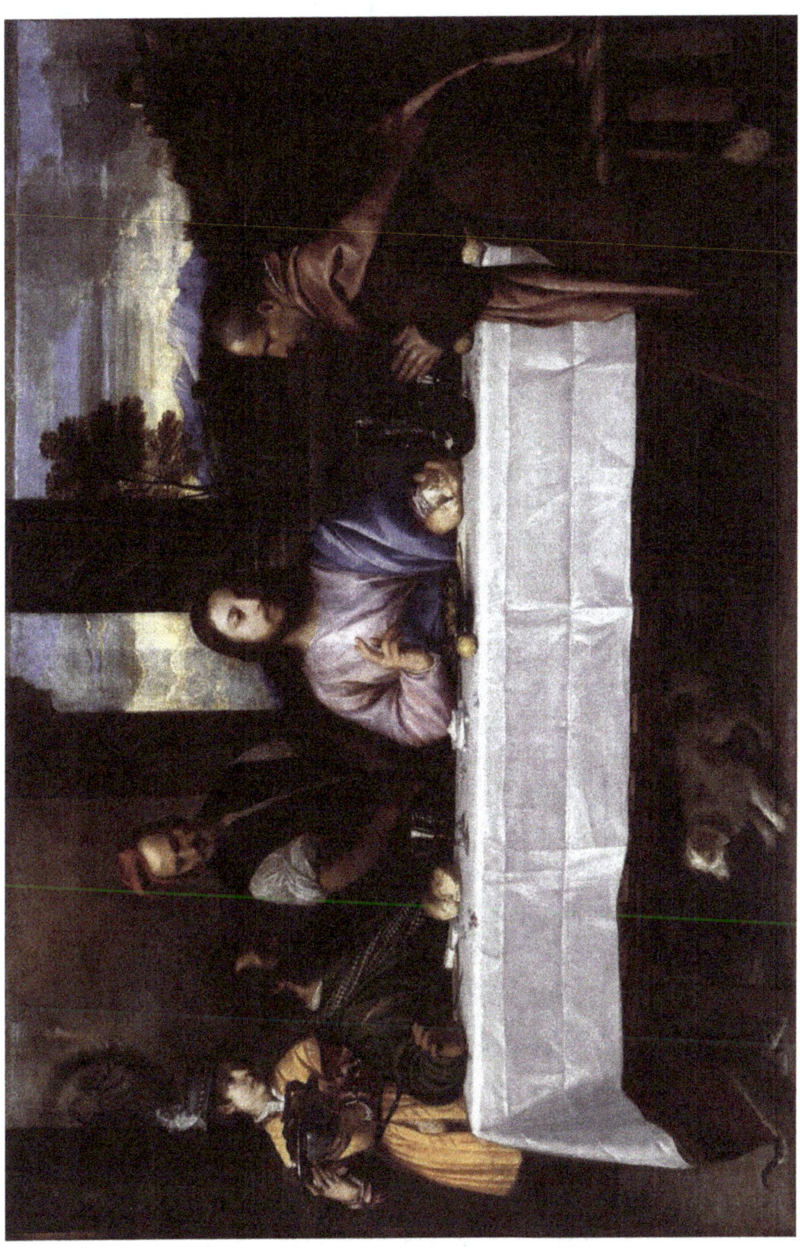

Fig. 27 Tiziano Vecellio, known as Titian. *Supper at Emmaus* circa1530 Louvre, Paris © PD The Athenaeum.

The Supper at Emmaus[152] was painted during a period in which Titian's work noticeably changes in manner. This is clear from the juxtaposition of these two images. Whether Titian's personal circumstances[153] had anything to do with this marked change we cannot know of course. There is a noticeable restraint in the use of color with the pale shades of the Emmaus work contrasting dramatically with the vivacity of colour in image twenty–six. The *Supper at Emmaus* may be less exciting than the glory of the *Assumption* but it quietly draws our attention to the intimate drama of the moment. *The Assumption of the Virgin* is a great shout of acclamation at the external drama. It is the *Hallelujah Chorus* as compared to the aria *I Know that my Redeemer Liveth* in Handel's *Messiah*. This is entirely appropriate to a scene in which the despondent disciples are about to "know" the living Jesus. However, there is no sense of Titian's engagement with that charged moment of recognition that is, surely, the vital climax of the biblical narrative. The character stage-right of the table is receiving close attention by the host and his magnificently attired servant. Lounging back in his splendid green robe, he is relaxed and aristocratically self-assured. There is little hint of the dusty pilgrim about him. When we learn that the "disciple" in question is thought to be a depiction of Nicola Maffei matters begin to clarify. Nicola Maffei was a count in the Mantuan aristocracy and an art collector. He had also commissioned the painting from Titian who clearly would have had other things on his mind than probing the hermeneutics of the gospel account. Pleasing his patron who was a military captain and diplomat serving Federico Gonzaga the ruler of Mantua would have been his primary concern. The man stage-left of the table whilst perhaps showing more interest in Christ's activity shows no more deference. "Humility" does not immediately come to mind. He is also splendidly dressed and it is suggested that the figure, in fact, represents Federico himself. Titian is at pains to demonstrate the range of his painterly skills. This would, no doubt, encourage his patron to congratulate himself on his connoisseurship. It would also guarantee some influence upon the patron's elevated circle of connections to whom he would proudly display his latest acquisition. Impressing wealthy patrons does seem to have been a motivation that greatly exercised Titian. His success in so doing supported his lavish life style. In *The Supper at Emmaus* this circle of viewers, I suggest, would have their wonder aroused by the white tablecloth with its every crease and fold

152. c. 1530. Now in the Louvre Museum, Paris.

153. Titian's wife had died in 1530.

exquisitely rendered. The still-life items of salt-cellar, decanter, glasses, and bread are so realistically depicted as to seduce the viewer with the sense that they might be lifted from the table and inspected at close quarters. Certainly, there is an ethereal quality to the depiction of Christ's face and gaze, but the poise of the aristocratic "pilgrims" is in no way disturbed by the cosmic magnitude of the event recorded in the biblical narrative.

MANNERISM

Throughout his long life in Venice, Titian remained essentially true to a conservative manner of subject representation but there was a developing movement away from strict adherence to the classical ideal in northern Italy. Correggio[154] worked largely in Parma.

154. 1489–1534. Antonio Aliegri was born in Correggio and named after the small town in Emilia.

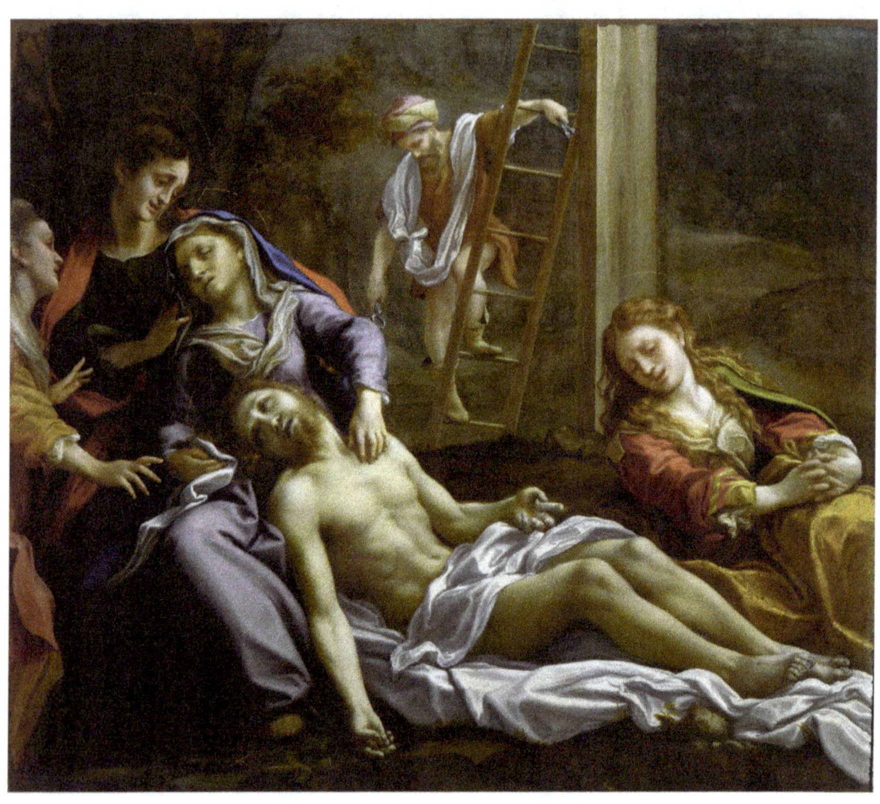

Fig. 28 Correggio *Lamentation over the Dead Christ* **circa 1524–25**
National Gallery, Parma © PD The Athenaeum.

His *Lamentation over the Dead Christ*[155] is remarkable on many levels. The nobility of the figures demonstrates a connection with the past but the intensity of overwhelming emotion offers glimpses of the later Baroque style. In Florence, things were changing more dramatically.

155. 1525. Galleria Nazionale, Parma.

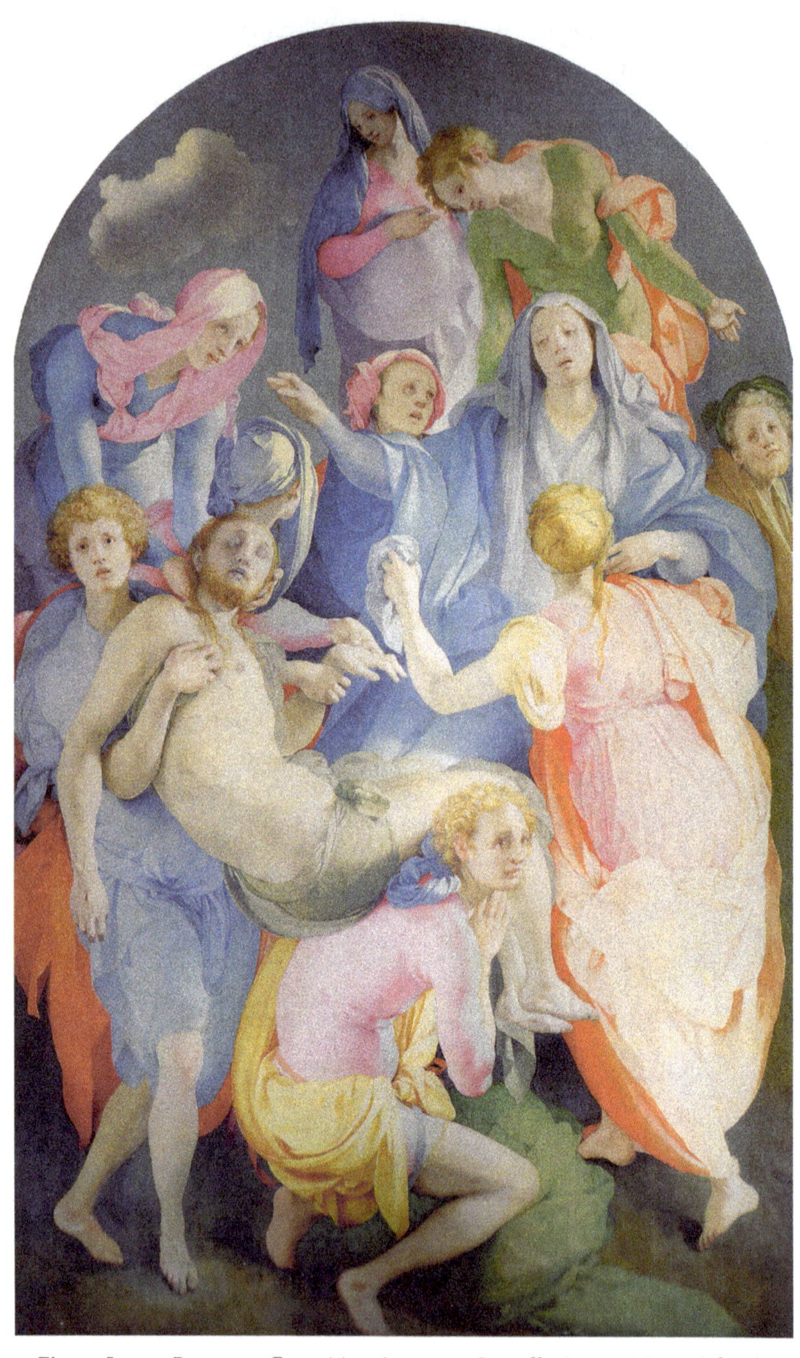

Fig. 29 Jacopo Pontormo *Deposition* circa 1528 Cappella Capponi Santa Felicità, Florence © PD Wikimedia Commons

The Deposition painted by Jacopo Pontormo[156] overwhelms by its audacity on all levels. The pink and blue colour tones surprise and intoxicate in a way that inhibits the viewers' attempts to unravel the knot of figures. Deciphering the subject is complicated by visual references to paintings of *The Lamentation* and the image of Christ's body draped over the lap of the Virgin in Michelangelo's *Pietà*.[157] The youth in the foreground of Pontormo's *Deposition* looking out towards the viewer with bewildered expression is ostensibly supporting the lower body of Christ. However, when we notice that he takes the weight on his bent toes or that he is, in fact, weightless, he becomes an ethereal presence. The painting is like a musical composition that relies on dissonant chords to make disturbing dramatic effects. We experience the awe on the faces of the angelic presences bearing the body of Christ, the soulful pity on the face of the Virgin, and that on the faces of the women who surround her. We see those emotions reflected on the face presented at an angle in parallel to that of the Virgin but depicted in contrasting dull brown shades stage-left of the Virgin.[158] We sense that we are experiencing, with the painter, a cathartic moment by participating in this deeply-felt painting. The challenge to the viewers' perceptions of everyday reality is certainly less demanding in Correggio's painting, but,

> both have imposed on classical inheritance a kind of energy of feeling that exceeds classical restraints and which demands a mobility of form that overrides classical prescriptions of constructed order.[159]

The Deposition by Jacopo Pontormo is widely referenced as an outstanding example of the style of painting that came to be called Mannerism. The term dates from the late 1700's and is attributed to the Italian art historian Luigi Lanzi. Mannerist paintings address the viewer through the style and technique or the manner in which they are visually presented. It is sometimes argued that style predominates over substance but this is unsatisfactory as a generalization. The style or manner of Pontormo's presentation whilst clearly challenging does not, I suggest, render it unsubstantial. The substance of a religious artwork or what Steiner refers to as the real

156. 1494–1557.
157. 1498/9 St. Peter's Basilica, Vatican City.
158. It is convincingly speculated that this is a depiction of the artist himself.
159. Freedberg. Ibid.,185.

presence[160] may be delivered by means other than the idealized naturalism of Leonardo, Michelangelo, and Raphael. Mannerist painters explore this possibility with effects that sometimes seem bizarre but may also be profoundly moving. Mannerist paintings can be a challenge to viewers today. However, today's viewer who has experienced modern expressionist paintings may find such works more accessible than those with the cultural experience of the original viewers were equipped to do. Paintings had up until this time sought to form an alliance with the viewers' daily visual experience. Suddenly, the viewer is presented with a painting that requires a psychological effort to overcome the initial recoil at the improbable nature of the presentation. I made reference to the fact that the downstage-centre figure's toes in Pontormo's *Deposition* appear to be accepting the weight of the lower body of the dead Christ. Such reactions have to be abandoned if we are to progress towards a participation in the painting. The whole painting, once the boundary of improbability is overcome, speaks of emotional or spiritual states rather than of physical states of being. We are confronted with non-rational expression. The balance and harmony of the High Renaissance is disturbed. In the period 1522–1525, Pontormo is recorded as resident in the Certosa[161]Galizzo near Florence where he was seeking refuge from the plague ravaging through Florence at that time. Whilst there, he worked on a fresco series of Christ's passion that survive in very poor condition. After the completion of the fresco cycle, Pontormo worked on a large oil painting for the monastery. This is in a good state of preservation.

160. Steiner. *No Passion Spent,* 33.

161. Carthusian Monastery.

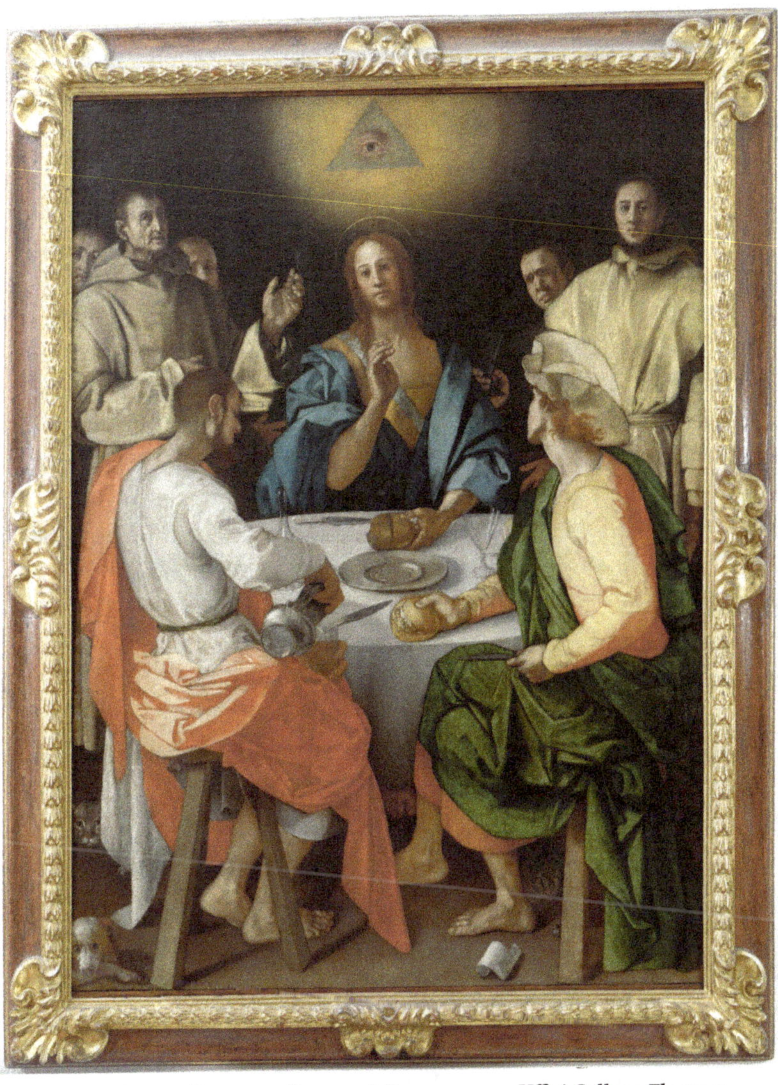

Fig. 30 Jacopo Pontormo *Supper at Emmaus* **1525 Uffizi Gallery, Florence.**
With grateful thanks to dr. Eike Schmidt for granting me permission to use this image.

Pontormo's *Supper at Emmaus* is often seen as having been influenced by the woodcut of Dürer. The figures are arranged in a similar fashion and the scene is thrust directly at us with no intervening space. There is more of a sense of that alliance with the viewers' daily visual experience than there is in *The Deposition,* painted three years later. This, of course, can be attributed to the subject matter in the Emmaus painting which is basically that of a domestic scene—supper. Here, the bread has not yet been broken but is being blessed prior to this act. What Pontormo builds is an atmosphere of expectation. The Carthusian monks either side of Christ convey this with the monk stage-right raising a hand as if receptive to what is about to take place. Two lay persons peer around his shoulders. The younger monk, stage-left, stares out entranced by the spirituality of the moment. Peering around the younger monk's shoulder, a lay figure has a deeply perplexed expression on his face as he struggles for everyday normality by proffering a glass that the table appears to lack. The two barefooted pilgrims being three-quarters on to the viewer create a visual triangle with Christ at the apex. The triangle is replicated by the later addition of the framed eye above the head of Christ. Apart from the technical function of their positioning, the two pilgrims are of great interest as part of the substance of the painting. They are like the lay bearers of the elements at the Eucharist. The stage-right pilgrim concentrates upon the act of pouring a glass of wine and the stage-left pilgrim grasps the bread as he looks fixedly upon the face of the soon-to-be-revealed Son of God. Central to this carefully constructed moment of tense expectation or apprehension is the calm face of Christ with his eyes focussed on a reality beyond the mundane world. The beautiful color tones of red, green, and blue that pick out the triangle of figures separate them from the tension and agitation that surrounds them. The viewers are, as in the Dürer woodcut, placed between the two pilgrims. We, with them, face the figure of Christ as he blesses the bread. Thus we are in the scene and apart from it at the same time. We experience on the one hand the tension and mystery evoked by the furtive peering of the human beings and animals.[162] On the other hand, we experience the anticipation at the table. Pontormo does not convey the passionate drama of earlier and later painters of *The Supper at Emmaus*. This might be expected to lessen its impact as a religious work of art. Pontormo relies on the power of aesthetic

162. To a contemporary viewer, the cats staring at them from the darkness under the chair and table would have been a reminder of the ever-watchful enemy of their souls and, by extension, of the importance of the sacred moment recalled in their Eucharistic observance represented in the painting.

sensation. This may have an effect that is as intense but more difficult to articulate than the power of passion demonstrated by characters involved in dramatic action. Perhaps to a greater extent than more literal approaches, the style of Pontormo's painting requires the participation of the viewer for its completion.

Jacopo Bassano was born in the small provincial town of Bassano del Grappa in 1510. He died there in 1592. His father ran a local artists' workshop and Jacopo would have been influenced by his involvement in his father's output of religious works in the local style. However, Jacopo seems to have been keen to expose himself to work much further afield than his limited travel would have made accessible. Although he is recorded as residing in Venice in the1530's becoming familiar with the works of Titian and Bellini, it is suggested that he must also have been influenced by the prints of work from such contemporaries as Tintoretto and Raphael in Italy to Dürer in Germany and Aertsen in the Netherlands. An appreciation of the intense spiritual debate affecting the mood of the public that Bassano was addressing with his work is essential in unlocking the morality that pervades his paintings. The necessity of catholic renewal was building well before Luther nailed his ninety-five theses to the door of the church in Wittenberg in 1517. The fifth Lateran Council[163] was warned by Giles of Viterbo[164] of the dire state of the church that threatened to undermine Christendom itself. Radical reform was urgently required. He spoke of personal reform to be undertaken by every individual Catholic soul. Luther's thinking was radically different: he saw the need to be for theological reform. The Church as an institution needed fundamental reform. Faith based on biblical teaching alone—*sola scriptura*—was the only pathway to salvation. Church tradition enshrined in doctrine was man-made and, therefore, lacking the divine authority that was possessed by scripture alone. Good works and priestly ministrations were at best a distraction. Cardinals Pole[165] and Contarini[166] were prominent in urging a middle way.[167]

163. 1512–17.

164. Created Cardinal in 1517.

165. 1500–1558. Last Roman Catholic Archbishop of Canterbury and papal legate to the Council of Trent.

166. 1483—1542. Prominent member of the Spirituali—a reform movement within the Roman Catholic Church from 1530's to 1560's. Diplomat and theologian, Contarini was an intellectual and an art aficionado and a collector. He was an advocate of the new Jesuit order.

167. The early Church fathers up to Augustine who died 430AD initiated an exegetical

The Jesuits[168] were advocates of *the vita mista*. They saw good works as outward and visible manifestations of the devout life and not as of spiritual justification in themselves. Institutional structures were an aid to a devout life and not a stumbling block on the pathway towards it. But such was the climate of the debate that extreme positions were taken up. Such positions uncomplicated by the niceties of debate are more easily made accessible to a mass audience. With personal charisma and a simple, straightforward message, a skilled orator can be a powerful force. Such an individual was the Florentine Dominican Prior, Girolamo Savonarola.[169] The necessity of a devout life and the condemnation of Church corruption was his simple message urged with uncompromising vehemence. It inevitably met with a like response from the established church authorities. After being excommunicated by the Borgia pope Alexander VI, he was burned at the stake. Ironically, after his death many Protestants as well as Catholics empathised with much of his teaching. Luther's rigidly-insisted-upon alternative way gave rise to like-minded exclusive communities such as John Calvin's in Geneva to which dissenters could attach their loyalty. The degenerate spiritual condition that reformers such as Savonarola railed against was that of *tepidity*. This was a lack of religious enthusiasm that could lead to the sin of sloth or *acedia*. *Tepid* used metaphorically derives from *The Book of The Revelation of St. John the Divine*:

> So then because thou art luke warm, and, neither hot nor cold, I will spue thee out of my mouth.[170]

This dire warning to the Church of Laodicea appears from the verses that follow it to have been brought about by self-complacency. A similar condition, so the reformers claimed, had been brought about, in their own communities. Religious observance had degenerated to mindless routine. Savonarola's emphasis is upon the spirituality of the individual as opposed

---

tradition of a dichotomy between the active life—*vita active*—as exemplifies by Martha in the Bible accounts and the contemplative life—*vita contemplative*—as exemplified by Mary. The *vita contemplativa* was regarded as the greater way. Gregory the Great—Pope 590–604—argued that the *vita mista* was demonstrated by the life of Christ as recorded in the Gospels. Thus it was the perfect way.

168. Ignatius of Loyola was ordained as a priest in Venice in 1557. He founded a new order *The Society of Jesus—The Jesuits* licensed in 1540 by Pope Paul III. This is a teaching order that was active in the Veneto and influential in Tridentine reform.

169. 1452–98

170. KJV. Revelations, 3. 16.

to public displays of good works. Long after his death, he was accorded the ultimate condemnation by the Counter Reformation. He was named as The Italian Luther.

Jacopo Bassano's work is notable for his introduction of genre[171] elements into his religious paintings. Peter Aertsen[172] was developing a type of painting in the Netherlands that involved mundane settings such as kitchens and markets with workaday folk engaging in routine activity alongside and apparently unrelated to the biblical scenes depicted. Even more surprisingly, these biblical scenes were overpowered in size by the foreground genre scenes. Sometimes, Aertsen's work has an eccentricity that can alienate the viewer.

171. The use of the term "genre" in this context is rather puzzling and it is difficult to pin down an entirely satisfactory definition of the term. It was not a term used by contemporary writers and does not appear to have been in use until the eighteenth century. It was then used to typify the work of certain painters of the Dutch Golden Age of the seventeenth century such as Vermeer and Jan Steen. These did not fit into the traditional genre classifications: historical, pastoral, still-life, landscape etc. In the seventeenth century it becomes, therefore, a genre of its own by default as it were. It is easier to give examples of its application than it is to find a definition of the term. Genre painting features unidentified humanity often engaging in humble human activity. In religious paintings it refers to elements involving mundane activity that does not have an obvious association with the central subject of the painting. The setting of these paintings tends to be down-to-earth: kitchens, markets, and taverns often feature. Such settings have sometimes led critics to regard genre paintings or paintings with genre elements to be second-rate. Thus "genre" became a term employed derogatively. Perhaps a comparison could be made with the use of the term to describe the "new-wave" drama of the 1960's that shunned the genteel drawing-room setting with which audiences were familiar: kitchen-sink drama. This term itself derived from an expressionistic painting by John Bratby in the late1950's.

172. 1508–1576

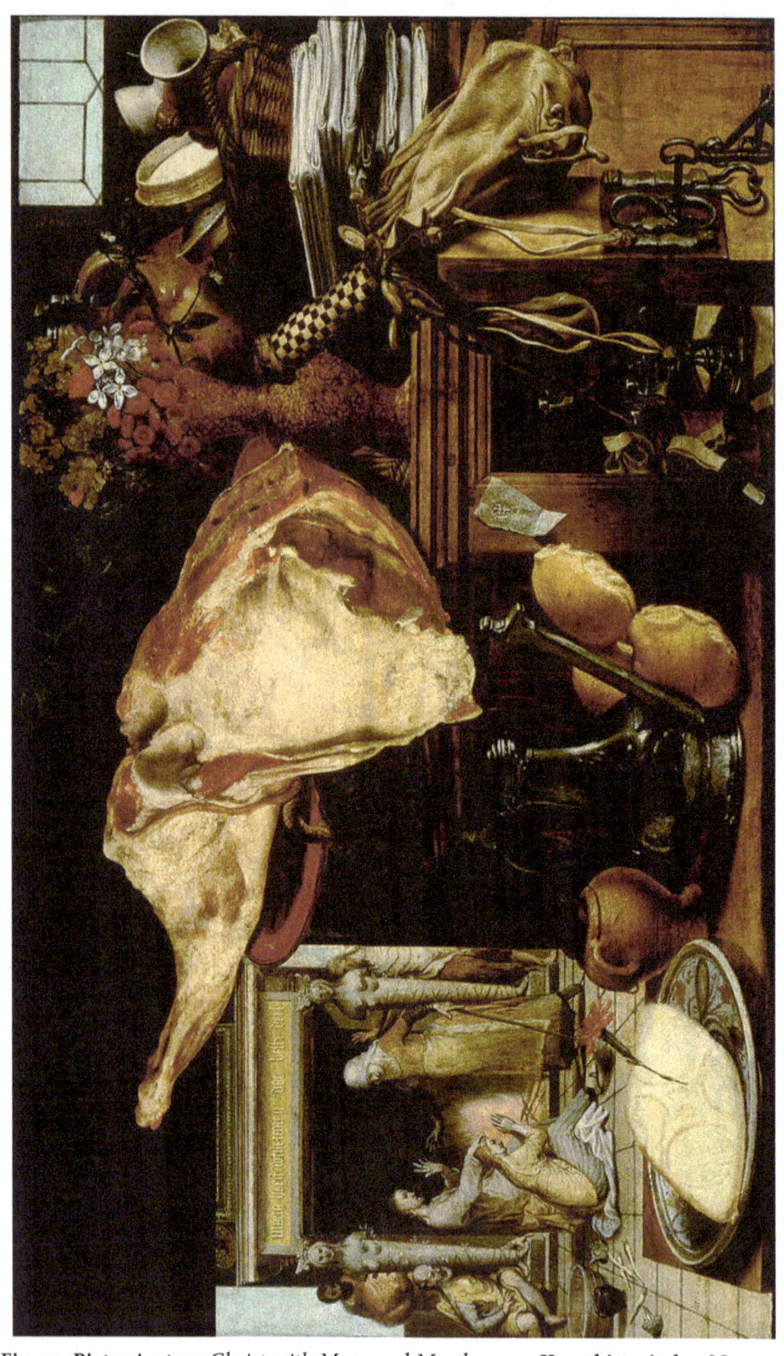

Fig. 31. Pieter Aertsen *Christ with Mary and Martha* 1552 Kunsthistorisches Museum, Vienna © PD The Athenaeum.

Christ with Mary and Martha is a case in point. The leg of venison grossly dominates the foreground still-life scene and it half-frames the biblical scene upstage right. Some cross-fertilization of ideas between the Netherlands and northern Italy no doubt took place, but the direction of flow and the extent of influence is a matter of debate.

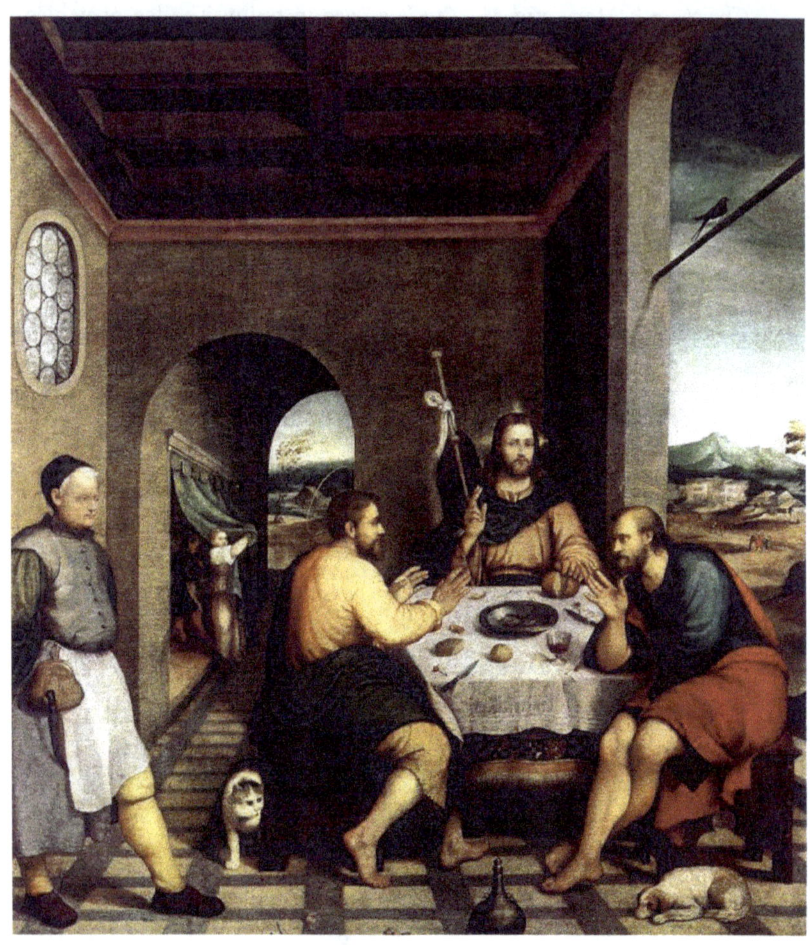

Fig. 32 Jacopo Bassano ***Supper at Emmaus*** **circa 1538 Duomo Citadella Italy.**

In the earlier of Bassano's two paintings of *The Supper at Emmaus*[173]the genre elements are naturally integrated with the subject matter. This painting was commissioned by the archpriest and aldermen of Cittadella to decorate the presbytery of the local church. Aikema[174] suggests that Jacopo was firstly a moralist and only uses genre elements to convey a message. Sometimes, Aikema suggests, the historians' focus on the genre elements of Bassano's paintings as if they were of primary interest detracts from the significance of Bassano's work. Public commissions such as this 1538 work, Aikema sees as essentially conforming to counter reformation orthodoxy. He sees those painted for domestic use as more reflective of christianity associated with evangelism. Figure thirty-two has the biblical element—the supper itself—prominently placed but it is off-centre. The still-life of the table top is meticulously portrayed and displayed by the improbable perspective of the table. Bassano displays the items on the table with great care. They are laid out before us like items on a tray in a party game that are then removed from the viewers gaze. The winner of the game is the one who can recall the greatest number of items. We are clearly meant to take note of them: bread, wine, fish, and cherries. The two pilgrims are totally engaged with what they have just experienced. Christ is no longer there as a physical presence. He is depicted iconically as the risen Christ with a cruciform nimbus. He holds a staff with an iconic white cloth of purity and peace knotted to it. He is not the pilgrim who accompanied them on the road as depicted in the far distance stage-centre-left. After blessing and breaking the bread "he vanished out of their sight."[175] What Bassano shows us the two pilgrims in animated conversation as they recollect.

> Did not our hearts burn within us, while he talked with us by the way, and while he opened to us the scriptures?[176]

The innkeeper is impatient to clear the table. He has his hands behind his back, his left leg forward with his well-filled belly over his apron. He is a figure of spiritual sloth. Standing downstage right, he is totally unmoved by what he appears to be witnessing. In contrast, the servant girl upstage urgently pushes the curtain aside sensing that there is something taking place that she does not want to miss. The poor and humble servant girl

173. 1538
174. Aikema. *Jacopo Bassano and his Public.*
175. KJV. Luke 24. 31.
176. Ibid. 32

is perhaps more spiritually receptive than the spiritually dull innkeeper weighed down by the burden of his worldly preoccupations. The cat is a traditional symbol of the devil always seeking whom he may devour. The dozing dog is totally off-guard against the furtively advancing cat. It is a very potent image of the vulnerability of the tepid Christian. Such an image would have been readily accessible to the contemporary viewer of Bassano's altar-piece The table display clearly refers to the Eucharist as an essential means of keeping the christian alert to diabolical assaults on his or her daily pilgrimage by becoming personally involved in Christ's sacrifice. The bread and wine are accompanied by a central platter of fish. The fish, of course, has many theological overtones. *ICHTHYS* is the Greek word for fish and the acrostic made from the word by early Christians was Jesus Christ, Son of God, Saviour—Iesous Christus Theou Yios Soter. Biblical baptism by total immersion was seen as being born again, fish-like, in water. Laid at each place on the table is a cherry. Cherries were often associated with the Madonna recalling Elizabeth's words to Mary:

> And she spake out with a loud voice, and said, Blessed art thou among women, and blessed is the fruit of thy womb.[177]

The sixteenth century *Cherry Tree Carol* demonstrates the popularity of the image.

Joseph was an old man,
And an old man was he,
When he wedded Mary
In the land of Galilee.

Joseph and Mary walk'd
Through an orchard good,
Where was cherries and berries
So red as any blood.

O then bespoke Mary,
So meek and so mild,
'Pluck me one cherry, Joseph,
For I am with child.'

O then bespoke Joseph
With words so unkind,
'Let him pluck thee a cherry
That brought thee with child.'

177. KJV. Luke 1. 42.

Then bow'd down the highest tree
Unto our Lady's hand:
Then she said, 'See, Joseph,
I have cherries at command!'

'O eat your cherries, Mary,
O eat your cherries now;
O eat your cherries, Mary,
That grow upon the bough.[178]

Cherries are often depicted in pairs as in *A Midsummer Night's Dream*[179] to symbolise a close female relationship. Mary and Elizabeth are both pregnant in supernatural circumstances. Bassano's 1538 *Supper at Emmaus* prominently displayed behind the altar from which the blessed bread and wine of the Eucharist was being served, was clearly intended to encourage the participant to accept in humility the miracle of the incarnation.

178. *The Cherry Tree Carol* c.1500. The original version of the Carol is much older still. It dates from the middle ages and it was performed in English sixteenth century mystery plays. Historians suggest that it is based upon a Syriac drama probably brought back from the middle east by twelfth-century crusaders.

179. Shakespeare. *A Midsummer Night's* Dream, 3: 2, 213–216.

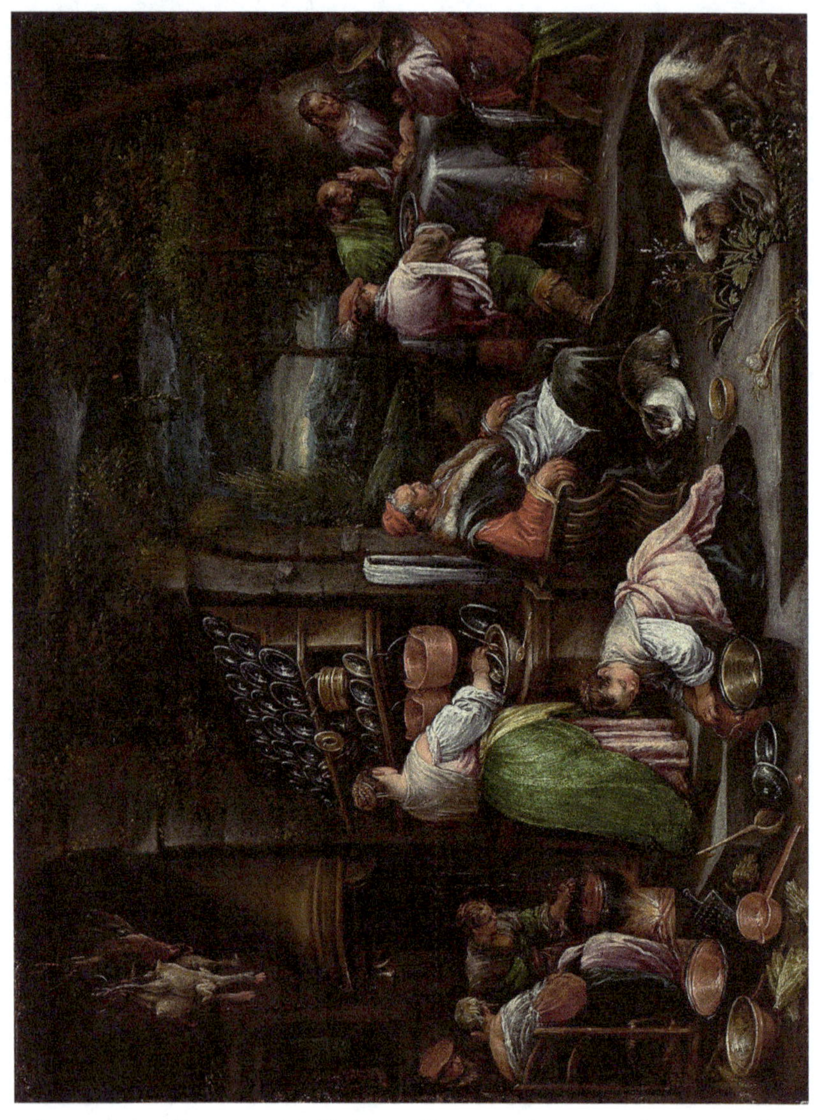

Fig. 33. Jacopo Bassano assisted by his son Francesco circa 1578 private ownership.
My grateful thanks to Clementine Sinclair of Christie's London for granting me permission to use this image.

In the late 1570's, Jacopo assisted by his son Francesco painted another version of *The Supper at Emmaus.*[180] It is clearly directed at an audience that differed from that of the 1538 version. The Bassano workshop produced many versions of this painting attesting to its popularity. It is thought that this particular version may well be the prototype. Evidently, Francesco was particularly skilled in genre painting and the kitchen scene with its clever details and colour palette suggest that it was by the hand of someone who delighted in the craft of painting and took pleasure in producing *meraviglia* or works that impressed rather than instructed. The cat and the dog appear as decorative components[181] rather than didactic elements. It has been suggested that Jacopo was responsible for the overall design that was then completed by Francesco although Jacopo himself appears to have been responsible for the figures at the table centre-stage-left and the horizon behind them with the three tiny figures of the pilgrims on their distant journey. The idea of life as a spiritual pilgrimage was very topical and these tiny figures totally overwhelmed by the size and prominence of the foreground figures are clearly meant to "speak" to the owners of the works as they contemplate the picture on a regular basis. They would be led toward this distant journey as their eyes move from the fascinatingly familiar bustle of the kitchen to reflect upon the miracle quietly taking place at the table. Stiff with gluttony and scarcely able to move, the Innkeeper presides over the comings and goings between the two worlds represented—the active world of the kitchen and the contemplative world of the table. He is enthroned and splendidly attired with a brilliant red cap and a fur-lined collar, the very picture of complacency as he glows with pride at the incongruous figure of his page dressed to impress with his feathered cap and tunic. That his presentation is pope-like is perhaps evangelically risqué given the period. In 1573, Veronese had painted a version of *The Last Supper* for a wall of the refectory of the *Basilica di Santi Giovanni e Paolo* that led to an investigation by the Roman Catholic Inquisition.[182] Church authorities on the Veneto

180. This Painting was sold at auction by Christies, London in 2010 to a private buyer. It was from the estate of the Earls of Erne, Crom Castle, Ireland.

181. Animal portraits were much loved by Venetians.

182. Irreverence, indecorum, and even heresy were suggested. The dog that appears very prominently downstage-centre and in front of the figure of Christ should be replaced by a more appropriate image. Mary Magdalene was suggested. The presence at the supper of drunken German "buffoons" seems to have particularly exercised the inquisitors. After all was not the land of Luther "infested by heresy" and very adept at ridiculing Catholicism in satirical pictorial propaganda without Veronese doing their work for

may have been actively checking artistic output post Trent but it seems that works aimed at private patrons attracted less precise scrutiny than works done in fulfilment of public commission. These might corrupt the morals of the ignorant masses. The table figures are such a contrast to the kitchen workers. The one cloaked in green bows his head in reverence as the bread is blessed. He partakes of the blessing as does the worshipper who receives the blessed bread at the Eucharist. The sunlit hill in background make the Psalmist's words irresistible:

> I will lift up mine eyes unto the hills from whence cometh my help.[183]

The table event stands out as an oasis of calm in the midst of the frenetic *busyness* of everyday life. The private owners of such works would, no doubt, have received much spiritual consolation from them.[184]

Tintoretto was born into this world of spiritual and artistic ferment in 1518. Luther had nailed his ninety-five theses to the Wittenberg church door the year before. Tintoretto was born in Venice where he carried out his lifetime's work. He was recorded as an independent painter in 1539.

> Counter to the old Titian, in these years it was Tintoretto who represented modernity in Venice and was the agent who converted much of Venetian painting to an aesthetic that was consonant with that of Mannerism.[185]

About five years after Bassano had painted his 1538 *Supper at Emmaus* in Cittadella thirty miles north-west of Venice, Tintoretto painted his version of the same subject.

---

them! Veronese compromised by changing the title of his work to *The Feast at the House of Levi*. This was also derived from the Gospels but it was not central to Catholic doctrine and the storm passed.

183. KJV. Psalm 121, 1.

184. Spiritual consolation can be rather expensive today. Christies' sale realized £312, 250.

185. Freedberg. Ibid., 352.

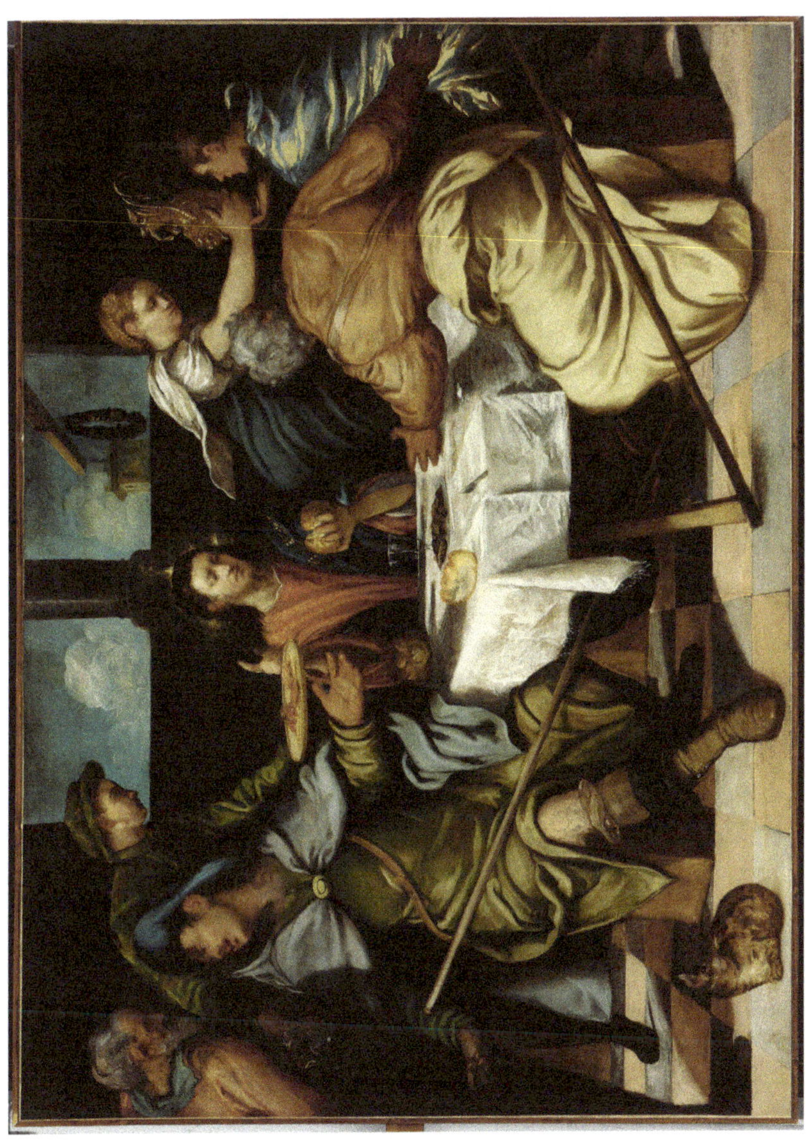

Fig. 34. Jacopo Robusti called Tintoretto. ***Supper at Emmaus*** **circa 1543 © Museum of Fine Arts Budapest.**

I find Freedberg's phrase, "an aesthetic consonant with that of Mannerism," tantalisingly accurate and at the same time irritatingly obscure. I think that it illustrates the tension that exists between the need felt by art historians to classify and the refusal of great creative artists to be so classified. Tintoretto was uniquely different. Attempts to understand this complex personality have been made perhaps most dramatically by Jean Paul Sartre's Marxist analysis:

> Born among the underlings who endured the weight of a superimposed hierarchy . . . the son of an artisan . . . (he) attacked the patrician aesthetics of fixity and being.[186]

Clearly, he was influenced by what was going on in the world around him. However, arguably, the greater external influence was the spirituality that was in the very air that Tintoretto breathed on his way to and from his studio on the Fondamenta dei Mori. Tintoretto's bottega was situated in the Canareggio sestiere in northern Venice as was his church *Madonna dell' Orto*. Alessandro Caravia[187] was resident there also. He was a poet and a reforming member of the poligrafi.[188] He worked as a goldsmith with a shop near the Rialto Bridge. This served as a distribution centre for writing that promoted the virtues of piety, humility, and charity. Caravia regarded the Venetian Scuole Grande as lacking these virtues. In particular, he targeted *the Scuola Grande di San Rocco*. Andrea Calmo[189] was another significant member of the poligrafi and he had a close relationship with Tintoretto. Calmo's father, Tadio, ran a dyeing business in Canareggio. In the first half of the sixteenth century there was considerable sympathy with Lutheran ideas amongst the *poligrafi* and in particular with the understanding that faith was the basis for salvation. Contarini[190] grew up as did Tintoretto along the Fondamenta dei Mori and they are both buried in *Madonna dell' Orto*. This does not imply a familiarity between the two men, that is unlikely, but

186. Sartre. *Le Séquestré de Venice*. Cited, Nichols. *Tintoretto Tradition and Identity*, 17.

187. 1513–1574

188. Traditionally, the term referred to a few versatile sixteenth-century intellectuals who were willing and able to write on any subject, hence the name: they were literary "hacks." It was applied to writers and publishers but expanded to describe a reformist network amongst the artisan community in Canareggio. Printing became an explosive industry in sixteenth century Venice undisturbed as it was by the wars of mainland Italy. It was three times less expensive to print in Venice than it was in Rome.

189. 1510–1571.

190. See note 166.

it does further suggest that Canareggio was an area where the reforming ideas of the *spirituali* would be difficult to avoid. Given this immersion and the passion as well as the subject matter of Tintoretto's work, the following conclusion is very difficult to accept.

> He was not a religious man; few artists were in this sixteenth-century Venice—half moulded in soul and dominions by the heretical or Islamic East; art was his religion, to which he sacrificed night and day.[191]

Tintoretto's paintings attracted both scorn and praise in inevitable comparison with the great venetian painter, Titian.[192] It was Tintoretto's speed of execution or *prestezza* that invited negative responses. Some criticised his lack of professional attention to the detail or finish of his work, others praised the spontaneity of his inspiration. He was contracted to his local church *Madonna dell' Orto* a few yards from his home and studio. His magnificent, dramatically-lit *Presentation of the Virgin Mary in the Temple*[193] is to be seen there along with several other works. Alphonsus Samerón[194] who was an influential figure at the Council of Trent arrived in Venice in 1537 where his preaching had a great influence on Christian thinking. He was a leading advocate for the consideration of Mary as co-redemptrix. This is a concept that dramatically informs Tintoretto's last great work *The Entombment*[195]. It has been suggested that Venice was somewhat isolated from the repercussions of the protestant reformation of northern Europe. Venice was governed by a merchant capitalist elite. Its mercantile ethos rendered it tolerant of divergent religious views and it was stubbornly resistant to papal domination. The mythology surrounding the transference of Saint Mark's body from Alexandria to Venice depicted in a mosaic above the southern transept of Saint Mark's Basilica gave Venice apostolic patronage rivalled only by Rome. It was the Doge Giustiniano Paticipzio who ordered the chapel built in his garden to receive the Saint's body. The cathedral up until 1807 was San Pietro di Castello. But from its inception the Ducal Chapel elevated as Saint Mark's Basilica took precedence. This was associated with the civil authority rather than the religious authority.

191. Durant. *The Story of Civilization*, 670.

192. 1488–1576.

193. 1553/6. Originally on the outside of the organ doors.

194. 1515–1585. A member of the newly-established Society of Jesus and close associate of Ignatius of Loyola.

195. 1592/3. San Giorgio Maggiore, Venice.

Thus, by focusing on the politics of Venice at the time of Tintoretto, it might be argued that Venice was somewhat isolated from reformation upheaval. However, within the lay confraternities such as San Rocco from which Tintoretto was seeking patronage, spirituality was demonstrably very much affected by tridentine events and the emphasis on the individual's responsibility for their own spiritual well-being. Tintoretto's works suggest that whilst the external influences of the contemporary art and religious movements were important, his stronger influence was his own personal vision that arrived on canvas via a passionate, dramatic and irascible personality.

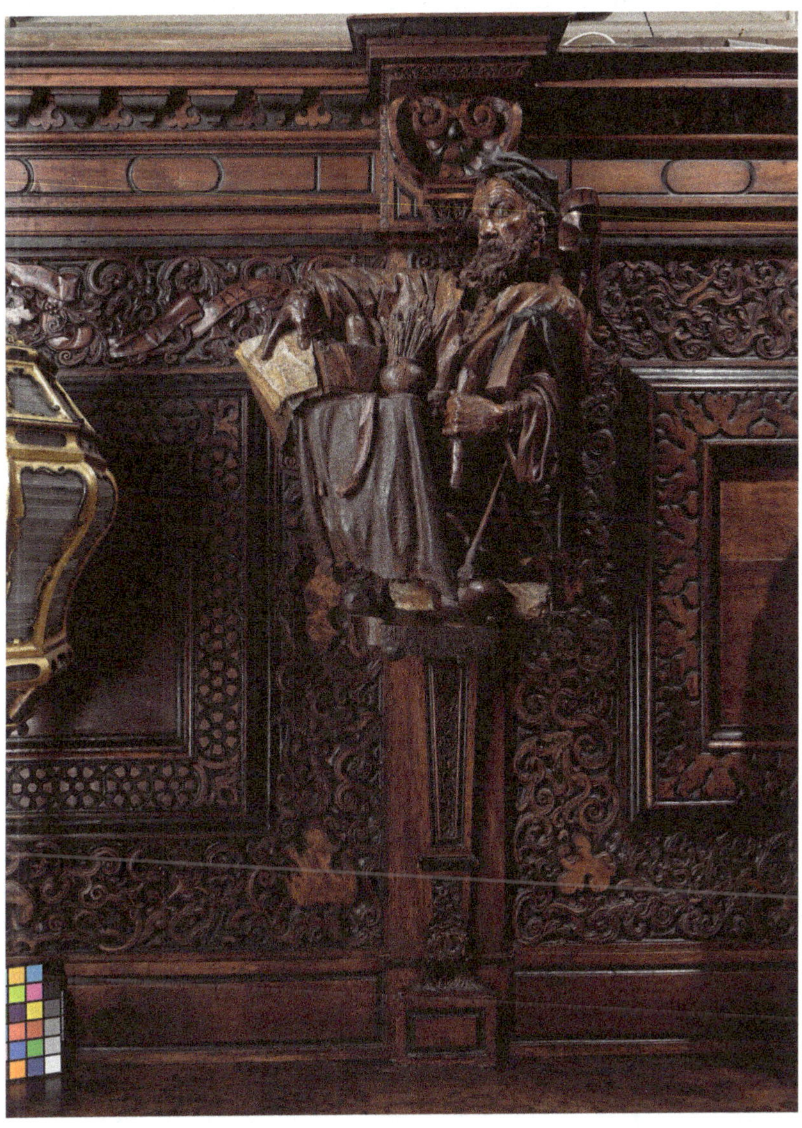

Fig. 35. Francesco Pianta. ***Tintoretto as 'Painting'*** **1657–58 Scuola Grande di San Rocco, Venice.**

My grateful thanks to the Guardian Grando for granting me permission to use this image.

Many anecdotes attest to the fact that Tintoretto was his own master and the wonderful wood carving: *Tintoretto as 'Painting'*[196] and the self-portrait suggest that he was a singular man.

196. Francesco Pianta the Younger. Second half of the seventeeth-century. Sala Superiore, Scula Grande di San Rocco, Venice.

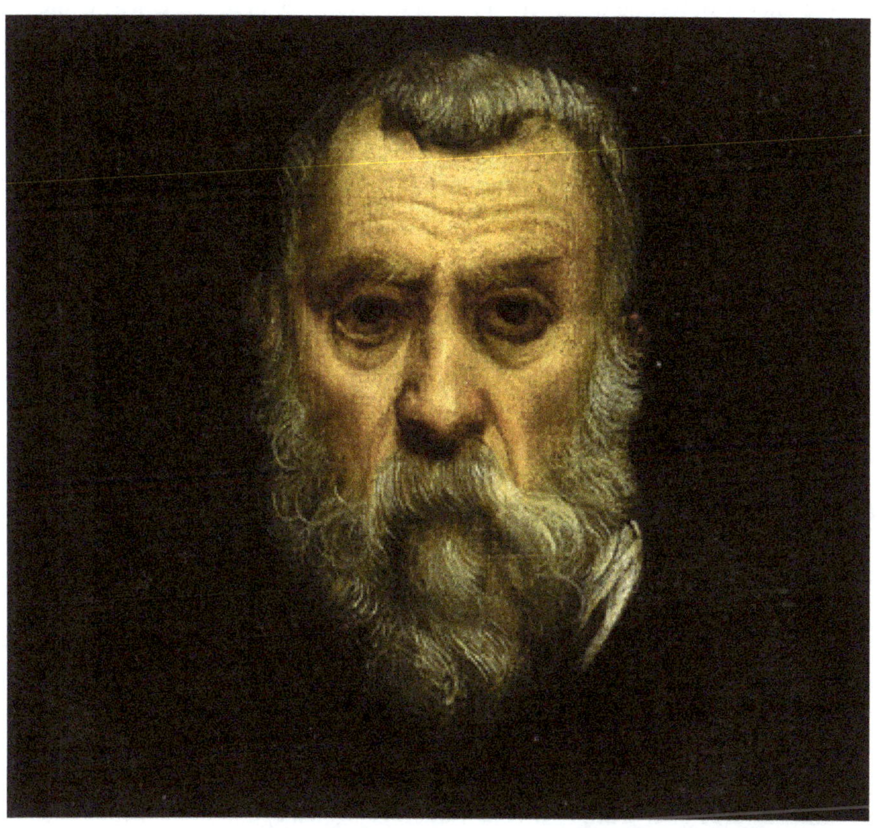

Fig. 36. Jacopo Robusti called Tintoretto. ***Self Portrait*** **date unknown Louvre, Paris © PD The Athenaeum.**

He was referred to by contempories as *Il Furioso.* This made reference to the speed and incredible energy with which he worked. Looking at *The Supper at Emmaus* one is immediately aware of a restless agitated energy: the energy of feeling of which Freedberg writes. The figure of Christ is the still centre of the painting as he blesses the bread. The only other still figure is the poor perplexed cat downstage right. It is as if the spiritual energy with which the creature is surrounded has caused it to abandon its ascribed diabolical role. There is no sense of tepidity here. Following the gospel story, we are to accept that Christ is no longer there as a physical presence. It is the miracle of that moment that Tintoretto captures. It disturbs. It disrupts. The painting is a very powerful presentation of disruption almost taken to the level of chaos. To chart the direction of movement in the painting is to describe a virtual catherine wheel. The stage-left pilgrim attempts to grasp something corporeal: how else to validate his experience? His companion stage-right twists his head violently to the right and his left arm in the opposite direction with a gesture of excited exclamation to a less-than-impressed bearded figure who is half-within the picture frame. Their agitation is given further emphasis by the stillness of Christ and the undisturbed routine of the serving figures to Christ's stage-right and left. It is a moment that is addressed to the two pilgrims personally and not a collective moment of united worship as expressed in a religious ceremony. The servants are still addressing a physical presence. The stage-right server presents food; the stage-left server reaches for a heavy jug of wine, just delivered by a third server. In that sense it goes right to the heart of the spiritual reform movement. It is a spiritual moment only for the two pilgrims who have personally laboured after truth or divine wisdom: *Haggia Sophia.* In their moment of a profound sense of abandonment, the miracle of the real presence of Christ is revealed to them. This cannot be grasped by human hands but it remains with them as they journey back to Jerusalem. The chaotic angle of their palmers' staffs that fronts the painting completes the overall sense of disorder, of things turned upside down. The beautiful subdued earth tones of Tintoretto's palette have a calming effect on the disturbed viewer in sharp contrast to Pontormo's use of colour in figure twenty-nine.

Although born in similarly humble circumstances in Verona, Veronese[197] appears to have been possessed of a very different personality and ambition to that of Tintoretto. He was the son of a local stonecutter, *spezapreda.* His mother was the illegitimate daughter of a member of the

197. 1528 Verona—1588 Venice.

Veronese nobility, the Caliari. Paolo preferred the pride of being associated with that name over the shame of his mother's history and adopted the name of Caliari as his own. Veronese had come to work in Venice in 1555. Titian, the acknowledged grand master of Venetian painting was focussed on commissions for foreign kings and emperors. Veronese competed with Tintoretto for commissions within Venice itself.

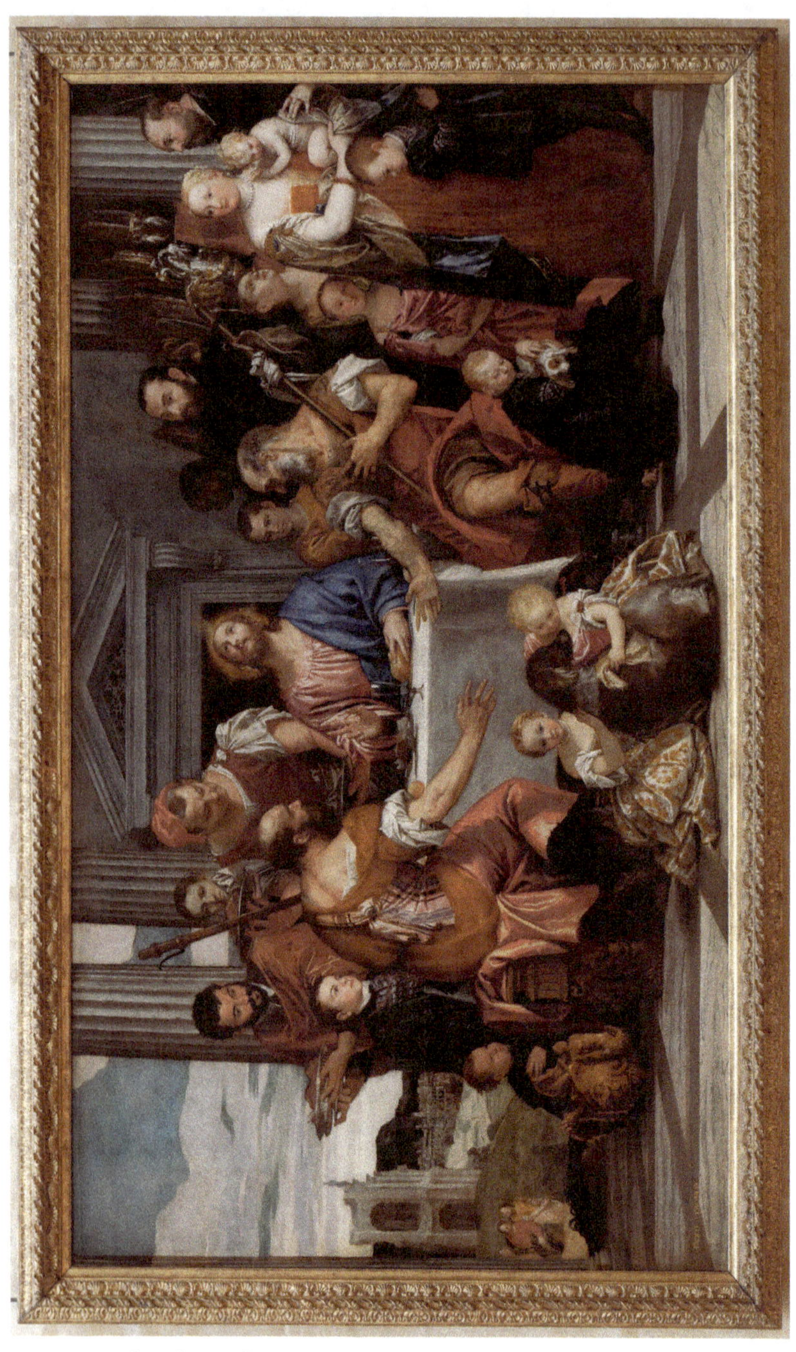

Fig. 37. Paolo Caliari called Veronese. *The Supper at Emmaus* 1559/60 ©Musée du Louvre. Dist. RMN-Grand Palais / Angèle Dequier.

At the time Veronese was painting *The Supper at Emmaus,*[198] Tintoretto's Mannerism was the predominant style of painting in Venice. However, Titian who was a generation older than Veronese appears to have been his greater influence. The two painters, Titian and Veronese, maintained a continuing adherence to the older classical style of painting. Placing prints of Tintoretto's and Veronese's *The Supper at Emmaus* side by side the briefest glance will show that although the subject is the same, something very different is taking place. This marked difference is of style. Veronese's figures are restrained and noble in manner. The two pilgrims have a sculptural elegance. Their emotion is only hinted at by a controlled right-handed gesture. The two children downstage-centre are immaculately posed and dressed as they caress a perfectly behaved dog. They could almost be in an Edwardian photographer's studio. Placed, as they are, directly below the figure of Christ and in direct contact with the viewers' eye line, they are, quite literally, the center of attention. The white tablecloth that backs them emphasizes this. The commissioner is unknown but the palatial setting of fluted columns and pediment over the door above the head of Christ seem entirely inappropriate to a biblical reading of the Emmaus story. It is true that to the stage right there is a visual reference to the disciples' journey preceding the supper, but this had become something of an iconic convention and cannot be taken as an example of Veronese's engagement with his subject. The inescapable fact is that the painting is a group portrait probably executed to satisfy the vanity of a wealthy patron. The beautifully rendered contemporary venetian costumes, in particular those of the two little girls confirm this opinion. The biblical account tells us that a miracle that is central to tridentine doctrine is taking place. The total lack of interest that is shown by those inappropriately present confirm that they are there for mere decoration. In these circumstances, Christ's raised eyes as he blesses the bread convey sanctimony rather than sanctity. One suspects that Savonarola would have consigned the painting to his bonfire of the vanities. The stage is laden with a superfluity of figures having no relation whatever to the subject. To accommodate them, the painting is approximately twice the width of Tintoretto's version and fifty per cent higher.[199] It is an example of the venetian genre of work known as *teleri*[200] that particularly appealed

198. 1560 Louvre.

199. 416cm X 242cm.

200. Large decorative painting. These gave Veronese ample opportunity to demonstrate his virtuosity in figure painting and use of colour.

to Veronese's inclination. He favoured large scale, long horizontal paintings that allowed him to demonstrate his virtuosity in presenting a variety of dramatic scenes on one stage decorated with complex architecture and intricate costume designs. The acme of his achievement is *The Wedding Feast at Cana*[201] that demonstrates the full fruition of Veronese's mastery of the genre.

Veronese's work suggests that his priorities as a painter were those of aesthetics rather than the passionate commitment to his subject matter demanded by the Council of Trent. His investigation by the Inquisition[202] substantiates this suggestion. Veronese was at pains to present the appearance of things whereas his contemporary and rival, Tintoretto, reached beneath the surface for a deeper truth.

Michelangelo Merisi da Caravaggio was seventeen years old when Veronese died. He was twenty–three at the death of Tintoretto. And his short life was like a detonation in the world of art.

> .... at my birth
> The front of heaven was full of fiery shapes,
> The goats ran from the mountains, and the herds
> Were strangely clamorous to the frighted fields.
> These signs have mark'd me extraordinary;
> And all the courses of my life do show
> I am not in the roll of common men.[203]

Perhaps Owen Glendower's boast regarding the signs that heralded his birth convincing him that he was "not in the roll of common men" is a somewhat exotic view of the thoughts that Caravaggio might have harboured concerning his own birth,[204] but he could well have regarded the timing of his birth as charged with significance. It was the feast day of the Archangel Michael. This was the occasion of his parents naming him Michelangelo. It just so happened that this was also the Christian name of the most famous Italian sculptor and painter of all time who had died seven years earlier. Eight days after Caravaggio's birth one of the most significant events in European history took place—the Battle of Lepanto. Cyprus, a long-standing and strategically important venetian possession had fallen to the Ottoman Empire. Pope Pius V joined forces with the venetians and

201. 1563. Louvre. 975cm X 670cm.

202. See note 182.

203. Shakespeare. *Henry the Fourth Part One*, 3, 1, 37–43.

204. 29th. September 1571.

recruited reinforcements from Spain and Portugal together with the states of Italy to form a Holy League for the defence of Christendom. The ensuing battle in the Gulf of Patraikos near Lepanto[205] was the last sea battle fought between galley-rowed ships. Eight thousand christians and many more muslim turks died in the battle. The ottoman fleet was destroyed. The fleet of the Holy League survived practically intact.

The Pope claimed that the Holy League had prevailed because of the Virgin Mary's intercession. Marian cults and devotion to the rosary reached unprecedented heights of popularity. Some fifty years earlier the christian western world had been torn apart by the Reformation. Some consolation might have been felt particularly on the catholic side of the division by the triumph of Lepanto. Even James VI of Scotland, no friend of the Pope, was moved to pen an epic poem celebrating the catholic victory. He made it clear in a modified preface that the hero of the battle, Don Juan of Austria, was still to be regarded as "a foreign papist bastard."[206]

Caravaggio's paternal grandfather, Giovan Giacomo Amatori was a highly respected member of the professional bourgeoisie. He was a surveyor and his work of land supervision meant that he had contact with the noble Colonna dynasty, a leading noble family of the region. The Sforza were another powerful and influential Italian dynasty. Constanza Colonna whose father Marcantonio Colonna was a hero of Lepanto as commander of the papal forces was married to Francesco Sforza. Margarita, Caravaggio's maternal aunt was a wet nurse to the Sforza children. It would seem that Constanza Colonna regarded Margareta's nephew, Michelangelo, born on the saint's name day and at a time of the great battle between christian and muslim forces, as endowed with good fortune. In the turmoil that was Caravaggio's life, Constanza Colonna was always a powerful ally. Caravaggio certainly needed support in his early years but he was not gifted with a personality that attracted it. These early years were spent between his native town of Caravaggio and the much larger city of Milan where his father, a stonemason by trade, had a workshop. When Caravaggio was five years old the bubonic plague devastated Milan killing about one-fifth of the population. Although the family moved back to Caravaggio, Michelangelo Merisi had lost almost every male member of his family to the plague. He was six years old.

205. Modern Navpaktos.

206. Graham-Dixon. *Caravaggio*, cited14.

Whether or not he needed it, one influence on Caravaggio's early years that he could not escape was that of Carlo Borromeo. He was to Milan what Savonarola had been to Florence a century earlier—a scourge although rather more successful than the Florentine and nobody would refer to him as an Italian Luther. Borromeo's uncle was Pope Pius IV and the Pope made his nephew a cardinal in his early twenties. He was a prominent presence at the Council of Trent and became archbishop of Milan in 1565. He brought to the role an evangelical sense of a god-directed mission to impose his rigid version of the tenets of christianity on the milanese people. To enforce this mission he claimed the ancient right of the Archbishop of Milan to maintain a private army—*famiglia armata*. Heresy, blasphemy, sodomy invited a dramatically unwelcome visitation. Phillip II the Spanish ruler of Milan gradually accepted the fact that Borremeo could be trusted to assume the rôle of the Spanish Inquisition in Milan. For his first twenty years, Caravaggio's heart, soul, and mind were controlled with those of all the other inhabitants of Milan by Borromeo's ascetic vision. The introduction of confessionals and the crucial role of minutely trained and closely supervised confessors loomed large among Borromeo's priorities. Milan's position bordering partly-protestant Switzerland made it a strategic outpost of the *true faith* and therefore it needed to be a brilliant and unequivocal example. When Borromeo survived a bullet in his back fired at close range by a disgruntled member of a religious order suppressed by Borromeo for what he deemed corruption, his conviction that he had been divinely approved was confirmed. Conviction of sin, imminent danger of damnation, the life-giving necessity of confession, and penance were deeply embedded within Caravaggio's psyche when he departed for Rome in his early twenties. Evidence of this is readily available from his paintings. It is highlighted by the following anecdote.

> One day he went into the church of the Madonna of Pilero with certain gentlemen, and the politest of them stepped forward to offer him some holy water. Caravaggio asked him what it was for and was told 'to cancel venial sins.' 'Then it is no use,' he said. 'Because mine are all mortal.'[207]

Borromeo had been influenced by Loyola's *spiritual exercises* that urged visualization of the life of Christ as essential for Christian empathy with the suffering of Christ. It was necessary to develop the sense of actually being

207. Graham-Dixon. Ibid., cited 28.

there as implied by the question of the African-American spiritual *Were you there when they crucified my Lord?* This was the aim of art and religious meditation in the medieval period and up to the early years of the sixteenth century. But the High Renaissance led by Michelangelo Buonarroti came to regard this type of painting as a kind of trickery aimed at deception. It was the Council of Trent at which Borromeo played a leading role that re-emphasised the need for artists to recognize that they had a duty to use their skills to enhance the public's spiritual education and to move them to penance. The role of penance was of particular emphasis in Borromeo's Milan. Failure to demonstrate adherence to these strictures would result in visits from the Archbishop's *famiglia armata.* In this, Borremeo was hearkening back to the fifteenth century as Michael Baxandall makes clear. He refers to a handbook for young girls—The Garden of Prayer—printed in Venice in the second half of the fifteenth century. The reader is encouraged to imagine places and people in a mental dramatization of the passion narrative. This, it is suggested, is helped if this mental drama is cast by the individual penitent from people from within their circle.

> When you have done all this, putting all your imagination into it, then go into your chamber. Alone and solitary, excluding every external thought from your mind, start thinking of the beginning of the Passion, starting with how Jesus entered Jerusalem on an ass. Moving slowly from episode to episode, meditate on each one, dwelling on each single stage and step of the story. And if at any point you feel a sensation of piety, stop: do not pass on as long as that sweet and devout sentiment lasts[208].

This exercise was developed further by the institution of the *Sacred Mountain* where a pilgrimage up a mountainside took place with various stopping points at which vividly presented tableaux from the life of Christ were displayed. The pilgrims thus moved with physical and emotional exhaustion from *the Fall* to G*olgotha* and *Christ's Cucifixion.* The presentations were deliberately and literally vulgar in an appeal to the common people. The influence of this 'gloves-off' appeal to basic human emotion is very apparent in the work of Caravaggio. Caravaggio's great originality for me is, paradoxically, that he embraced the idea of looking back to the past for inspiration when the trend was, and still is that things must continually evolve. The momentum is always to be forward. One of the most irritating introductory or concluding phrases to the sentences of contemporaries is

208. Baxandall. *Painting and* Experience, 46.

"going forward." But Caravaggio looks backward past the High Renaissance Classicism to the Middle Ages and his art came to be labelled Baroque.

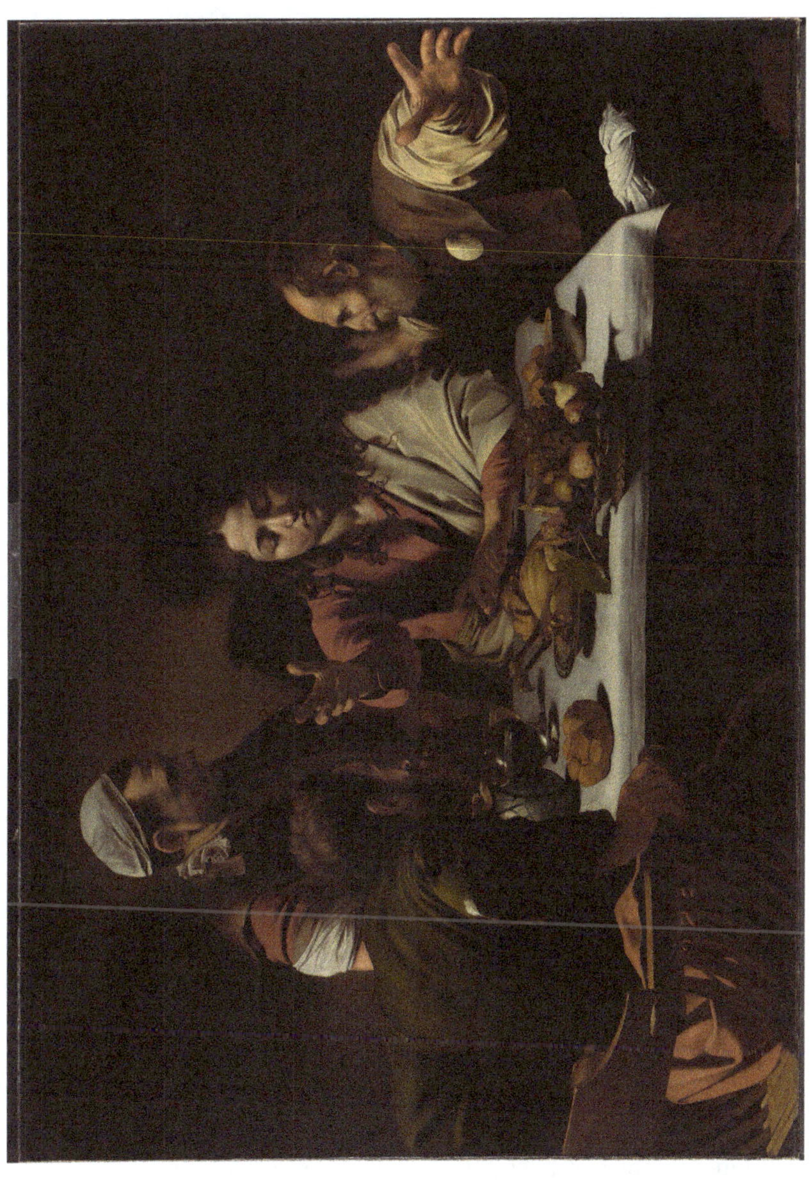

Fig. 38. Michelangelo Merisi da Caravaggio. *The Supper at Emmaus* 1601 courtesy of the National Gallery (London) Picture Library.

Caravaggio's first painting of *The Supper at Emmaus*[209] almost bursts out of the frame with the emotional energy of physical drama. Viewing it on the wall of the National Gallery in London's Trafalgar Square, one almost expects a uniformed attendant to ask it to make less noise. The chair of the pilgrim stage-right screeches against the floor as he pushes it backwards with a muscular spasm of heart-stopping shock. The bowl of fruit is about to topple off the table and clatter to the floor at the feet of the viewer. This sense of the painting invading the viewer's space represents a break in the tradition where the action takes place safely behind a barrier between the viewer's world and the world depicted in the painting. The hand of the pilgrim stage-left—marked out as a pilgrim by his finely depicted scallop shell—pushes through this barrier with his energetic gesture of amazement. The sleeve of the stage-right pilgrim appears to have been ripped as he pushes against this barrier. With Borromeo's emphasis on the need for christians to become personally involved with the drama of the life of Christ deeply embedded in his psyche, Caravaggio seeks to engage the viewer's five senses in response to his work. Instrumental in this, of course. is Caravaggio's revolutionary use of light. On the superficial level, the tension of the drama is increased by the use he makes of light and shadow or *chiaroscuro*. It is very atmospheric and conducive to a sense of mystery like the dimmed lights of a séance. But Caravaggio makes more subtle use of it than that. The bowl of fruit that so bothered Bellori[210] as it contained Autumn fruits and Easter is celebrated in Spring is used in the painting to develop a deeper purpose than that of the superficial naturalism so prized by Bellori. The rotting apple has obvious associations with inherited sin and therefore the necessity of confession as emphasized by Borromeo. The grapes refer to the essential nature of the Eucharist in line with tridentine doctrine. The magnificent pomegranate ripely bursting out and spilling the seeds of life as Christ has burst forth from the tomb bringing life to all believers is a long-standing allusion to the resurrection. This may be seen in the famous painting by Botticelli, *Madonna of the Pomegranate*.[211] But there are some less obvious, finer points. These are available to those following a life of spiritual meditation encouraged by the *Spiritual Exercises* of Ignatius

209. 1601 National Gallery, London.

210. Giovan Pietro Bellori (about 1616–1696) was an Italian art theorist and biographer.

211. c1487 Uffizi Gallery, Florence.

Loyola.[212] This disciplined approach to spirituality was very influential in Borromeo's thinking and teaching. *The Garden of Prayer*[213] speaks of the necessity for detailed looking for moments that might be individually selected as encouraging personal piety. There are such moments in Caravaggio's painting. The shadow cast on the tablecloth by the play of light on the fruit basket is very clearly shaped like the tail of a fish.[214] This might lead the faithful to the reassuring reflection upon the miracle of Emmaus as a revelation that Jesus Christ is indeed the son of God and their savior, a living presence in their world. There is another very fine detail that is presented with great skill and delicacy, so unexpected and moving from a man whose rough life was scarred by violence and uncontrolled passions. Bread and wine were standard elements and expected on depictions of the table of the Emmaus supper commonly associated with the Eucharist. Here the carafe next to the jug is of pure water. This facilitates the light passing through it to reflect a pool of pure white light on to the tablecloth. Given the emphasis on Mariology at The Council of Trent and its influence on catholic art, this might well be taken by the devout as an invitation to meditate upon the Immaculate Conception.[215] Alphonsus Samerón was an influential figure at the Council of Trent. His writings show him to have been, in particular, a leading advocate for the consideration of Mary as co-redemptrix. He refers to the mother's "co-suffering, co-misery, co-sorrowing" and suggests that she was "co-crucified."[216] By meditating upon Caravaggio's pool of white light within the context of the painting, the faithful might reflect with awe that the light of the world came to us through the medium of Mary's self-effacing obedience and thereby reflect upon the condition of their own faithfulness. The spirituality of the painting was often concealed from the eyes of contemporaries by what they regarded as the coarseness of his physical portrayals. Poussin, the great classical French baroque painter, who was noted for his "good taste" and the nobility of his characters, thought that Caravaggio was destined for hell because of the ugliness of his. Caravaggio, it might be argued, had a vested interest in "the worldliness of

212. Spanish theologian, one of the most influential figures in the Roman Catholic Counter-Reformation in the sixteenth century, and founder of the Society of Jesus (Jesuits).

213. See note 208.

214. See page 56.

215. The Immaculate Conception refers to the birth of Mary the mother of Jesus. The virgin birth refers to the birth of Jesus.

216. Miravalle. *With Jesus*. 106/7.

grace."[217] Certainly, his characters are of this world. He is reported as having caused something of a scandal by using as his model for Mary in his *Death of the Virgin*[218] the bloated corpse of a prostitute. In this Emmaus painting, Caravaggio depicts Christ as a podgy-faced, beardless youth. The two pilgrims, one with an impressively broken nose, are rugged men of toil. The innkeeper does not feel it necessary to remove his rather greasy-looking cap in the presence of such men. Hibbard rather pompously sees him as representing those who

> See(s) and understand nothing (and) the world of pagans and heretics who do not recognize Christ and his Church.[219]

However, Hibbard graciously allows:

> Nevertheless the innkeeper casts a shadow that seems to form a negative halo around the brilliant head of Christ, as if to indicate that we honor the Savior even while ignoring or denying him.[220]

Might the human shadow appearing to rest on the back of Christ symbolize the weight of human sin borne at the Crucifixion by the man who is before us awaiting our recognition?

217. See note 141.

218. 1602 Louvre, Paris.

219. Hibbard. *Caravaggio*, 80.

220. Ibid.

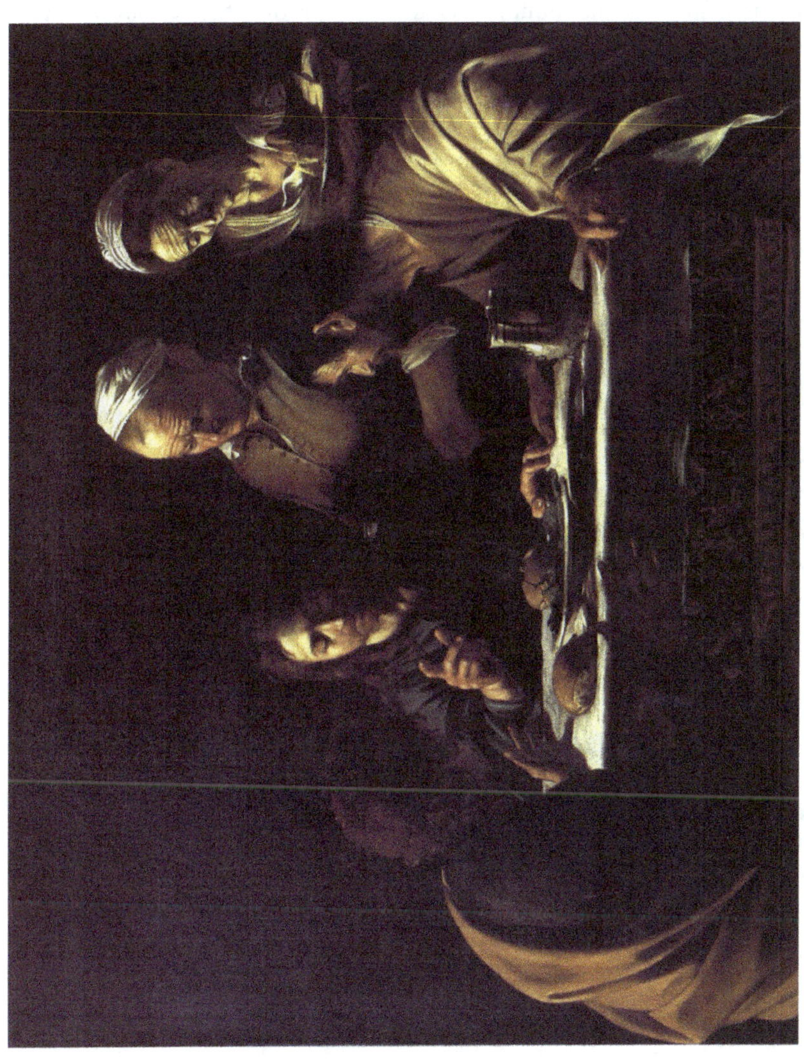

Fig. 39. Michelangelo Merisi da Caravaggio. *The Supper at Emmaus* 1606 Pinacoteca di Brena, Milan © PD The Athenaeum.

Caravaggio's second painting of *The Supper at Emmaus*,[221] painted some five years later is more subdued in tone. The painting conveys an overwhelming sense of aching need. If the earlier work shouts with the excitement of having found, this painting sighs over the despair of having lost. Caravaggio was painfully aware of personal loss at this period of his troubled life. He had killed a man and had been sentenced to indefinite exile from Rome. His sentence granted anyone who discovered him within the papal states the right to kill him with impunity. They were encouraged to do so by a bounty being offered to anyone bearing his severed head. Never had Caravaggio been so in need of the protection offered him by the Constanza family. In May 1606, Caravaggio had engaged Ranuccio Tomassoni in a duel. The details are rather obscure but it would seem that some form of sexual insult was the occasion of the duel and that Caravaggio, in attempting to castrate Tomassoni, cut his femoral artery and he died of blood loss. Caravaggio, badly wounded, escaped to the Palazzo Colonna and sought the protection of the Marchesa. She spirited him away to a remote town outside Rome owned by the Colonna family. It was at this time that Caravaggio painted his second version of *The Supper at Emmaus*. Although of a similar size to the original painting, the scene appears darker, enclosed and claustrophobic as opposed to the expansive energy of the former painting.

221. 1606 Pinacoteca di Brena, Milan.

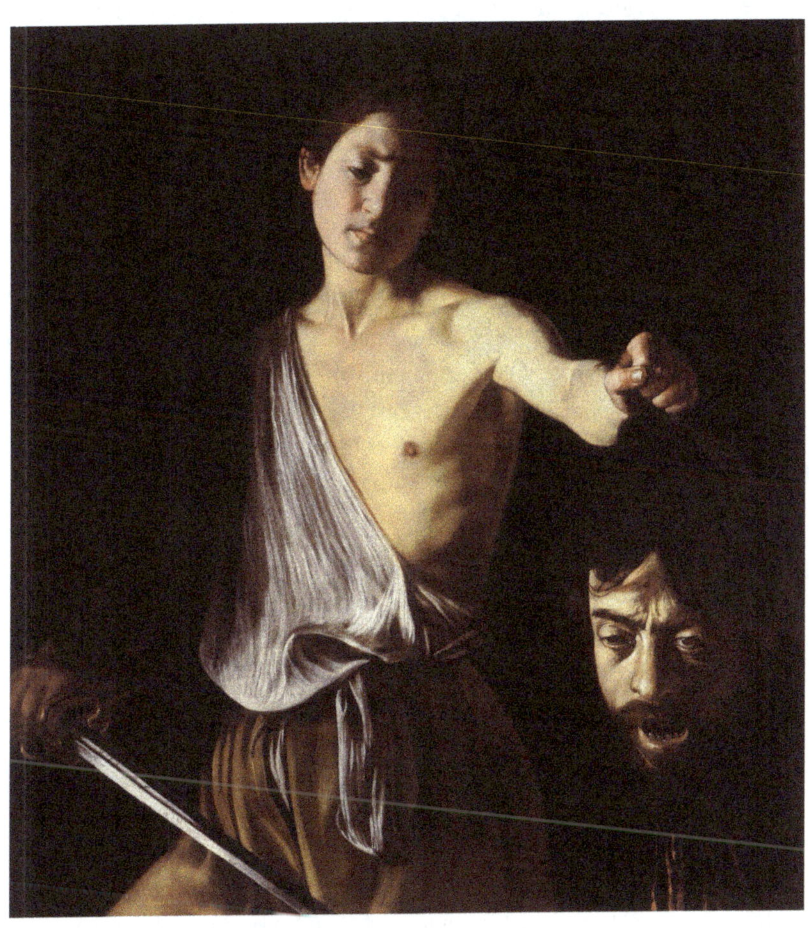

Fig. 40. Michelangelo Merisi da Caravaggio. *David with the Head of Goliath* **1606 Galleria Borghese, Rome PD Wikimedia Commons.**

Caravaggio frequently paints a self-portrait into his work, most notably in the painting, *David with the Head of Goliath*[222]. This was painted in the same period as the later of the two Emmaus works. It is plausibly suggested that Cecco, Caravaggio's "boy," who accompanied him in exile, is the model for David and the head of Goliath is a Caravaggio self-portrait. The head that has a bounty placed upon it is here being delivered. Caravaggio's life has perhaps left his faith and hope hanging by the threads of hair clutched by the Cecco/David figure dangling the head of the Caravaggio/Goliath figure in the *David with the Head of Goliath* painting. This painting has attracted much interesting speculation.[223] The gaze of David at the head of the monster he has slain is so full of pathos that it startles and puzzles the viewer. The original viewers would have been well aware of the orthodox understanding of the Old Testament story as alluding to the victory of Christ over Satan. There is no sense of triumph in the painting. There is, rather, a profound sense of melancholy reflection upon the tragedy that has led to such a conclusion. This substantiates the suggestion that the painting's reference is personal rather than historical.

The tone of Caravaggio's second painting of *The Supper at Emmaus* seems to be set by the serving woman whose scrawny face is creased with misery and despair. It is as if there is nothing on earth that could lift the gloom. It is tempting to think that the poor soul with the platter of meat is, if not a self-portrait, a soul mate of the painter himself as he reflects on his need for reconciliation with God. Permanently exiled from Rome, maybe he fears that he has also been permanently exiled from God. The dish of scraggy lamb that she bears emasculates the traditional allusion to "The Lamb of God." The wiry pilgrim stage-left clutches the table as if hardly daring to allow himself to believe. An atmosphere of gloom weighs heavily on the subject matter. Christ is depicted in a more traditional manner than in the earlier painting. He is a bearded, sombre character. The hand that blesses the bread is tired. In the earlier painting, the hand is raised shoulder high and it reaches out energetically. Here, the arm barely carries the hand above the table and that lack of energy is reflected in the responses. There is a sense of dare-we-believe about the work. Instead of the ecstatic arm-spread of the stage-left disciple in the former painting, we have a lean, tense figure gripping the table and craning his neck with prominently stretched tendons almost begging for revelation. Recalling Caravaggio's earlier years

222. 1606 Galleria Borghese, Rome.

223. See, for example, Dixon. Ibid., 332/3.

under the influence of Borromeo with his emphasis on the essential nature of the confessional, the painting does take on the nature of a plea for the mercy of forgiveness. The drudgery of unbelief that marked out the pilgrims on their journey is conveyed by the innkeeper's sceptical examination of Christ's action. A crucifying weariness also burdens Christ as he strives with those identified by Stephen as,

> Ye stiffnecked and uncircumcised in heart and ears, ye do always resist the Holy Ghost: as your fathers did, so do ye.[224]

The same weariness leads Christ to rebuke rather than sympathise with the two pilgrims he encounters on the road to Emmaus. The painting is a challenge to the viewer as a kind of "cliff hanger." What will the response be when the bread is broken? Perhaps there is something here upon which fellow pilgrims experiencing the dark night of the soul might meditate.

Although Caravaggio's reputation was widespread during his lifetime, it faded to near obscurity after his death. Many of his now famous works were attributed to other painters. It was as if his awkward and often alarming presence in life could not be ignored because it attached to so many startlingly new and challenging works of art. Now that presence removed by death could be comfortably expunged from memory if the works were divorced from his name. It is quite remarkable to discover that the superb *Taking of Christ*[225] was attributed to the Dutch painter Gerrit van Honthorst until 1990.

224. KJV Acts 7, 51.

225. 1602. National Gallery of Ireland.

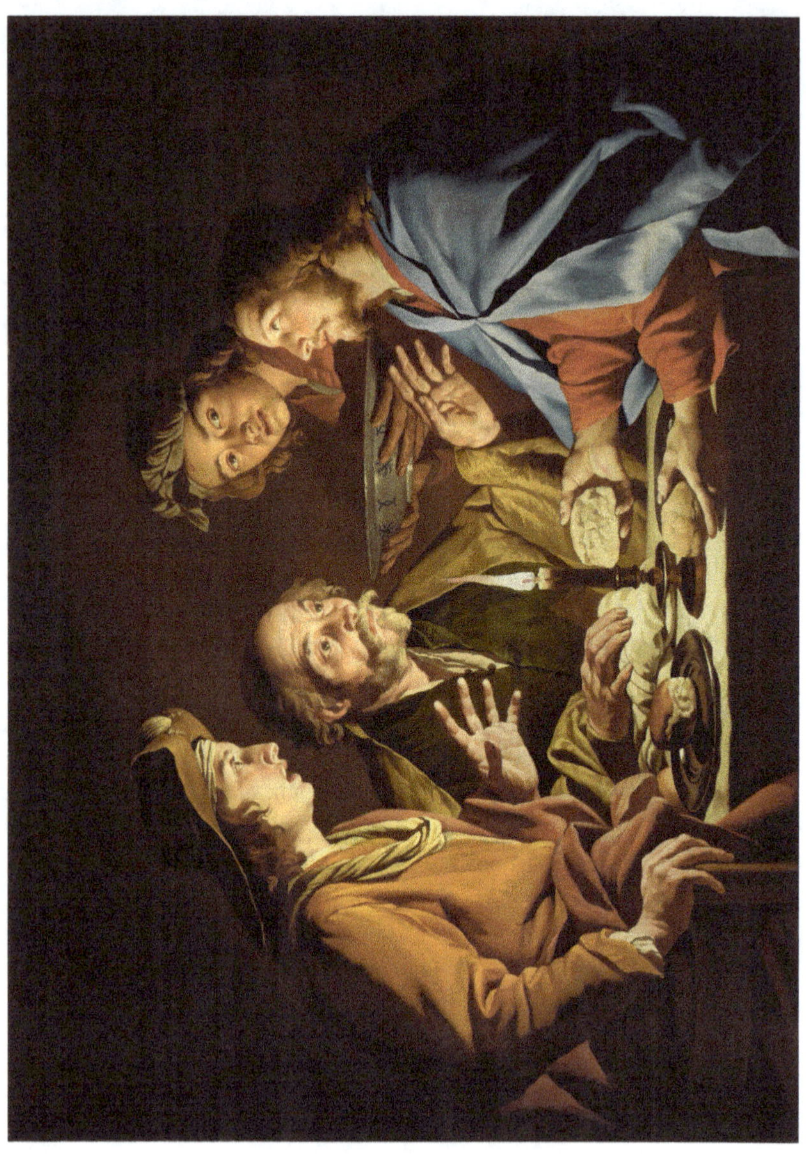

Fig. 41. Matthias Stom (Stomer). ***The Supper at Emmaus*** **1633–1639 Museo Nacional Thyssen-Bornemisza (Madrid).**

My grateful thanks to Laura García Oliva of Archivo Fotográfico & Área de Restauración for granting me permission to use this image.

A group of painters known as the Caravggisti were enthusiastic practitioners of what they saw as Caravaggio's style of painting. One of these was Matthias Stom,[226] another was Trophime Bigot.[227] Both of these painters have their names attached to a version of *The Supper at Emmaus* although Bigot's somewhat more tenuously it seems. It is quite clear from these two works that what captured these two so-called followers of Caravaggio was his dramatic lighting technique. For me the two paintings in question also illustrate the limitations of the comparison with Caravaggio. That by Matthias Stom[228] seems to be lacking in the qualities that the Caravaggisti so admired in their mentor—naturalism and drama. In fact, the painting has more in common with Jan Cornelius Vermeyen born a century before Bigot and seventy years before Caravaggio in the northern Netherlands. In Vermeyen's painting of *The Marriage at Cana*[229] the faces of the characters are underlit melodramatically, the light ostensibly emanating from the candles on the table. Similarly with the Stom and Bigot paintings the lighting full on the faces of the characters is used only to increase the sense of a rather vacuous drama. There is nothing naturalistic about it, no attempt at modulation as in Caravaggio's work. The effect is of a group huddled around a bonfire. The face of Christ is idealized in a manner quite alien to the work of Caravaggio. The passionate religious energy conveyed by lighting-enhanced symbolism that is so essential in Caravaggio's work is completely absent here. How could it be anything else. The style of Caravaggio's work was unique to the man. It appears to have been developed organically from the need to express the profound psychological impact that his chosen subjects exerted upon him. He did not establish a workshop or any other evidence of a mission to spread his painterly ideas. Quite simply, Matthias Stom was not Caravaggio, neither was Trophime Bigot.[230]

226. 1600–1650. Sometimes referred to as Stomer. Born in the Nerherlands. He was active in Italy finally settling in Sicily where he died.

227. 1600–1650. Born in Arles, France died in Avignon.

228. 1633—1639.Museo Nacional Thyssen-Bornemisza, Madrid.

229. c1530. Rijkmuseum, Amsterdam.

230. c.1600, Arles—1650, Avignon.

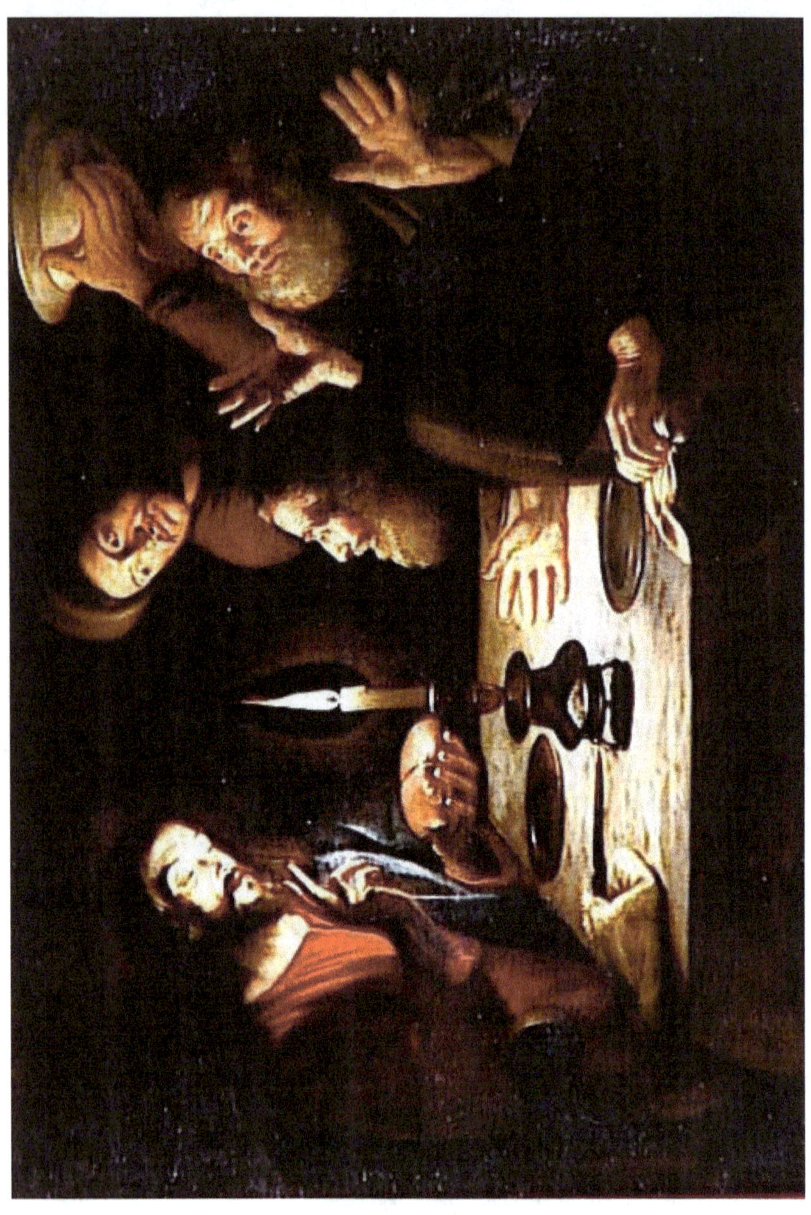

Fig. 42. Trophime Bigot 1600–1650. *The Supper at Emmaus* date unknown Musée Condé, Paris PD Wikimedia Commons

Bigot's *The Supper at Emmaus*[231] makes a similar use of lighting effect to that of Stom. Again the light is ostensibly from a central candle. The characters lean into it to make sure they are well-lit rather as if they are posing for a "selfie." The stage-left character strikes a ridiculous pose of amateur-theatrical surprise. The figure of Christ leans over the bread like a stage magician about to perform a spectacular trick. The servant stares fixedly at the loaf of bread as if expecting to be visually amazed. If we compare the presentation of the servant with those in Caravaggio's two versions, the contrast is very marked. Caravaggio's servants have a crucial role to play in the impact of the painting as a whole. The servants in both Bigot's and Stom's presentations underline the point that these paintings are Caravaggesque only at a very superficial level. Caravaggio's style serves his deeper purpose and as such contributes to the impact of his work in a very moving manner.

Bernard Berenson[232] thought that of all Italian painters with the exception of Michelangelo Caravaggio had the greatest influence on subsequent artistic development. Being influenced by a mentor, of course, is one thing, attempting to copy that person's style is something entirely different. Those who tried to paint *like* him were bound to fail. Peter Paul Rubens[233] was a man of immense talents and achievements. He was an artist, diplomat, scholar and humanist excelling in all of his many roles. He was the Baroque period's Renaissance man. Rubens' father was a Calvinist. With his wife and four children he left Catholic Antwerp in the southern Netherlands for Siega in Germany to escape religious persecution. When Rubens was ten years old he returned to Antwerp with his Roman Catholic mother where his formal education and apprenticeship began. In 1598 at the age of twenty-one he was admitted to the painters' guild in Antwerp. There followed visits to Italy where, in Venice, works by Titian, Tintoretto and Veronese were to be seen. The radiance of color in these paintings seems to have left a lasting impression on Rubens. This is evident in his *Supper at Emmaus.*[234]

231. Date unknown. Musée Condé, Paris.

232. American art historian, 1865—1959.

233. 1577, Siegen, Germany–1640 Antwerp, Spanish Netherlands now Belgium.

234. 1638, Museo Nacional del Prado.

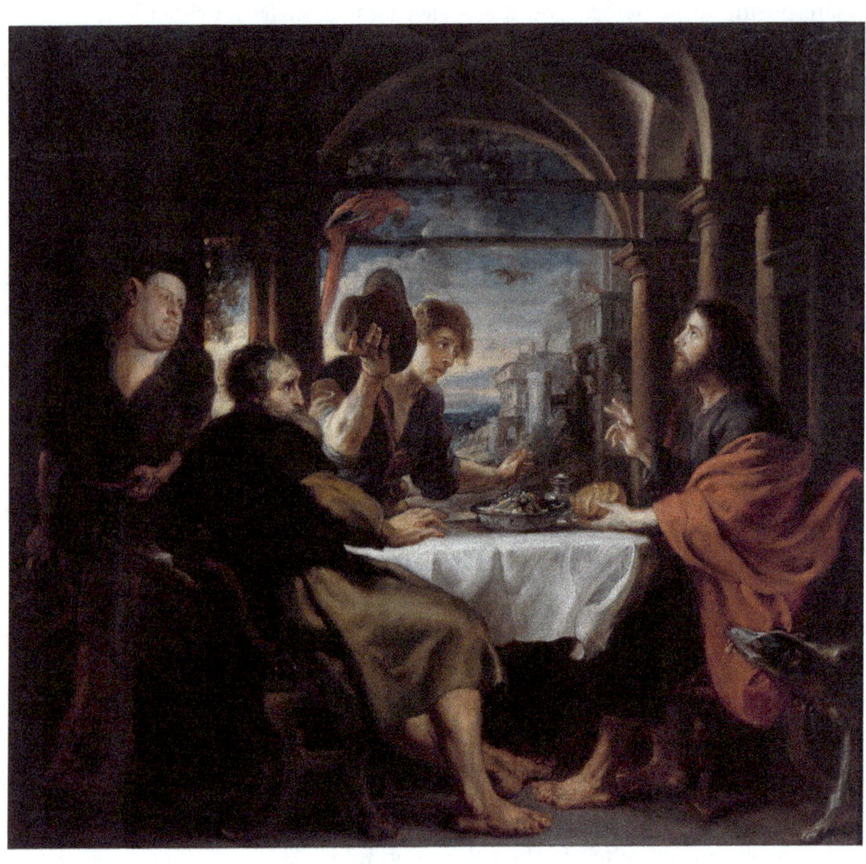

Fig. 43. Peter Paul Rubens. *Supper at Emmaus* **Museo Nacional del Prado.**
Image made available under the Creative Commons Attribution-Share Alike license.

In Rome, the works of Caravaggio with characters and events aggressively rooted in earthy reality made an impact on Rubens as did the heroic forms of Michelangelo and Raphael. But, unlike Stom and Bigot, Ruben's towering intelligence enabled him to absorb these influences and make them his own. In 1608 his mother's illness brought him back to Antwerp. Although his mother had died before he arrived, he accepted a commission to paint an *Adoration of the Magi* for the town hall. This was an important civic commission to celebrate a truce between the protestant Dutch separatists to the north and Spanish catholic Flanders to the south. Rubens' fame was established and this led to him being appointed as court painter to the Spanish Habsburg regent of Flanders. It also meant that his ambition to return to Italy was thwarted. Instead, he moved into an impressive townhouse with an extensive studio attached. As well as directing the artistic output of his large and very productive workshop, Rubens became a high-level and well-travelled civil servant in the diplomatic service of his country. Rubens had "arrived" without, apparently, making a great effort so to do. Caravaggio never did "arrive" after, apparently, making great effort so not to do. Two men so temperamentally different it would be difficult to imagine. The domestic life of Rubens was harmonious and a great support. It was to be shattered on the death of his wife in 1626. His diplomatic career supplied diversion from his grief sending him to England that was an ally of the Dutch Republic with which Flanders was seeking settlement. The 1630 peace treaty between England and Spain was largely the result of his finesse. Rubens received an honorary MA from Cambridge University. Shortly before his return to Antwerp, as a final accolade, Charles the first knighted Rubens. So he was able to return to Antwerp and take up once more the work to which he was most devoted, that of painting. In 1630, he married sixteen-year-old Helena Fourmat with whom he produced four children.

Rubens painted *The Supper at Emmaus* at this final tranquil period of his life. The setting is suggestive of his joyful exposure to Italian artists in his formative years. The background is an open view of a distant fortress with a Baroque balcony over which a figure leans. The softly-lit warm colors of the clothing and the way in which the expressions of the characters "talk" to the viewer all pay tribute to the assimilative intelligence of Rubens. But the interpretation of the biblical text that inspired the work belongs, of course, to Rubens alone. It is the interpretation that exercises us as viewers. The central character leaning across the table towards the figure of Christ responds in an endearingly simple and straightforward manner: he raises his hat. It is eloquently inadequate and such a comfortably-human touch to place at the centre of an otherwise overwhelmingly spiritually charged moment. In old testament terms it is a burning-bush moment.[235] The satyr-like, lumpen innkeeper stares with tight-lipped and uncomprehending brutishness. He looks like the kind of creature that was seen as an impediment to later revolutionary ideas.[236] Perhaps he senses that the figure he stares at, although completely unfathomable to him, is an unstoppable force. The figure seated stage-right of the table is an incredible creation. The body is twisted in a kind of paroxysm of tense angst. With the staring eye and the furrowed brow Rubens gives us a face contorted with awe. This is a physically powerful man, probably a fisherman used to wrestling unfazed with turbulent seas. But that with which he is confronted, although presented as a young, gentle-faced figure quite overwhelms him. An exotic, long-tailed parrot views the scene from above and a dog with a bone looks up from below in confirmation that we are in an everyday world albeit one where divine intervention takes place for those enabled to perceive it. The life of Rubens was not freighted with the burden carried by Caravaggio; how could it be? However, the contrast in this case is particularly extreme as demonstrated by a brief comparison of the two biographies. The weight of Caravaggio's burden charges the impact of his work in a uniquely powerful way. An attempt to achieve a similar impact through purely technical means is bound to be ineffectual. However, to be influenced by it as Rubens having seen it in Rome inevitably was is a different matter entirely.

Diego Rodriguez de Silva y Velázquez was born in Seville, Spain in 1599. He died in Madrid in 1660. He was allowed to set up his own studio in 1617 at the young age of eighteen. Initially, he was producing traditional religious works and *bodegones* or scenes of everyday life. Sometimes the religious and secular were combined. This suggests that the young Velasquez had some knowledge of the innovations of Peter Aertsen in the Netherlands and Jacopo Bassano in northern Italy. He was certainly alert to and influenced by the work of the older but contemporary Caravaggio in Rome. In 1623 the reputation of Velasquez was such that he was summoned to the court of Philip IV in Madrid to paint the king's portrait. This led to him becoming one of the court painters, a position he held until his death. After this appointment the subject matter of his paintings was predominantly

235. Exodus 3: 2.

236. Lumpenproletariat is a word coined by Karl Marx and Friedrich Engels in the 1840s in reference to the unthinking lower classes.

portraiture notably displayed in equestrian portraits. The earlier work of Velasquez does suggest that Caravaggio's dramatic lighting or *tenebrism* was an influence but the path he followed at court suggests that he was a much calmer, more restrained character. His father-in-law under whom he was apprenticed—Francesco Pacheco—said of him,

> After five years of education and training, I married him to my daughter, moved by his virtue, integrity and good parts and by the expectations of his disposition and great talent.[237]

237. Britannica online.

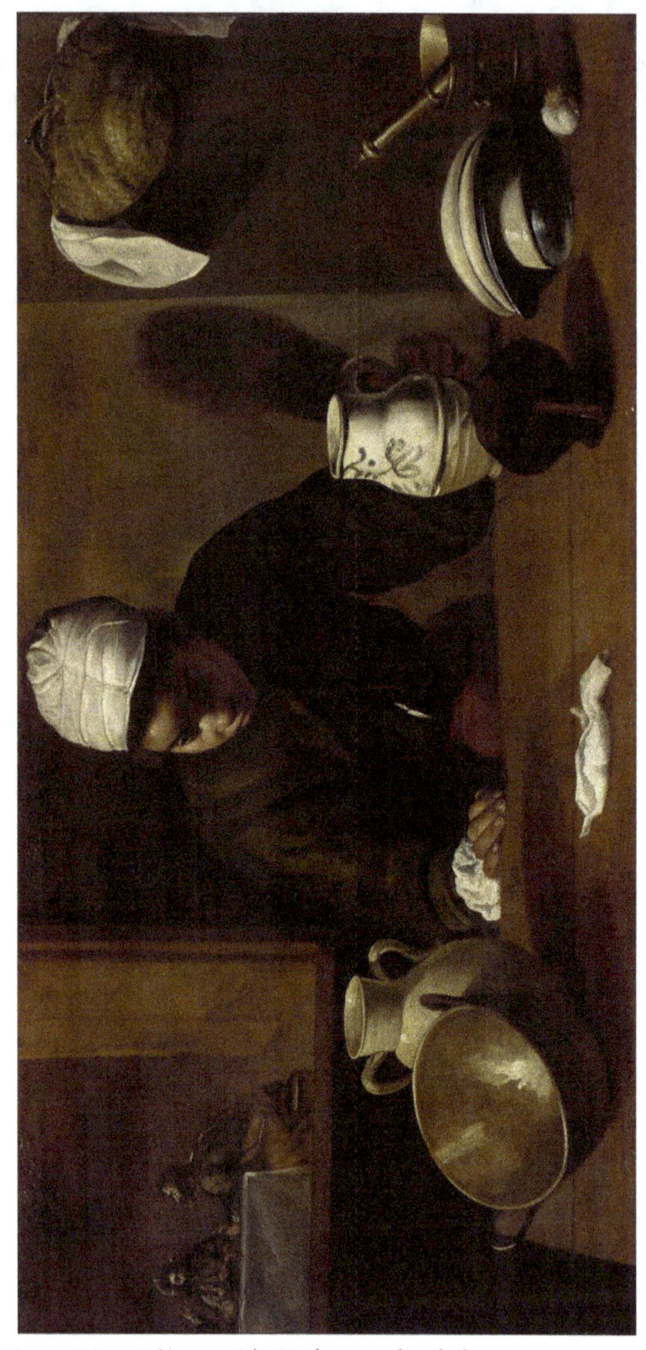

Fig. 44. Diego Velázquez. ***The Kitchen Maid with the Supper at Emmaus*** **1618 PD Wikimedia Commons.**

The two paintings concerning the Supper at Emmaus are early works[238] painted when he was free to select his subject matter. The first one—*The Kitchen Maid with the Supper at Emmaus*—is a remarkable meditation on the narrative in the gospel of Luke. It was painted in the period known as the golden age of Spanish culture, *Siglio de Oro*. Cervantes was living and writing in Madrid as was Lope de Vega, often compared to his English contemporary, Shakespeare. Like Shakespeare, Lope de Vega was a poet and a prolific playwright. Both Cervantes and Lope de Vega softened cynicism with good humor to attack the ancient attitudes and institutions of their country and their work was very well received. Cervantes published the second part of *Don Quixote* in 1615. The first part had been published in 1605 to immediate success. The book satirizes with great humor and humanity the Spanish love affair with stories of swashbuckling romance and derring-do. This had fuelled the conquistadors' conquests in Latin America and the Philippines. The attendant human suffering resulting from these events was now being questioned. Cervantes himself had fought very bravely in 1571 as part of the Holy League in the Battle of Lepanto. He had insisted on staying on the deck of his ship although suffering from fever, choosing, as he put it, rather to die for his God and king than to take cover. He was wounded with two gunshot wounds to the chest and one that rendered his left arm permanently useless. However, the brutality of the conquistadors and their treatment of indigenous populations as virtual slaves could not be ignored by the clerics who were there to give the enterprise the gloss of a catholic mission. The Dominican friar Bartolomé de las Casas petitioned the Spanish court on behalf of the suffering Latin American Indians. New laws were passed in Spain to protect the captives but the colonists proved resistant to them. In Peru, the viceroy attempting to implement the new dispensation was beheaded by local consent. The Spanish court was forced to bow to the reality of what had been unleashed and revoked the offending clauses in the new laws. The debate in Spain had become heated at the time that Velasquez was painting his meditations. I use "meditations" as by choosing to place a mulatto maid[239] at the forefront of his work, Velasquez is allowing his imagination to recognize that there has to be a kitchen with someone undertaking the drudgery of preparing and serving the food. This is usually unseen in the background. Velasquez dramatically reverses this,

238. 1618 and 1620.

239. Clearly of Moorish and Caucasian descent. The expulsion of the Muslim Moors from Spain was effectively completed by 1614 during the reign of Philip III.

prioritising the maid's predicament. The people at supper are in the obscure upstage-right background. It is important though to note that the breaking of bread and the miracle of recognition has not yet taken place. Yet in the kitchen, the attentive attitude of the maid and her expression of humbling awe clearly tells us that something profound has stirred within her innermost being. Velasquez catches the mood so brilliantly that the viewer is almost compelled to rehearse the maid's internal debate themself. This provoked Denise Levertov[240], to imagine that the Maid can hear at least a voice that she recognizes. She is having an internal dialog. It is not just the voice but also the way he looked at her when she handed him the bread. And there was something about his hands, his healing hands. She repeats the word "surely" three times in the poem as if pinching herself: he has risen from the dead! Clearly, Velasquez is entering the debate that is taking place in his country: how, as a Christian country, can the enslavement of human beings be justified? They have souls capable of responding to the presence of God. Velasquez ponders the fact that the gospel from which the narrative of the supper is taken suggests that a person from the lowly station of an African maid may be more open to the presence of Christ than the disciples who had lived in daily proximity to him and who are now sharing the table with him, the "fools and slow of heart."[241]

240. American poet 1923–1997. *The Servant-Girl at Emmaus (A Painting by Velázquez).*

241. KJV Luke 14, 25.

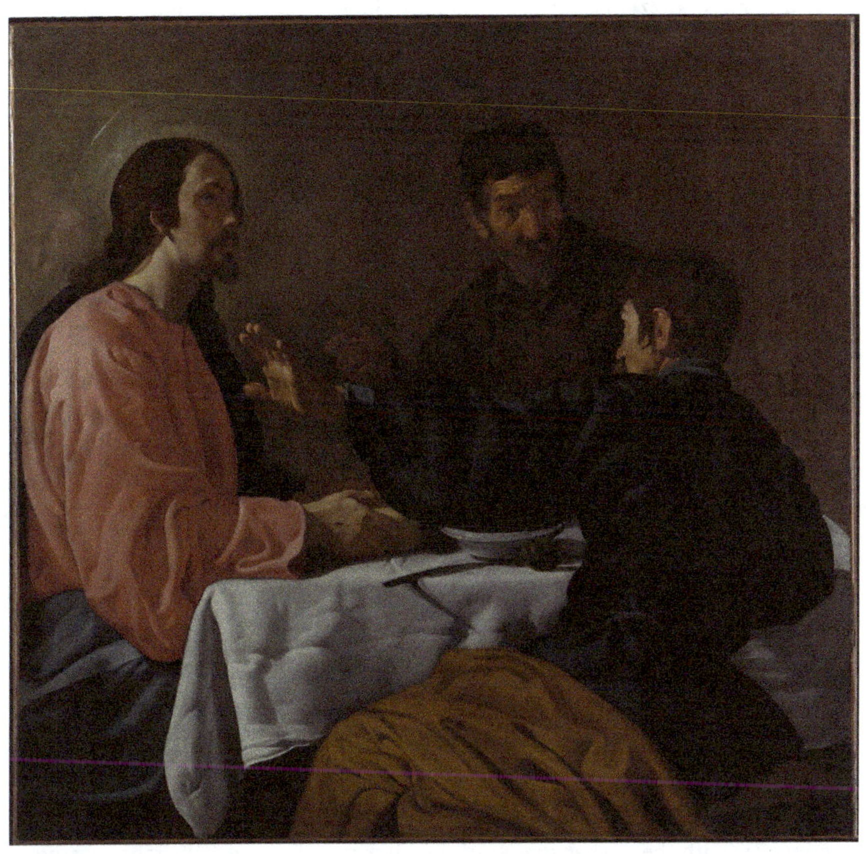

Fig. 45. Diego Velázquez. *The Supper at Emmaus* 1622–1623 Metropolitan Museum of Art, New York © PD The Athenaeum.

The second painting focuses exclusively on three figures at a table. Velasquez provides us with the stabilizing feature of a white-covered table that clarifies the very dramatically active arrangement of the painting with its otherwise dizzying variety of angles. Stage-right is the figure of Jesus identified by a diaphanous halo. A full-faced depiction of one pilgrim is at the centre and a figure with his back towards us and a face in partial profile is stage-left. The painting is thought to have been completed in 1622/3 most probably in Seville before Velasquez transferred to Madrid to paint the king's portrait. The presentation of the trio in such a confined space creates a strange, almost impertinent aspect to the painting. Christ is a dignified and aloof figure with the fresh nail-wound showing on the back of his right hand that rests upon the table-top. The two pilgrims are in animated conversation as if Christ is not there. And, of course, to the two pilgrims, he isn't. The miracle has not yet taken place: the bread remains unbroken. The attitude conveyed by the faces and body language of the two men as with that of the maid in the previous painting is so brilliantly "caught" by the painter that the viewer is compelled to speculate. The left hand of the stage-left pilgrim almost touches the body that they are discussing. The center figure casually jerks his thumb towards it. The impersonal pronoun seems appropriate here as clearly they are not aware of a sentient being: animation has for the moment been suspended. It is as if two surgeons are discussing the body of an anaesthetized patient. One recalls the isolation of Christ as prophesised in Isaiah 53. The faces of the pilgrims are those of serious opinionated men: you do not pull the wool over the eyes of these two. The humility conveyed by the kitchen maid is not on show here. The otherness of Christ is emphasized by the delicate coral pink of his garment that contrasts with the darker shades of the pilgrims' clothing. The light coming from behind the head of Christ seems to be a transfiguring element. And the "light of the world" is about to dawn on the pilgrims and confound the "wisdom" that they are so proudly displaying.

The century in which Rembrandt lived was, like the same period in which Velasquez worked in Spain, known as a golden age. In 1648 the *Peace of Westphalia* had recognized the division between the southern Spanish-dominated Netherlands—largely today's Belgium—and the northern provinces, the Dutch Republic. The Republic achieved world status in science, military might and art. It was largely protestant as opposed to the catholic south. Although the Hague was the seat of government, Amsterdam became one of the leading ports and commercial centers in the world.

Rembrandt was born in Leiden in 1606 but he moved to Amsterdam in 1631. He seems to have been temperamentally independent with his own opinions and sense of direction. He was,

> a most temperamental man [inclined to] disparage everyone. The ugly and plebeian face with which Rembrandt was ill-favoured was accompanied by untidy and dirty clothes, since it was his custom, when working, to wipe his brushes on himself, and do other things of a similar nature . . . When Rembrandt worked he would not have granted an audience to the first monarch of the world who would have to return again and again until he found him no longer engaged.[242]

Clearly, Rembrandt made little attempt to cultivate personal popularity. His focus was on his artistic life. This, he pursued on his own terms. He was briefly a student at Leiden's internationally acclaimed university but his studies there failed to engage his interest and he moved to Amsterdam in 1631. He eschewed the conventional route followed by many young painters of the time of travels in Italy to study italian art. He studied prints of such work and conversed with colleagues who had returned from their travels. The dramatic lighting effects of Caravaggio in Rome were, to use the modern term, "trending." But the tridentine catholic energy that exercised Caravaggio was not stirring within Rembrandt. There is no evidence that Rembrandt himself belonged formally to any one church. His independent personality was perhaps a barrier to that. His mother was a Roman Catholic but his father belonged to the Dutch Reformed Church. The Dutch Republic was strongly protestant. Art commissions from the protestant church and religious institutions were not forthcoming. Private commissions tended to be for portraits. Wary of catholic emphasis on visual representations of Mary, Jesus and sacred events that to the protestant mind led to idolatry, still life and pastoral scenes became the market-favoured works of art. Rembrandt who focussed on religious themes had to rely upon similarly inclined and artistically informed clients and private students for his steadily growing income. However, Caravaggio's sense of drama heightened by contrasts of light and dark seems to have intoxicated Rembrandt in his early work. This may be seen in his 1629 version of *The Supper at Emmaus.*[243]

242. Badinucci, cited Rosenberg. *Rembrandt Life and Work*, 33.

243. Musée Jacquemart-André, Paris.

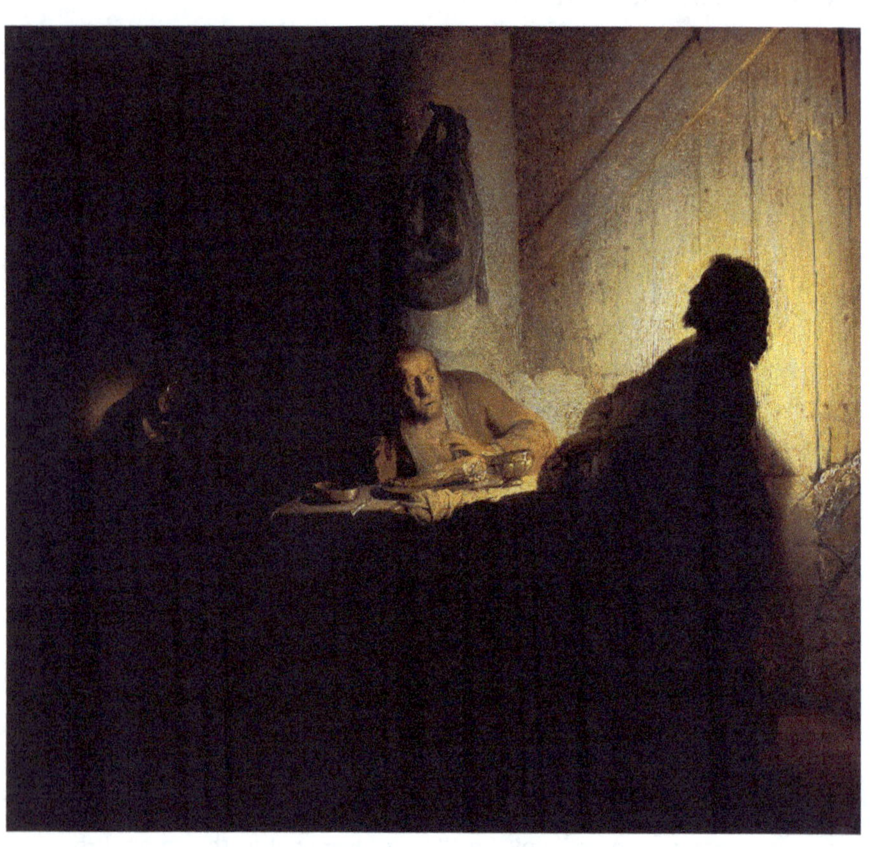

Fig. 46. Rembrant Harmenszoon van Rijn. ***The Supper at Emmaus*** **1629 Musée Jaquemart-André, Paris PD Wikimedia Commons.**

Rembrandt boldly depicts Christ in harsh silhouette against a brightly lit scene depicting an awe-struck character on the opposite side of the table. He cowers, completely overawed and apparently petrified. The head of Christ is thrust back in a rather imperious manner as he breaks the bread. The fellow pilgrim stage-right has fallen to his knees kicking his stool backwards. His position against the dark shadow of the table is impossible to see in prints of the painting. To the upstage-right in her own pool of light is the kitchen maid busy in her kitchen. The lighting effects serve a purely dramatic purpose: they create an unreal and quite alarming atmosphere. The scene around the table is turbulent and disorienting. Quite literally, we do not know where we are. The distant glimpse into the ordinary world of the kitchen suggests by contrast that we are being presented with visions of two different worlds. It is difficult to escape the feeling that we would rather be in the kitchen. Rembrandt was twenty-three when he completed this version of *The Supper at Emmaus* so to a large extent it must be considered an experimental work and on that level very impressive. But it is such a relief to turn to his 1649 version painted when he was forty-two and settled in Amsterdam with his reputation established.

Along with his artistic reputation, Rembrandt's life experiences had been such as to shape his perception and priorities. On moving to Amsterdam in 1631, Rembrandt quickly gained a reputation as a portraitist. He astutely lodged with an influential art dealer and three years later married the art dealer's cousin, Saskia van Uylenburgh. This was a socially advantageous marriage. Saskia's father had been a lawyer and mayor and was, therefore, well connected. In the same year Rembrandt became a burger of Amsterdam and a member of the local painters' guild. Saskia and Rembrandt moved into a fine new house in a fashionable neighbourhood. For a time they were financially secure. The couple had lost a son and a daughter in infancy. In 1640 a second daughter died at a few weeks old. Titus the fourth child lived into adulthood. However, soon after his birth, his mother died in 1642. Geertje Dicx was employed as a nurse for Titus. She became Rembrandt's lover. Geertje later sued Rembrandt for breach of promise to marry her and was awarded alimony. But Rembrandt contrived to have her committed to a lunatic asylum for twelve years. Towards the end of the 1640s Rembrandt embarked on a relationship with his maid Hendrickje Stoffels. She was considerably younger than Rembrandt and in 1654 they had a daughter, Cornelia. The Dutch Reformed Church charged Hendrickje with "whoring" with Rembrandt and she was banned from receiving communion. Rembrandt was not troubled by the church of which he was not a member. As with his social skills it seems that his talent as an artist was not matched by his financial management skills and his fortunes declined. He sold his house and moved into barely adequate accommodation. Hendrickje died in 1663. Titus died in 1668 leaving a baby daughter. Rembrandt died in 1669 and was buried in poverty. Quite clearly, Rembrandt did not enjoy a tranquil or happy private life.

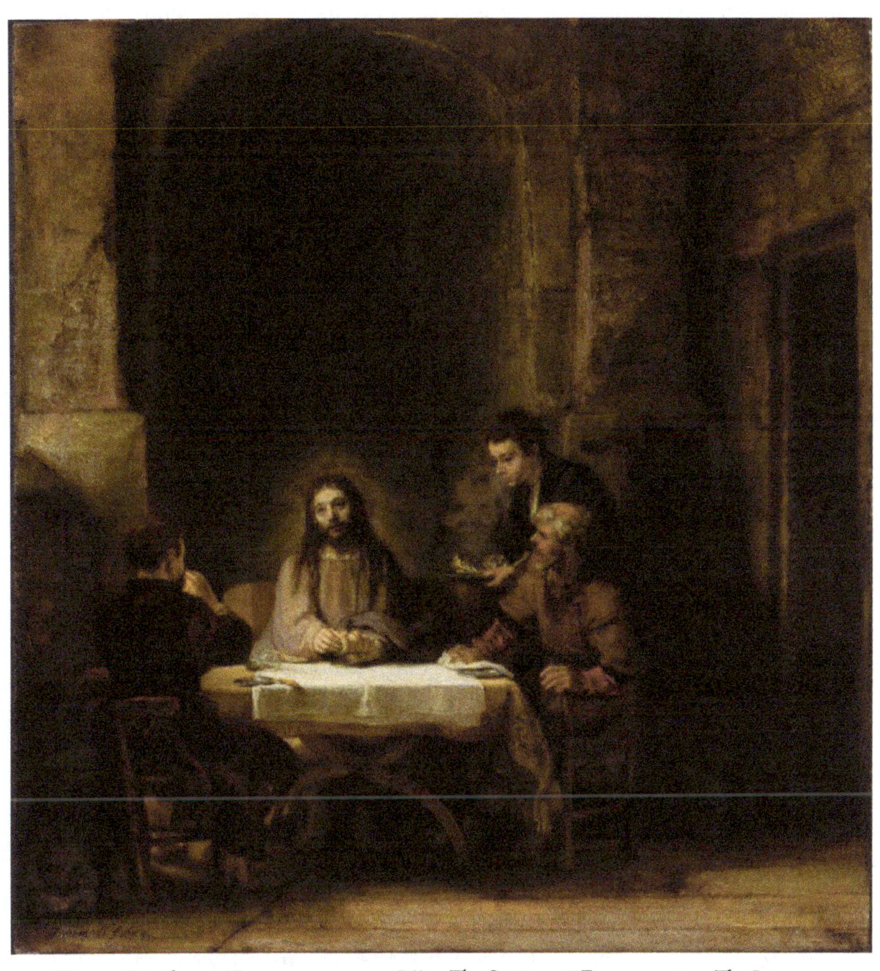

Fig. 47. Rembrant Harmenszoon van Rijn. *The Supper at Emmaus* 1649 The Louvre, Paris © PD The Athenaeum.

When Rembrandt painted the 1649 version of *The Supper at Emmaus* he had lost three children and a wife to whom he was apparently devoted.[244] His romantic entanglements since these tragic events were somewhat turbulent. But the Emmaus subject seems to have had a special significance for Rembrandt as he returned to it on several occasions. The calm and tranquillity that pervades this painting is quite amazing given the background of Rembrandt's life at this time. When compared with the drama and agitation that some painters have brought to the scene—not least Rembrandt himself in his 1629 version—it is a most moving experience. If Caravaggio's 1602 version in London's National Gallery is a shout, this version by Rembrandt is a whisper. It brings to mind lines from the beautiful Christmas hymn by Phillips Brooks,[245] "O Little Town of Bethlehem."

> How silently, how silently
> The wondrous gift is given!

There is an atmosphere of humility conveyed by the every-day nature of the scene, particularly in the portrayal of Jesus. The idealised form that we see, for instance, in Veronese's depiction[246] is in sharp contrast with what we see here. Rembrandt was a very close observer of humanity, its attitudes, expressions and moods. As mentioned earlier, he did not travel to study the works of other painters as did many of his contemporaries. He stayed at home and observed people. The fruits of these observations are abundantly rewarded in his incredible etchings. But here it is illustrated in his depiction of Jesus. Rembrandt was living in the Jewish Quarter of Amsterdam at the time. What he gives us here is the face and demeanor of a young Jewish man: "a man of sorrows and acquainted with grief."[247] The far away look reflecting on past sorrow and suffering must have been readily observable for Rembrandt. Many of the Jewish population in Amsterdam were fleeing pogroms and uprisings attendant upon the thirty years war[248] in central Europe. These were the Ashkenazi Jews. The Sephardic Jews from the Iberian Peninsula had been expelled from Spain in 1492. Seeking a home in Portugal, they were given the choice in 1497 of conversion to catholicism or death for heresy. This weight of sorrow and suffering would have been

244. The moving drawings of Saskia on her death bed suggest as much.

245. 1835–1893.

246. Image 37.

247. KJV. Isaiah 53:3.

248. Between 1618 and 1648.

seen and reflected upon by Rembrandt on a daily basis. Apart from it feeding into his intrinsic sensibility, it must also have made him aware of the pernicious effects of religious zealotry. Somehow, Rembrandt manages in the midst of this ordinariness of which Jesus partakes to make him stand out as an extraordinary presence. Light emanates from him and his gown is given a luminous sheen by the subtle modulation of colours. All counter-reformation zeal is missing here. No symbolic elements cover the table and we are left to focus on the bread and the hands of Christ. The two pilgrims are portrayed in calm meditation as the light dawns upon them. For the stage-right figure with his cupped hands to his mouth this is a moment of profound understanding beyond words. The more mature figure stage-left seems to be acquiring another layer of wisdom to his understanding of the Christ whom he has followed but not understood at this level. The young serving boy, although unaware of the revelation taking place, is depicted as aware that he is entering sacred space. He could easily be imagined as advancing on tip-toe. This is a very protestant painting in its emphasis on the inner, personal spiritual experience. What Rembrandt so skilfully manages to paint are the thoughts of Christ and the pilgrims. It is like an advent painting: the coming of a deeper experience gently taking hold of the two disciples. By setting the scene against the background of the opening in a monumental alcove, a sense of emptiness is conveyed. This recalls the sense of utter desolation in the grip of which the disciples were when Jesus encountered them on the road to Emmaus. It is, of course, the filling of that great void that the Emmaus experience consummates. The soft brown earth tones in which the scene is bathed console along with the humanity of the scene as the essential divinity of Christ serenely shines over it with an inner light.

Jan Steen was also born in Leiden in 1626. His family were brewers and long-standing hosts of a local tavern. They were financially secure but as catholics they were, post-Reformation, not eligible for political advancement. Jan followed the pathway of his older contemporary, Rembrandt, through the latin school and an unremarkable attendance at Leiden University. From an early age he was presented with the daily human drama of people at uninhibited play. His work suggests that he viewed the spectacle with a benign eye, sometimes critical but mitigated by a humorous awareness of his own involvement in the drama. He studied art in Utrecht and in 1648 he co-founded the Guild of Saint Luke and worked with the artist who, in 1649, was to become his father-in-law. After five years he moved to Delft to take charge of the brewery the lease of which had been gifted to him by his father. 1654 was not a very auspicious year to arrive in Delft as it was the year of The Delft Thunderclap.[249] The brewery was not a success, the art market was depressed, and Steen moved on to a little town to the north of Leiden. From there he moved to Haarlem with his wife, Margriet with whom he produced eight children. In 1670, Margriet died and Jan moved back to Leiden where he lived until his death in 1679. He married again in 1673 and produced another child. In 1674, he was appointed president of The Guild of Saint Luke. Steen's work suggests that he liked to tell stories of daily life in his paintings. Because of his own life-style and situation this daily life tended to be focused on the less elevated activities that occupy humanity. Sometimes, his paintings contained elements of gentle satire as in his versions of *As the Old Sing, so Pipe the Young*. This was a popular proverb reminding the adult population of their responsibilities towards the next generation. However, in the middle of the drunken levity that this painting presents to us, a self-portrait of Steen is to be seen happily participating in the jolly dissolute behaviour. His popularity as a commercial artist[250] is suggested by the fact that a common subject of his paintings passed into a Dutch proverb that still holds currency today: *een huishouden van Jan Steen*.[251] The disorderly nature of such a household was common knowledge. This admittedly entertaining aspect of Steen's work is not the whole story.

Steen's art suggests that beneath what often appears to be a frivolous surface there was a genuine depth to his character. This is to be detected in the affection he demonstrates for children in his paintings. Incidental images of children are scattered throughout his works. In *Peasants before an Inn*[252] for example two young children are unobtrusively placed in the center of the scene. They are totally and endearingly absorbed in their private world. A young boy with a caged bird laughs knowingly to himself at a couple of his "elders and betters" flirting drunkenly with a stubbornly uninterested woman.

249. A gunpowder store exploded destroying a great part of the city and killing over one hundred people and injuring thousands more.

250. Steen produced approximately 800 paintings.

251. A Jan Steen household.

252. 1653. Toledo Museum of Art.

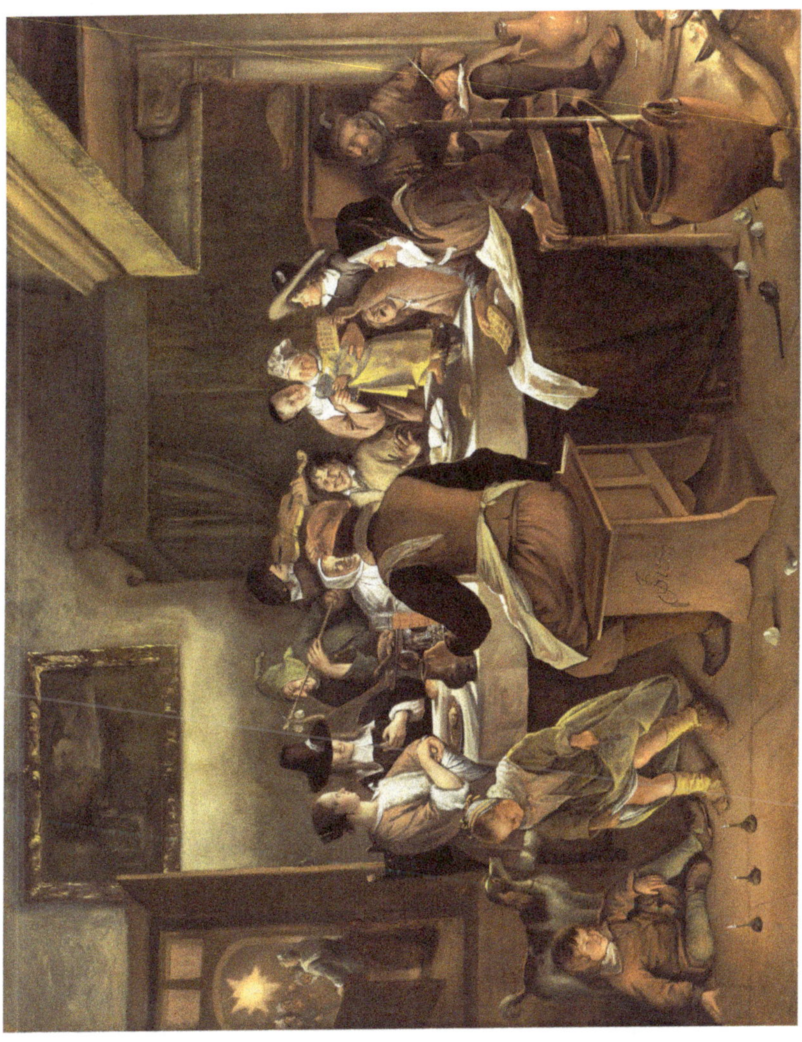

Fig. 48. Jan Havicksz Steen. ***Twelfth-Night Feast*** **1662 Photograph © November 2019 Museum of Fine Arts, Boston.**

In *Twelfth Night*[253] Steen features a festival frowned upon by the protestant burghers of Leiden but celebrated by catholics in homes and taverns. The figure enjoying the fun at the center of the table facing out appears to be a self-portrait. The fun includes an incongruous couple center-stage-right being discomfited by the jester dangling a sausage and eggshell mock-up of male genitalia before their eyes. The householder's hospitality appears to have been extended to protestant, here possibly quaker, neighbours and the scene makes a nice reference to the prevailing relaxed neighbourly relationships that Steen favoured. Steen places two innocents prominently downstage-right. They are playing at jumping over the three candles representing the three kings of the advent story. Again, they are completely engrossed in their private world. In a typically Steen touch, the little boy neglects his concentration on the game by gazing at the little girls naked legs that she is revealing by lifting her skirt. This gentle, reflective side of Steen's nature is called to the fore in his religious works.

253. 1662. Museum of Fine Arts, Boston.

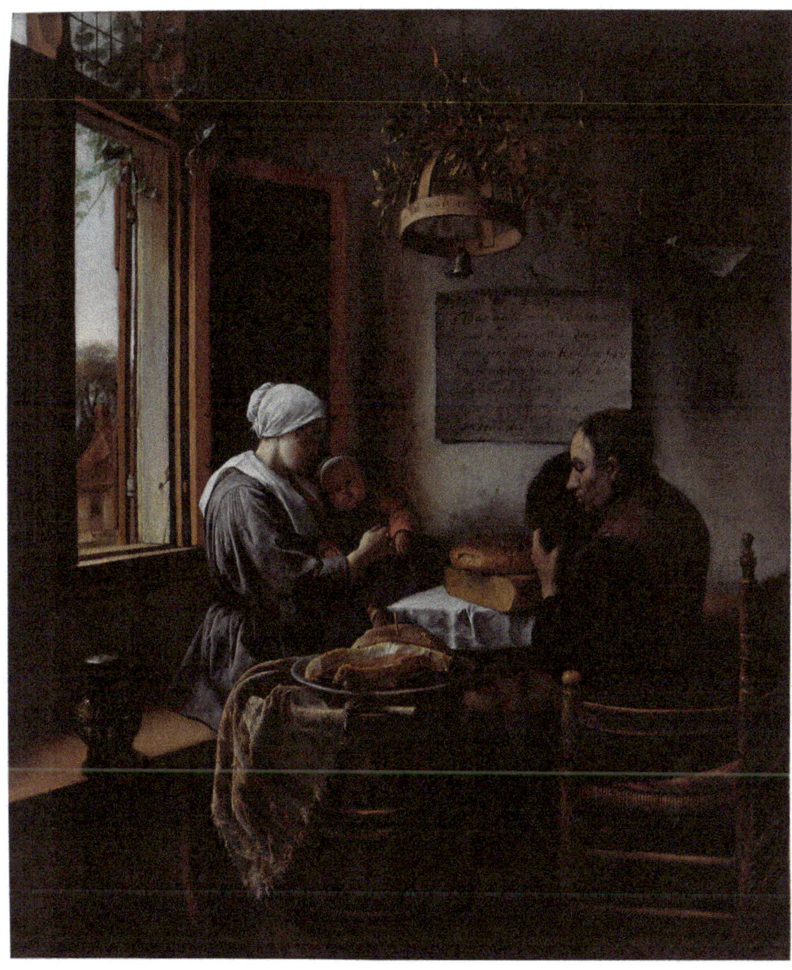

Fig. 49. Jan Havicksz Steen. *Prayer Before the Meal* **1660 image courtesy of The Leiden Collection, New York.**

I acknowledge with gratitude the efforts of Scarlett Rose Atkinson of Sothebys London in securing this image.

The Prayer before the Meal[254] depicts a humble domestic interior. A man, a woman, and their young child sit at a simple table before a meal of bread, cheese, and the cheap cut of ham that is largely fat. The man reverently removes his hat to give thanks for the provision of food. The inscription displayed on the wall is based upon a biblical passage.[255]

> These things I desire and no more/Above all to love God the Father/Not to covet an abundance of riches/But to desire what the wisest pray for/An honest life in this vale/In these three all is based.

On the shelf in the upstage-left corner of the painting are symbolic reminders of the transience of life and the promise of the Resurrection: wheat that must die, be buried, and rise again, an extinguished candle, and a skull. On the wall beneath the shelf it may clearly be seen that the image of a crucifix has been obliterated. The cynical explanation for this might be that Steen was aiming for a wider market as the crucifix was anathema to the protestant community. I think that on the evidence of Steen's work, devout Catholic though he was, he was also impatient of the artificial barriers erected between his community and that of his fellow christians who happened to belong to a different way of celebrating what was a shared faith, The pious humility of the painting and the care in execution are very moving and quite remarkable within the context of the work for which Steen is commonly celebrated. But it is a timely reminder that, as Hamlet discovered, too much emphasis on what *seems* can deceive us and that sometimes we should try to see into that which is within and passes show.[256]

254. 1660. Now in the Leiden Collection, New York.

255. Proverbs 30: 7–9.

256. Shakespeare. Hamlet, 1: 2, 80 and 89.

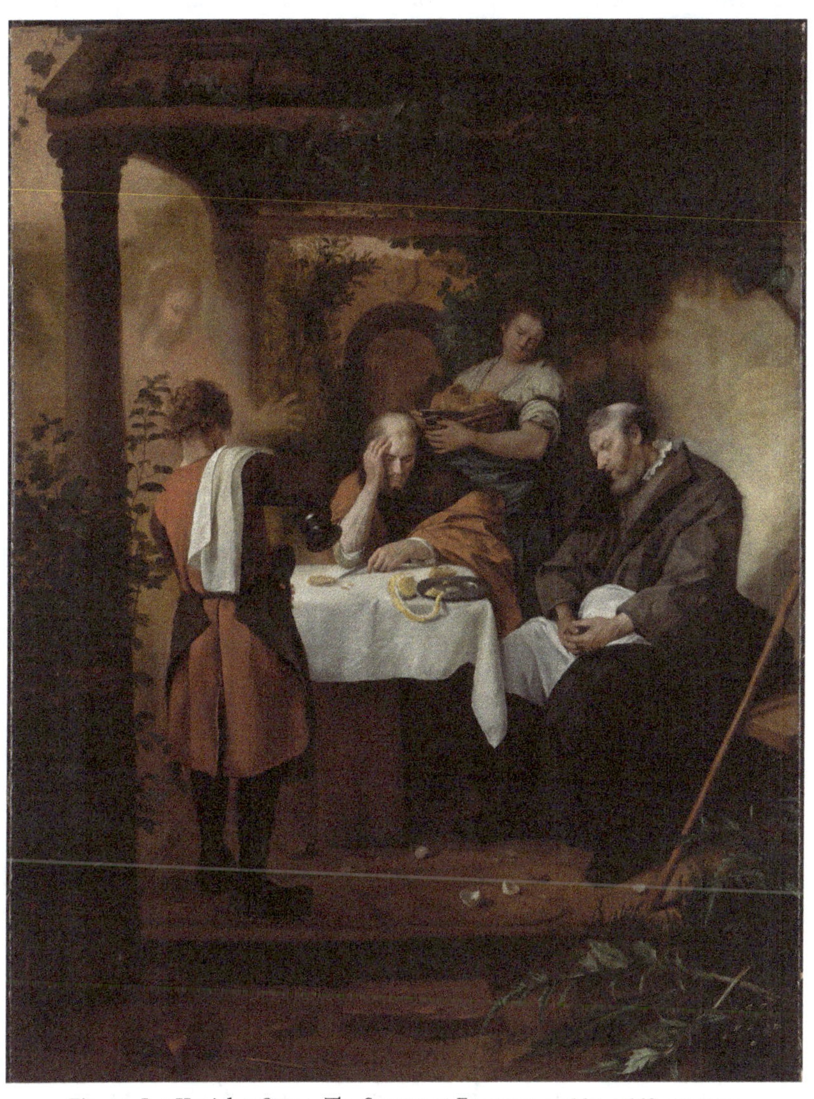

Fig. 50. Jan Havicksz Steen. ***The Supper at Emmaus*** **c 1665–1668 courtesy Rijksmuseum, Amsterdam.**

This is, I suggest, clearly demonstrated in Steen's *Supper at Emmaus.* At first, it looks like another disorderly house with two over-indulged burghers sleeping off a meal the debris of which scatters the floor. But the faint ghostly apparition reaching out a hand of blessing to the two diners reminds us that we are looking at Steen's depiction of *The Supper at Emmaus* and that the two at the table are pilgrims at prayer. It is a startlingly idiosyncratic presentation of the moment when the risen Christ reveals himself to the two pilgrims who have met him unrecognized on the road to Emmaus. What Steen has evoked very effectively is the moment when we are told that Christ revealed himself to the pilgrims as he broke the bread and simultaneously "vanished out of their sight."[257] What Wheelock refers to as "the weighty dignity of the painting."[258] is enhanced by the use made by Steen of the two servers. They deliver the bread and wine with a solemnity that suggests that they have been momentarily elevated above their role of tavern servers. They are in effect the bearers of the elements of the Eucharist. The two supplicants, deep in prayer are participating in the Eucharist with the real presence of Christ extending his hand of blessing into the grape arbor. The simple table with the half-peeled lemon, and the broken egg shells on the floor suggest interruption and abandonment of routine. Other symbolic associations may be attributed to them as with the thistle and the situation within the grape arbor but the simplicity of the scene overrides such intellectualizing. The atmosphere of humble spirituality that Steen evokes in *Prayer before the Meal* is present in this work also. I suggested that Rembrandt's 1649 version of *Supper at Emmaus* is a very protestant painting in its emphasis upon the inner, personal experience. Steen's work seems to me to share this emphasis and yet it is arguably, a very catholic painting. So, I clearly disagree with the conclusion of Schmidt-Degener and van Gelder that Steen's painting lacks the "depth of inner life"[259] displayed in Rembrandt's 1649 version of *The Supper at Emmaus.* I suggest that the work of Rembrandt and that of Steen both demonstrate that the two painters discover and convey very clearly "the net within the gross."[260] Perhaps that is what prompts Wheelock's conclusion,

257. KJV Luke, 24: 31.

258. Wheelock. *Jan Steen,* 200.

259. Scmidt-Degener. *Forty Reproductions,* 123.

260. See note 10.

> (Steen's) *Supper at Emmaus* remains the most daring and provocative religious painting in Dutch art.[261]

Steen dared to suggest, perhaps by inspiration rather than intention, that the division between the two branches of western Christianity are artificial. To sift through the lemon peel and eggshells of Sheen's painting is to be seduced by the "intentional fallacy.[262]

As many of us in the west now live in largely secular societies, it may be of interest to look at a painter ostensibly without religious faith and yet driven to devote a significant amount of his creative life to very specifically Christian subjects including *The Supper at Emmaus*. The Age of Enlightenment as the eighteenth century in Europe came to be labelled developed ideas that undermined the authority of monarchy and church and culminated in The French Revolution of 1789 that had brutally ushered in the brave new world of the first French Republic. It was into this revolutionary melting-pot that Eugene Delacroix was born in 1798 in Charenton-Saint-Maurice, near to Paris, France. After a classical education during which he demonstrated a talent for drawing, he began training as an artist in 1815 at the age of seventeen. His early work demonstrated empathy with suffering humanity by focussing on the plight of the ordinary Greek people in their war for independence from Turkish domination.[263] He faced criticism for evoking the pathos rather than glory of battle that was more appealing to the revolutionary times in which he lived. In 1825 Delacroix visited England where he developed an interest in depicting emotionally charged scenes notably those inspired by the romantic poet Byron whose work he greatly admired and also by those inspired by the novels of Walter Scott.

261. Wheelock. Ibid., 200.

262. Term of twentieth-century literary criticism to suggest that it is a mistake to base judgments on works of art upon assumptions concerning the intention of the artist.

263. 1821–1830.

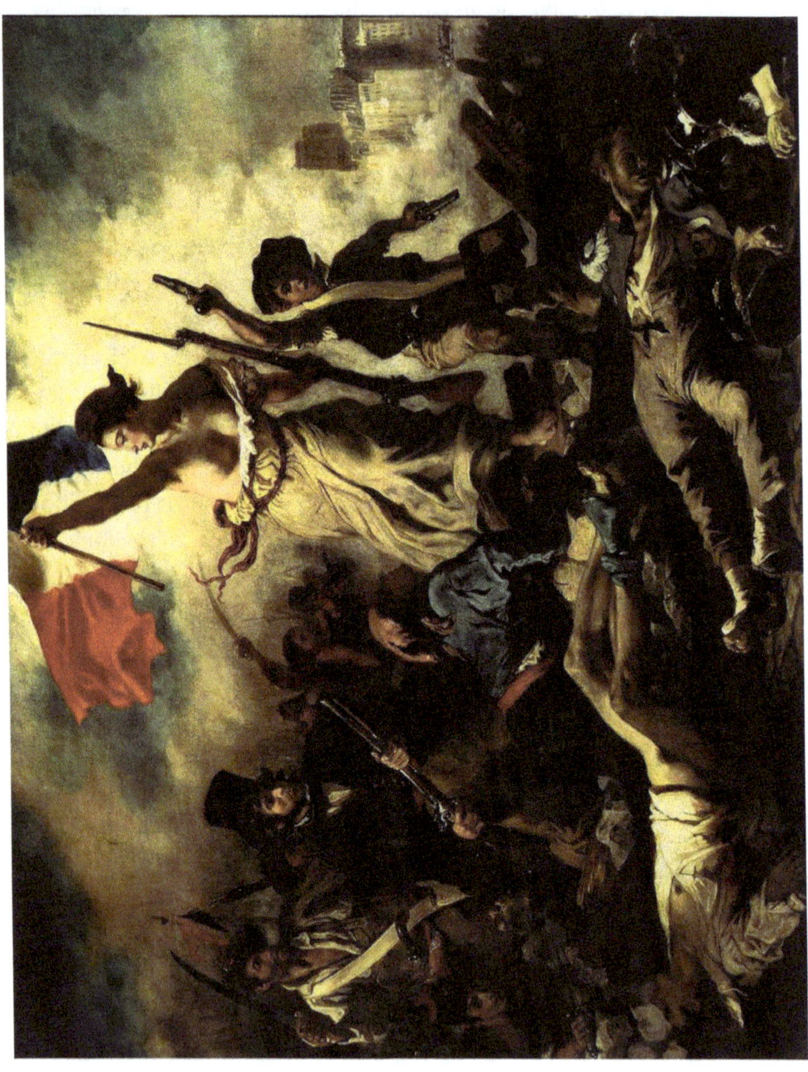

Fig. 51. Eugène Delacroix. Liberty Leading the People 1830 Louvre Museum, Paris PD Wikimedia Commons.

Perhaps Delacroix's best-known Romantic painting is *Liberty Leading the People.*[264]The personification of Liberty leads the common folk onward under the banner of the tricolour. The nobility of the implied cry of "liberty, equality, and fraternity" is counterpoised by the pile of corpses in the foreground. The pathetic suggestion is that the man in the top hat and the young boy, a pistol in each hand, are both doomed to be added to the pile very shortly. The chief result of the 1830 revolution that inspired the painting, apart from the carnage, was, ironically, to change kings from Charles X to Louise Philippe. The Paris uprising of 1832 that sought to overturn this unsatisfactory result was featured in Victor Hugo's novel *Les Misérables.*[265] The character of Gavroche in his novel was, so many believe, inspired by the young pistol-waving boy in Delacroix's painting. During this period, Delacroix was also painting religious subjects but with no indication that his secular philosophy was in any way compromised. Rather, he seemed to be determined to convince would-be clients and the public at large that he was working within the tradition of the Renaissance artists of the previous two centuries. The way in which the mind of Delacroix was set may be clarified if we consider his background. He was orphaned at the age of sixteen and had to navigate his way through the prevailing climate of ideas to which he was exposed. The secular principles that dominated the intellectual climate were inevitably anti-clerical. Delacroix, classically-educated and highly intelligent, found the atheism of Diderot engaging. He read Voltaire and Jean-Jaques Rousseau and their attacks on catholicism. Perhaps more interestingly he was deeply impressed by the logical search for God in the writings of Descartes. This suggests that, for whatever reason, he wanted to go where his mind refused to follow.

> Can it be possible that He does not exist? . . . If the universe had been produced by chance, what would *conscience* mean or *remorse*, or *devotion*? O! If only, with all the strength of your being, you could believe in that God who invented duty, all your doubts and hesitations would be resolved.[266]

This entry in the twenty-four-year-old Delacroix's journal is very revealing. It demonstrates that Delacroix was driven by spiritual forces the source of which puzzled him. Those forces could not find comfortable habitation within the secular revolutionary fervor of his time. This is

264. 1830. Louvre, Paris..

265. 1862

266. Norton. *The Journal*, 9.

demonstrated in the perceived ambiguity of *Liberty Leading the People*. The religious paintings suggest that those spiritual forces find a resting place at the heart of christianity but not as presented by the church of Delacroix's experience.

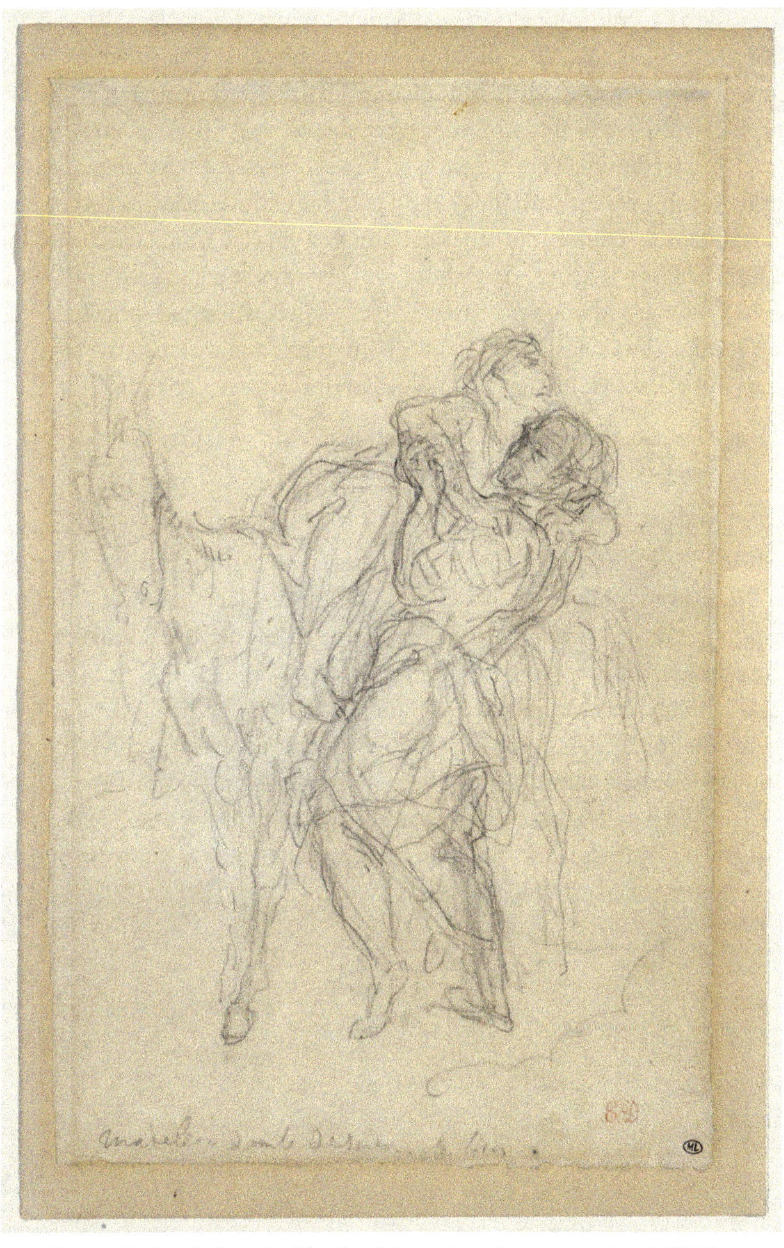

Fig. 52. Eugène Delacroix. ***The Good Samaritan*** **circa 1849–1850 © PD The Athenaeum.**

The 1850 version of *The Good Samaritan* presents a clear demonstration of this. The muscular physicality of the presentation, in which many have observed the influence of Rubens, is like a wrestling match as the Samaritan leans backwards straining every sinew to ease the burden of his injured and traditional enemy gently on to his horse. The passage in Genesis where Jacob wrestles with the angel[267] comes to mind. Delacroix received a commission to paint a mural based upon this passage from Genesis for the church of Saint-Sulpice in Paris in 1849. This was not completed until 1861. So he was engaged upon the Saint-Sulpice project whilst painting *The Good Samaritan.* The Genesis story has been interpreted in various ways over the years but Delacroix focuses on one straightforward explanation:

> This struggle is regarded by the holy books as a symbol of the trials that God sometimes sends his chosen ones.[268]

It does not take a great effort to see *The Good Samaritan* work as symbolising the christian recognition of the need to cast the burden of sin on to the Savior of Mankind. It can also be seen as placing emphasis on the requirement of a strong faith to be able to surrender oneself in absolute trust to the deliverer as the injured man clearly does in the painting. We may, perhaps, be able to hear Delacroix exclaiming with Hamlet, " . . . ay, there's the rub."[269] Disappearing out of the picture downstage left is a monk deeply engrossed in a devotional text. Such prioritising of word above deed is clearly seen by Delacroix as misplaced. The preparatory graphite drawing that Delacroix undertook shows how concerned he was to render the image of faith and total surrender effectively.

267. Genesis32:24—32.

268. Dunn, Ahley, cited Metrpolitan Museum of Art website.

269. Shakespeare, *Hamlet* 3: 1, 66. Delacroix drew inspiration from the works of Shakespeare.

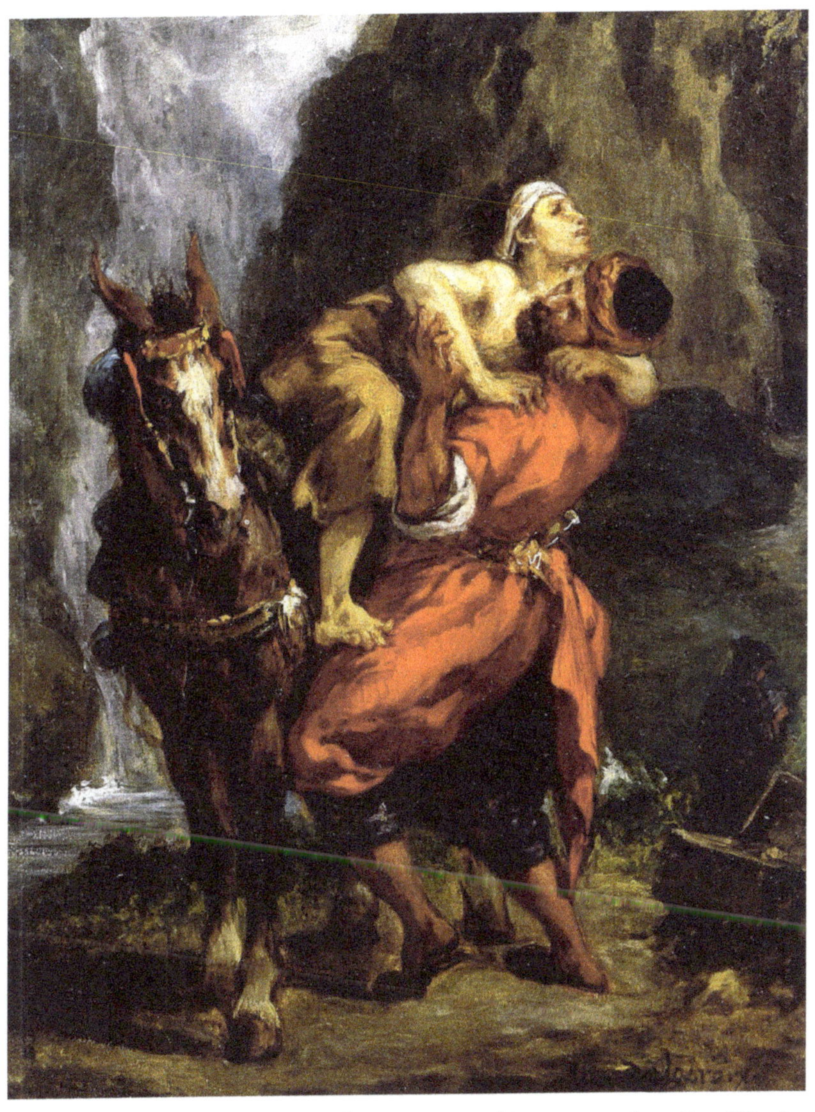

Fig. 53. Eugène Delacroix. ***The Good Samaritan*** **graphite on paper circa 1849 ©Musée du Louvre.**

The creative potential between religion and art, of course, had been recognised for many centuries and the mere engagement with a religious subject, of itself, tells us little about a painter's personal convictions. However, the intensity of feeling conveyed by Delacroix's later work causes one to question a common response that his religious works were simply paintings based upon well-known themes from a great artist who had no religious convictions. It does seem to be a plausible argument that Delacroix's early-demonstrated empathy for suffering humanity directed his choices regarding the precise moments of the life of Christ that he depicted rather than any sense of Christ's divinity. However, it does seem more difficult to fully embrace that viewpoint when looking at the many variations of *Christ on the Cross* that Delacroix painted towards the end of his life. A brief look at one of these paintings is sufficient to demonstrate this point. Delacroix takes the iconography for this painting from the Fourth Gospel:

> 25 Now there stood by the cross of Jesus his mother, and his mother's sister, Mary the wife of Cleophas, and Mary Magdalene.
>
> 26 When Jesus therefore saw his mother, and the disciple standing by, whom he loved, he saith unto his mother, Woman, behold thy son!
>
> 27 Then saith he to the disciple, Behold thy mother! And from that hour that disciple took her unto his own home.
>
> 28 After this, Jesus knowing that all things were now accomplished, that the scripture might be fulfilled, saith, I thirst.
>
> 29 Now there was set a vessel full of vinegar: and they filled a spunge with vinegar, and put it upon hyssop, and put it to his mouth.
>
> 30 When Jesus therefore had received the vinegar, he said, It is finished: and he bowed his head, and gave up the ghost.[270]

270. KJV. Jn. 19, 25–29.

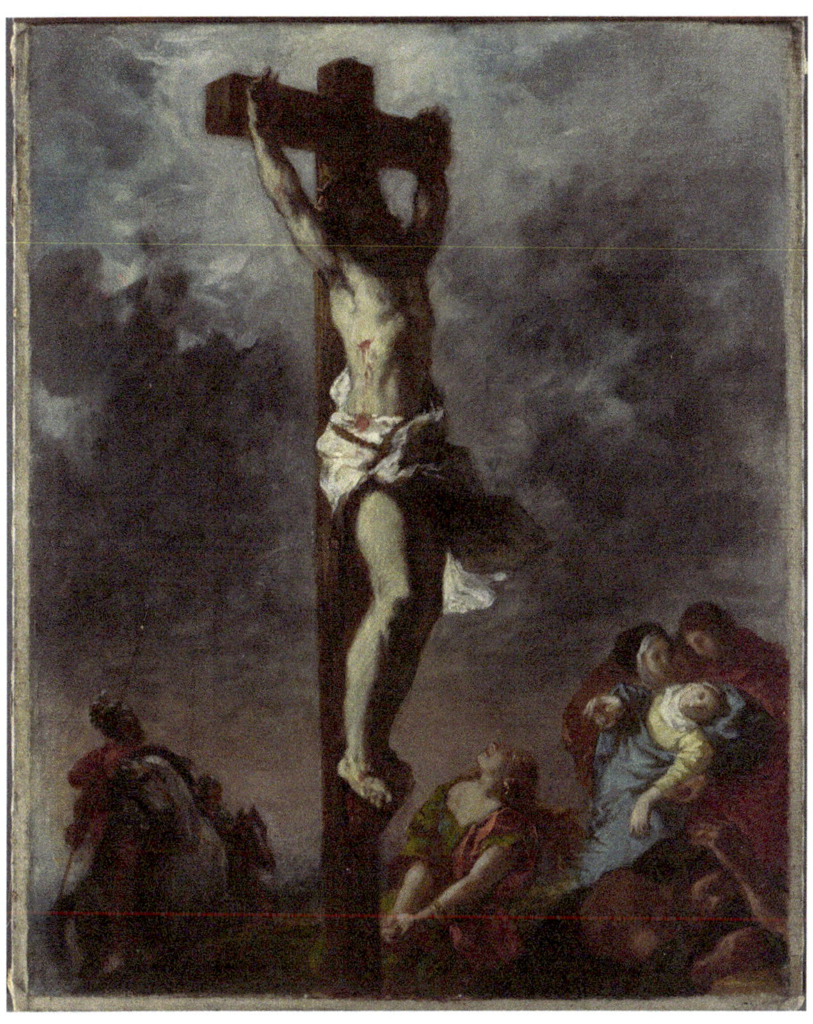

Fig. 54. Eugène Delacroix. ***Christ on the Cross*** **1853 courtesy of the National Gallery (London) Picture Library.**

Delacroix had painted several images of Christ on the Cross but here he takes a new approach. The scene becomes a family drama by the inclusion of the Virgin and her sister-in-law Mary. This Mary is the wife of Cleophas who is the brother of Joseph. John the beloved disciple helps Mary support the Virgin. Mary Magdalene wrings her hands in prayerful anguish as she looks up at her departed savior whose side has been pierced by the lance of the Roman soldier below. The dark, overcast sky speaks of the cosmic nature of the event. Extreme downstage-left, Delacroix, in a uniquely personal touch, presents the anguished figure of Judas Iscariot. We, the viewers, are with the group at the foot of the cross as the narrow landscape width has us looking up with them to the pallid figure of Christ. In this way we become part of the bereft human family. This reflects Delacroix's realization of the words of Christ in the biblical passage upon which the passage is based: " . . . he saith unto his mother, Woman, behold thy son!/ Then saith he to the disciple, Behold thy mother! . . . "[271] The family is extended to become a universal family. The deeply felt despair of being excluded from that universal family of loving care for each other is conveyed by Delacroix's inclusion of the despairing Judas. Maybe Delacroix, himself, feels something of that emptiness.

In the winter of 1862 a very sick Delacroix who was to die the following year still managed to carry out what he called his daily prayer: *nulla dies sine linea.*[272] He produced ten drawings all of which were focussed upon the life of Christ. They have a remarkable expressionistic quality. In the simplification that conveys a sense of urgency[273] Delacroix manages to get to the essence of his subject.

271. KJV. John. 19, 26/7.

272. Not a day without a line drawn.

273. Three of the drawings are dated the same day.

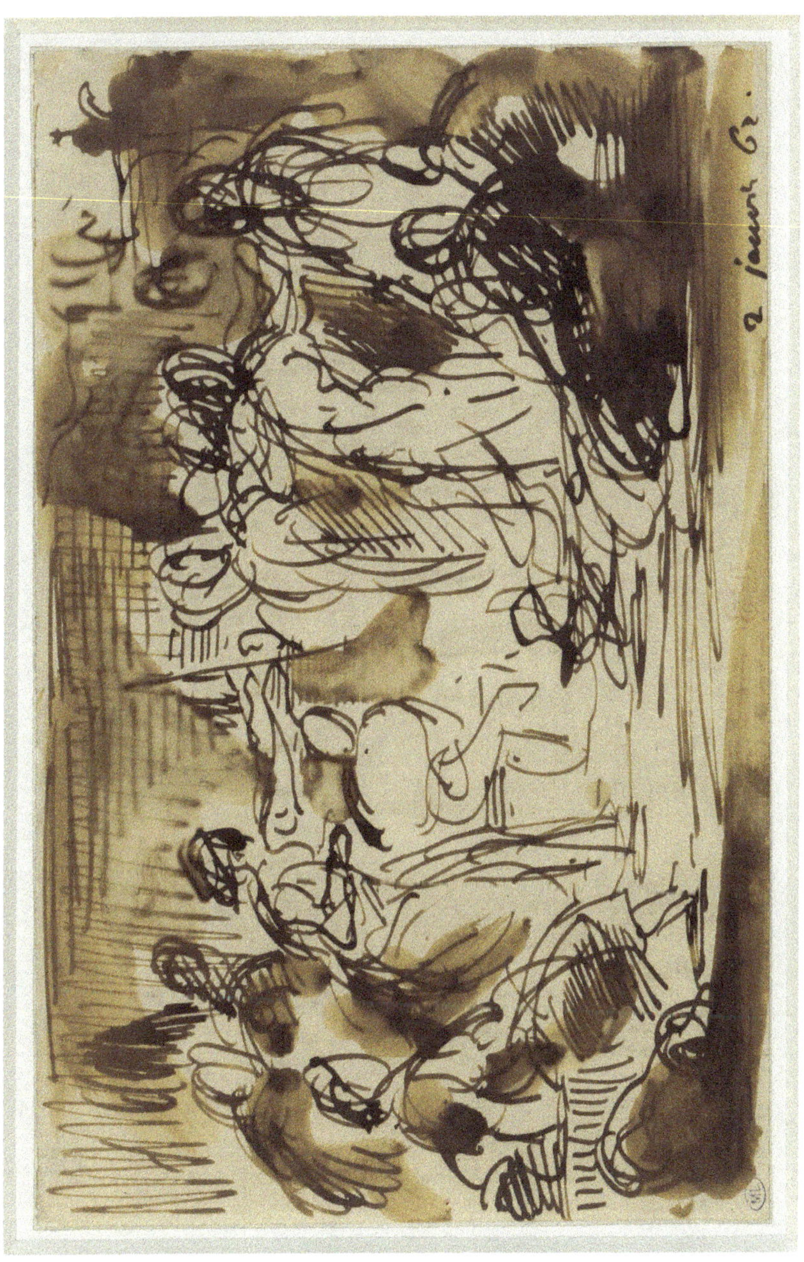

Fig. 55. Eugène Delacroix. ***The Denial of Saint Peter*** **1862 Pen, brown ink wash Photo© Muséedu Louvre, Dist. RMN-Grand Palais / Martine Beck-Coppola.**

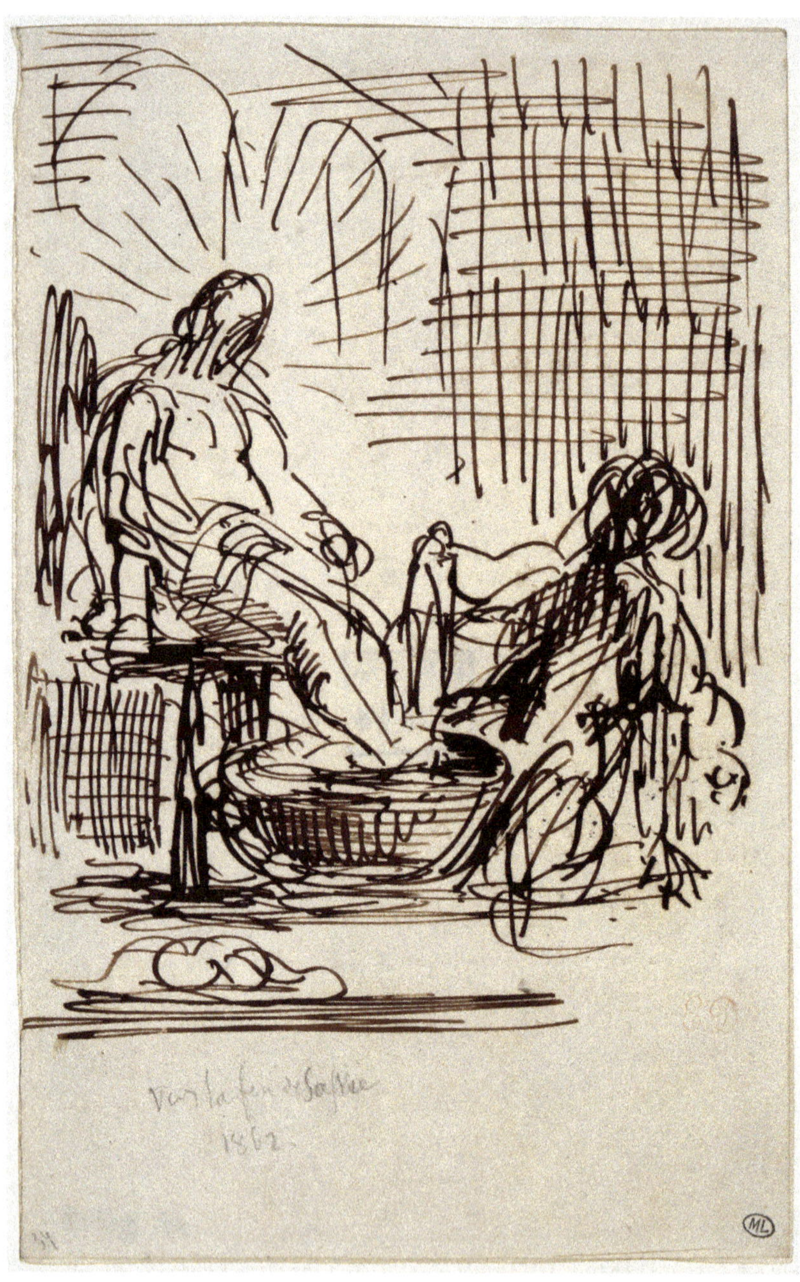

Fig. 56. Eugène Delacroix. *The Madeleine at the feet of Christ* 1862 Pen, brown ink wash Photo© Musée du Louvre RMN-Grand Palais / Michèle Bellot.

In *The Denial of Peter* Delacroix identifies a specific moment[274] by placing a symbol of a crowing cock in the upstage left corner of the drawing. We see aggression, recoil, confusion, and panic—all of the emotions associated with the chaos released by betrayal. It is like an image of the nightmare in the head of Judas introduced in Delacroix's painting of *Christ on the Cross.*

Mary Magdalene at the Feet of Christ conveys a vision that acts as an antidote to this nightmare. Forgiveness and love shine from the portrayal of this intense moment. Christ is set in space empty apart from the rays around his head suggesting radiance almost too much for Mary Magdalene to look upon as she leans back into the shadows. The expressive power and intensity of feeling in these final statements from Delacroix suggest a dying man's legacy of wisdom beyond words.

274. Mtt. 26: 33—35; Mk. 14; 29—31; Luke. 22; 33/4; Jn. 13; 37/8.

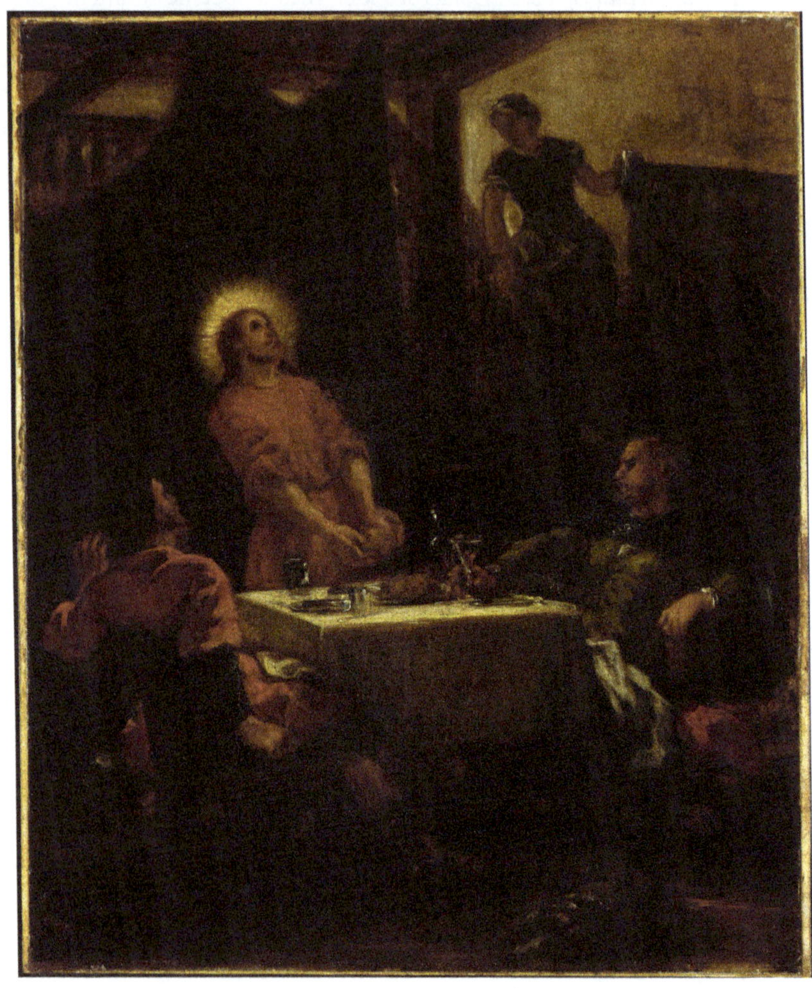

Fig. 57. Eugène Delacroix (French, 1798—1863). *The Disciples at Emmaus, or The Pilgrims at Emmaus (Les disciples d'Emmaüs, ou Les pèlerins d'Emmaüs).* **1853, Oil on canvas, 21 ¾ x 18 ½ in. (55.2 x 47 cm).**
Brooklyn Museum, Gift of Mrs. Watson B. Dickerman, 50.106. (Photo: Brooklyn Museum).

In the same year as *Christ on the Cross,* Delacroix painted his version of *The Supper at Emmaus.*[275] In correspondence, the painter refers to his work as *The Pilgrims at Emmaus.* The emphasis as with his *Christ on the Cross* is upon the human element: what must it have been like to be present? *How* would I have responded? Delacroix had made a close study of Rembrandt's many versions of *The Supper at Emmaus* and he was clearly deeply moved by Rembrandt's work. He even produced a copy of one of Rembrandt's paintings that he entitled *The Pilgrims of Emmaus After Rembrandt.* The realism of the work under consideration reflects Delacroix's study of Rembrandt's approach but it does not arrive at the same resting place. Here it is a rather startling, if not a shocking presentation. The stage-left pilgrim lounges back in his chair, fingers his glass of wine and looks rather crossly at Christ breaking the bread. The stage-right pilgrim reacts more in accordance with traditional presentations: his left hand is raised in surprise as he leans back in an awe-struck pose. The staircase upstage-left down which a maid carrying a jug descends creates along with the dog downstage-left a perspective of depth to the presentation. There is a powerful energy to the scene that counterbalances the literally laid-back attitudes of the pilgrims. In fact the collective physical movement is backwards, away from the center. This gains emphasis from the slant of the staircase. But whereas the pilgrims are as it were lounging backwards, the figure of Christ is taken backwards by a powerful energetic charge generated through his arms to the grasp of the bread. The large powerful hands are not so much breaking the bread as kneading it. The action is rather like a potter kneading a mass of wet clay. The downward energy has a compensating release in the burst of radiance that surrounds the head of Christ. This illuminates the central space vacated by the backward movement. Within this space the table is placed. This particular table is, however, unremarkable. It is not laden with symbolic elements. It is a very ordinary domestic table bearing the rudimentary utensils of a simple meal. The stage-left pilgrim is the puzzling and puzzled feature of this painting. Placed within the context of the period in which Delacroix painted, it is perhaps more easily understood. The pilgrim may be seen as a product of what Baudelaire referred to as a century of nonbelievers, a century, paradoxically, of enlightenment where belief in something that challenged the limits of human rationality had become virtually impossible. Perhaps Delacroix is suggesting that the radiance of Christ is in the eye of the beholder. Maybe we can see Delacroix

275. 1853.

himself in the stage-left figure, conflicted at being asked to abandon everything his education has taught him regarding the pathway to truth and to surrender himself to what is before him as the man who fell among thieves surrendered himself to the love and care of the Good Samaritan. Delacroix sets his scene in a downstairs room, a lower room. This sets up a contrast in the biblically focussed mind with the upper room of the last supper[276] at which many Christians believe the Eucharist was established. The stage-left pilgrim as a disconsolate disciple of Christ is being challenged by this Emmaus experience, as it were, spiritually to mount the stairs and re-enter that upper room where he had been in the presence of the living Christ whom he has seen die on a cross three days ago. It is a very big ask.

CONCLUDING REMARKS

From the middle of the thirteenth-century, books of hours were available for the aristocracy. They were originally developed from the Psalters that monks and nuns were required to recite as determined by certain canonical hours, hence the classification. They were adapted and simplified as personal prayer books for the secular population who were able to afford them. The books were visually adorned, sometimes with exquisite examples of miniaturist art alongside the text. Such people would have led more leisurely lives than common folk.

Most of us lead very busy lives today with little time to "Stand and stare" the importance of which the welsh poet W. H. Davies (1871–1940) celebrated in his poem *Leisure*. Davies asked the question, "What is this life if, full of care/We have no time to stand and stare?" Without suggesting that this book in any way shares the status of a book of hours, I suppose I do offer the wonderful works of art that it contains as worthy of a stare in scattered moments. Quentin Letts is a very familiar name in the UK. He is an English Journalist and Theatre Critic leading a very busy life. He found time to rush a post card off to me referencing my previous book *The Continuing Dialogue* that featured five magnificent paintings of *The Wedding at Cana*.

> At church yesterday we had the second lesson and sermon on the wedding feast at Cana. As a result of your fine book I found myself

276. KJV, Mark. 14: 15. "And he will shew you a large upper room furnished and prepared : there make ready for us."

> unusually engaged by the story—and even paid attention to the sermon. Unusual! Thank you.

The post card made me realize what I had been hoping to achieve and what I am hoping to achieve with this work. I trust that it may enable such moments for you.

Bibliography

Aikema, Bernard. *Jacopo Bassano and his Public: Moralizing Pictures in the Age of Reform, ca1535–1600*. Princeton: Princeton University Press, 1996.

Andreopoulos, Andreas. *Art as Theology: From the Postmodern to The Medieval.* London: Equinox, 2006.

Austin, Michael. *Explorations In Art, Theology And Imagination*. London: Equinox, 2005.

Ayrton, Michael. *Giovanni Pisano*. London: Thames and Hudson, 1969.

Badinucci, Filippo, cited Rosenberg, Jakob. *Rembrandt Life and Work,* third edition. New York: Phaidon, 1968

Balthasar, Hans Urs von. *The Glory of the Lord: a Theological* Aesthetics (Vol 1). Translated by Erasmo Leiva-Merikakis. London: T & T Clark, 1989.

Barth, Karl. *Protestant Theology in the Nineteenth Century*. London: Student Christian Movement, 1972.

Baxandall, Michael. *Giotto and the Orators: Humanist Observers of Painting in Italy and the Discovery of Pictorial Composition*. Oxford: Oxford University Press, 1986.

———. *Painting and Experience in Fifteenth Century Italy*. London: Oxford University Press, 1988.

Begbie, Jeremy S, ed. *Sounding the Depths: Theology Through the Arts*. London: Student Christian Movement, 2002.

Bellosi, Luciano. *Giotto*. New York: Riverside, 1999.

Bentley, Hart David. *The Beauty of the Infinite:The Aesthetics of Christian Faith.* Grand Rapids: Eeerdmans, 2003.

Britannica Online http://www.britannica.com/ebc/article-9021901

Burch Brown, Frank. *Religious Aesthetics: A Theological Study of Making and Meaning.* Princeton: Princeton University Press, 1989.

Camus, Albert. "On Nihilism." Discussing his stage adaptation of Dostoevsky's *The Possessed,* 1959. Available on You Tube.

Christiansen, Keith. *Duccio and the Origins of Western Painting.* New Haven: Yale University Press, 2008.

Clark, Kenneth. *Civilisation.* London: BBC and John Murray, 1971.

———. *Moments of Vision*. London: John Murray, 1981.

Cole, Bruce. *The Scrovegni Chapel, Padua: Great Fresco Cycles of the Renaissance*. New York: George Braziller, 1993.

Daganello, Georgio, ed. *Giotto.* Padova: Razzodini, 2007.

Dawkins, Richard. *The God Delusion*. London: Black Swan, 2007.

Derbes, Anne and Sandona, Mark, eds. *The Cambridge Companion to Giotto*. New York: Cambridge University Press, 2004.

Dillenberger, John and Dillenberger, Jane, eds. *Paul Tillich on Arts and Architecture.* New York: Crossroad, 1989.

Dixon, John W. *Art and the Theological Imagination*. New York: Seabury Press, 1978.

———."Painting as Theological Thought: The Issues in Tuscan Theology." http://www.unc.edu/~jwdixon/articles/tuscan.html

Drury, John. *Painting the Word: Christian Pictures and Their Meanings*. London: Yale University Press in association with National Gallery Publications, 1999.

Durant, Will. *The Story of Civilization: The Renaissance*. New York: Simon and Shuster, 1953.

Eliot, T. S. *The Waste Land*.

Freedberg, S J. *Painting in Italy*, 1500–1600. Harmondsworth UK: Penguin, 1971.

Gallagher, Daniel B. "The Analogy of Beauty and the Limits of Theological Aesthetics." Theandros 3 no 3, 2006. www.theandros.com/beauty.html

Garcia-Rivera, Alex. "Creator of the Visible and the Invisible: Liberation Theology, Postmodemism, and the Spiritual." *Journal of Hispanic/Latino Theology* 3, no. 4, 1996, 35–56.

Graham-Dixon, Andrew. *Caravaggio, A Life Sacred and Profane*. London: Penguin, 2011.

Hagiioannu, Michael. "Giotto's Bardi Chapel Frescoes and Chaucer's *House of Fame*: Influence, Evidence, and Interpretations." *The Chaucer Review* 36 no 1, 2001, 28–47.

Harrison, Charles. "The Arena Chapel: Patronage and Authorship." In Diana Norman ed. Case Studies 2: *Siena, Florence and Padua: Art, Society and Religion 1280–1400*. New Haven: Yale University Press, 1995, 82–103.

Hibbard, Howard. *Caravaggio*. London: Thames and Hudson, 1988.

Hunter, G. K. *Dramatic Identities and Cultural Tradition*. Liverpool: Liverpool University Press, 1978.

Keats, John. *Ode to a Nightingale*.

Lessing, G. E. *Theological Writings* cited Barth. *Protestant Theology*.

Maginnis, Hayden B J. *Painting in the Age of Giotto: A Historical Re-evaluation*. University Park: Pennsylvania State University Press, 1997.

Malraux, Andre. *The Metamorphosis of the Gods*. Translated by Stuart Gilbert. New York: Doubleday, 1960.

Miravalle, Mark. *With Jesus: The Story of Mary Co-redemptrix*. Goleta: Queenship, 1993.

Moore, Henry. "Introduction." In Michael Ayrton, *Giovanni Pisano*, London: Thames and Hudson, 1969.

Nichols, Tom. "Tintoretto , *prestezza* and the *poligrafi:* a study in the literary and visual culture of Cinquecento Venice." *Renaissance Studies* 10 no 1, 71–99.

———. *Tintoretto, Tradition and Identity*. London: Reaktion, 1999.

Norman, Diana, ed. *Siena, Florence and Padua: Art, Society and Religion 1280–1400*. New Haven: Yale University Press, 1995.

Norton, Lucy, trans. *The Journal of Eugène Delacroix: A Selection*. Edited Hubert Wellington. London: Phaidon, 1951.

Offner, Richard, "Giotto, non-Giotto." *Burlington Magazine*, 74, 1939, 96–113.

Otto, Rudolph. *The Idea of the Holy*. Translated by John W. Harvey. London: Oxford University Press, 1996.

Radke, Gary. "Giotto and Architecture." In Derbes, *The Cambridge Companion to Giotto*, 76–102.

de la Pava, Sergio. *A Naked Singularity*. University of Chicago Press, 2012.

Rosenberg, Jakob. *Rembrandt Life and Work*, third edition. New York: Phaidon, 1968.

Sartre, Jean-Paul. *Le Séquestré de Venice*, 1957 (unfinished). Cited, Nichols, Tom. *Tintoretto Tradition and Identity* London 1999 Reaktion Books

Schmidt-Degener, F and van Gelder, H. E. *Jan Steen: Forty Reproductions in Photo-gravure of the Artist's Principle Works, with a Critical Study.* London: John Lane, 1927.

Steiner, George. *No Passion Spent: Essays 1978–1996.* London: Faber and Faber. 1997.

Sherry, Patrick. *Spirit and Beauty: An Introduction to Theological Aesthetics.* London: Student Christian Movement, 2002.

Stubblebine, James H, ed. *Giotto, the Arena Chapel Frescoes.* New York: W. W. Norton, 1996.

Stiles, Kenton M, " In the Beauty of Holiness: Wesleyan Theology, Worship, and the Aesthetic." http://wesley.nnu.edu/wesleyan_theology/theojrnl/31–35/32–2-10.htm

———. "Ultimate Concern." In Dialogue with Mackenzie Brown Second Dialogue. http://www.religion-online.org

Taylor, Mark C. *Disfiguring: Art Architecture and Religion.* Chicago: University of Chicago Press, 1992.

Thiessen, Gesa Elsbeth ed. *Theological Aesthetics: A Reader.* London: Student Christian Movement, 2004.

Tillich, Paul. "One Moment of Beauty." In John and Jane Dillenberger eds. *Paul Tillich on Art and Architecture.* New York: Crossroad, 1987.

Viladesau, Richard. *The Beauty of the Cross: The Passion of Christ in Theology and the Arts from the Catacombs to the Eve of the Renaissance.* Oxford: Oxford University Press, 1999.

Ware, Timothy. *The Orthodox Church.* New York: Penguin, 1997.

Wellington, Hubert, ed. *The Journal of Eugène Delacroix: A Selection.* Translated by Lucy Norton. London: Phaidon, 1951.

Wheelock, Arthur K, Jr. *Jan Steen: Painter and Storyteller.* New Haven: York University Press, 1954.

White, John. *Art and Architecture in Italy* 1250–1400. Third edition. New Haven: Yale University Press, 1993.

Yeats, William Butler. *The Second Coming.*

———. *Easter 1916.*

INDEX

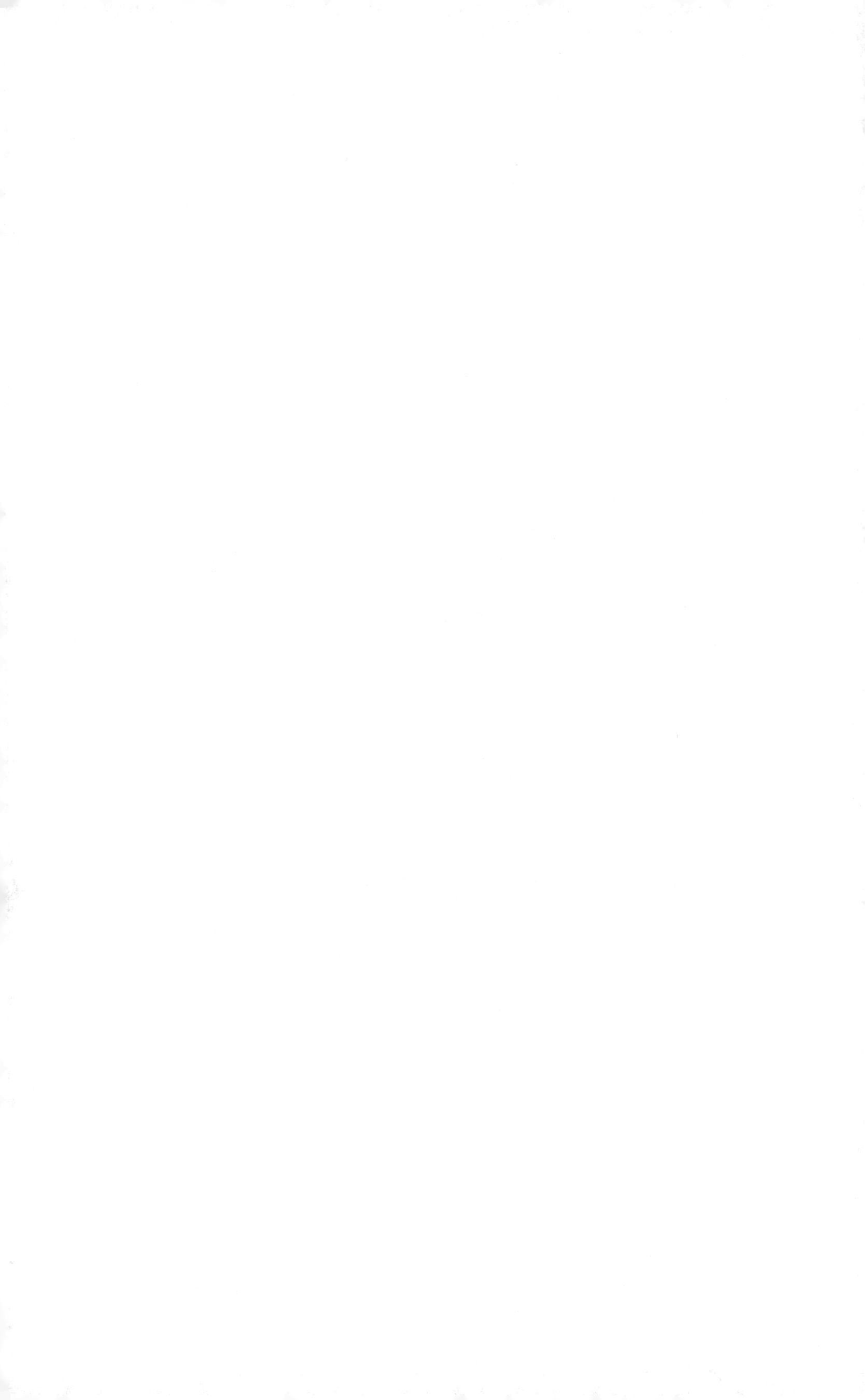

www.ingramcontent.com/pod-product-compliance
Lightning Source LLC
LaVergne TN
LVHW012328100826
845148LV00017B/538